RISK

OCRACY

Propaganda in the US and Australia

TAKING THE RISK OUT OF DEMOCRACY

PROPAGANDA IN THE US AND AUSTRALIA

ALEX CAREY

EDITED BY ANDREW LOHREY

UNSW
PRESS

Published in Australia by
UNIVERSITY OF NEW SOUTH WALES PRESS LTD
Sydney NSW 2052 Australia
Telephone (02) 398 8900
Facsimile (02) 398 3408

National Library of Australia
Cataloguing-in-Publication entry

Carey, Alex
    Taking the risk out of democracy: propaganda in the US and Australia

    Includes index.
    ISBN 0 86840 358 X.

    1. Corporations — United States — Political activity.
    2. Corporations — Australia — Political Activity.
    3. Corporations — Social aspects — United States.
    4. Corporations — Social aspects — Australia.
    5. Business and politics — United States.
    6. Business and politics — Australia. I. Title.

322.3

Available in Singapore, Malaysia & Brunei through:
Publishers Marketing Services
Singapore 1232
Tel: (65) 256 5166
Fax: (65) 253 0008

Printed by Southwood Press, Sydney
Text: Garamond 3 11.5/12.5

CONTENTS

FOREWORD
BY NOAM CHOMSKY

In our book *Manufacturing Consent*, devoted to the subordination of the major media to the interests of state-corporate power, Edward Herman and I opened with a dedication to the memory of Alex Carey. This was far more than a testimonial to a close personal friend and valued co-worker. It was also a bare and inadequate way to try to express our indebtedness to him for his uniquely important work on 'the ideal of a propaganda-managed democracy' that the highly class-conscious business community in the United States has sought to achieve, with the dedicated support of major segments of the intellectual culture. His contributions to the thought and understanding of those fortunate enough to have known and worked with him can at last be sensed by a larger public, though only partially, with the publication of some of his major essays, preliminaries to a major work on the role of propaganda in democratic societies that he never completed, to the great loss of all who care about freedom and its enemies.

'The twentieth century', Carey writes, 'has been characterized by three developments of great political importance: the growth of democracy, the growth of corporate power, and the growth of corporate propaganda as a means of protecting corporate power against democracy'. That the growth of corporate power would undermine freedom and democracy had been understood by classical liberal opinion well before the contours of the future industrial capitalist society could be clearly discerned. In his later years, Thomas Jefferson warned that the newly rising 'banking institutions and moneyed incorporations' would destroy the freedoms won in the American revolution, becoming the foundation of a 'single and splendid government of an aristocracy' if given a free hand. So they were, to a degree that exceeded Jefferson's worst nightmares, though not through the expression of popular will: rather, primarily by courts and lawyers, acting in 'technocratic insulation' from the annoying public, to borrow some of the lingo of World Bank recommendations.

The establishment and growth of democracy has always been a prospect greatly feared by 'the masters of mankind', who understand that it can only impede the pursuit of their 'vile maxim': 'All for ourselves, and nothing for other people' (Adam Smith). Smith had in mind particularly the 'merchants and manufacturers' who were 'by far the principal architects' of policy in his day, designing it so that their interests were 'most peculiarly attended to', whatever the impact on others, including the people of England. In later years the institutions of the masters have taken new forms, and the problem of ensuring that the levers of state power remain firmly in their hands has arisen in new ways as well. But basic themes persist in different guise.

At the time of the first modern democratic revolution in seventeenth-century England, the self-described 'men of best quality' expressed deep concern that the 'rascal multitude' might seek to enter the public arena, aroused by pamphleteers, itinerant preachers, and other riffraff who had 'made the people thereby so curious and so arrogant that they will never find humility enough to submit to a civil rule', one eminent intellectual warned. Particularly disturbing was their outspoken wish to be ruled neither by King nor Parliament, the official contestants in the civil war, but 'by countrymen like ourselves, that know our wants'. 'It will never be a good world while knights and gentlemen make us laws, that are chosen for fear and do but oppress us, and do not know the people's sores', their subversive pamphlets declared. Such sentiments echo through the centuries, always arousing contempt and fury and if necessary ample terror and violence, on the part of the men of best quality, who rule by right. They were willing to grant the people too certain rights, but within reason, and on the principle that 'when we mention the people, we do not mean the confused promiscuous body of the people', as another seventeenth-century authority explained. 'Day-labourers and tradesmen, the spinsters and dairymaids' must be told what to believe, John Locke observed after the democratic upsurge had been quelled: 'The greatest part cannot know and therefore they must believe'.

The 'crisis of democracy' of the seventeenth century brought into sharp relief a distinction between 'aristocrats' and 'democrats' that was drawn by Thomas Jefferson as he pondered the fate of the American democratic experiment. Jefferson's 'aristocrats' are 'those who fear and distrust the people, and wish to draw all powers from them into the hands of the higher classes'. His 'democrats', in contrast, 'identify with the people, have confidence in them, cherish and consider them as the honest & safe, altho' not the most wise depository of the public interest'. The aristocrats, in this sense, include Smith's 'merchants and manufacturers' and their successors who gained control over the economy and political system, developments that Jefferson viewed with dismay because of the obvious contradiction between democracy and capitalism, whether in the state-guided Western model, or some other. Also among Jefferson's 'aristocrats' are the twentieth-century progressives whom Alex Carey discusses in the essays that follow, including the distinguished 'public intellectuals' and founders of contemporary academic social science who urged the 'responsible men' of the community to recognize the 'ignorance and stupidity [of] … the masses', not succumbing to 'democratic dogmatisms about men being the best judges of their own interests' (Walter Lippmann, Harold Lasswell). The general public, mere 'ignorant and meddlesome outsiders', must not intrude in the management of public affairs; for their own good, they must keep to their 'function' as 'interested spectators of action', not 'participants', though they may be permitted to select periodically among the 'responsible men' whose task it is to analyse, decide, and rule. As explained by William Shepard in his presidential address to the American Political Science Association in 1934, government should be in the hands of 'an aristocracy of intellect and power', not directed by 'the ignorant, the uninformed, and the anti-social elements'. 'The public must be put in its place', Lippmann admonished, so that the 'responsible men' may 'live free of the trampling and the roar of a bewildered herd' as they do their necessary work, for the common good.

Remaining unspoken, to be sure, is a hidden premise: the 'responsible men' gain this impressive status by virtue of their service to the interests of those who truly own and manage the society. It was not because of a low IQ that the leading figure in the American labor movement, Eugene Debs, was sentenced to ten years in jail while such thoughts as these were gaining respect and prominence in the ideological institutions.

The spectrum of 'aristocrats' extends from the liberal and progressive thinkers to those who are still more extreme in their disdain for the rabble. Reactionary statists of the Reaganite variety, absurdly called 'conservatives' in contemporary Newspeak, are typical examples. Unwilling to grant the public even the role of 'interested spectators of action', they favour clandestine operations — secret from no one except the domestic public — and harsher censorship to protect the powerful state they nurture as a welfare state for the rich; and, of course, greater power in the hands of the protected and publicly subsidized 'private sector', which operates in virtual secrecy. Another version of the same basic doctrines is the Leninist variety of Marxism, founded on the belief, put into operation at once as the Bolsheviks took state power, that the stupid and ignorant masses must become a 'labor army' subordinated to the revolutionary intellectuals, who will drive them to the future designed by their betters — as always, in the interests of the bewildered herd.

To ensure that the 'ignorant and meddlesome outsiders' have the proper beliefs has become a task of growing importance, as their struggles have gradually expanded the scope of democratic institutions. The basic problem is one that had intrigued David Hume, who, in considering his First Principles of Government, expressed his puzzlement over 'the easiness with which the many are governed by the few' and 'the implicit submission with which men resign their own sentiments and passions to those of their rulers'. 'When we enquire by what means this wonder is brought about', Hume concluded, 'we shall find, that as Force is always on the side of the governed, the governors have nothing to support them but opinion. 'Tis therefore, on opinion only that government is founded; and this maxim extends to the most despotic and most military governments, as well as to the most free and most popular'.

Hume seriously underestimated the capacity of the powerful to control the rabble by force, lessons that are constantly being taught in gruesome ways, though generally kept from the public eye unless some power interest can be served by lamenting properly selected evil works. The matter was considered in an important conference organized by Jesuits and lay associates in San Salvador in January 1994, unreported in the United States. Reflecting on the consequences of the recent state terrorist projects that Washington had organized and directed in its Central American domains' with the Church a prime target, they took special note of 'what weight the culture of terror has had in domesticating the expectations of the majority vis-a-vis alternatives different to those of the powerful ... '; the destruction of hope, they recognized, is one of the great achievements of the Free World doctrine of 'low intensity conflict', what is called 'terror' when conducted by official enemies.

Nonetheless, Hume's basic point is well taken, and is of particular significance with the decline of traditional means to keep the public arena safely under proper management.

Alex Carey's enquiries unravel the story as it has unfolded through the twentieth century, in its manifold aspects: advertizing devoted to creation of artificial wants; the huge public relations industry with its goal of diversion to meaningless pursuits and control of 'the public mind'; academic institutions and professions, today under renewed assault from private power determined to narrow still further the spectrum of thinkable thought; the increasingly concentrated media, in which, as one leading academic media scholar wrote a few years ago, 'the taboo against criticism of the system of contemporary enterprise is, in its unspoken way, almost as complete ... as criticism of communism is explicitly forbidden in the Soviet Union' (Ben Bagdikian).

'The public mind' was recognized long ago by corporate leaders to be 'the only serious danger confronting' their enterprises, and the major 'hazard facing industrialists', along with 'the newly realized political power of the masses', which had to be beaten back. From the early nineteenth century, it was no small task to impose capitalist values on human beings, with very different conceptions of a decent existence — ideas that found expression in the lively working-class press, as they had in the classical liberal thought that has long been rejected and forgotten. In the early days of industrial capitalism, the independent press condemned the 'degradation and the loss of that self-respect which had made the mechanics and laborers the pride of the world', as the system of wage labor was imposed and free people were forced to sell themselves, not what they produced, becoming 'menials' and 'humble subjects' of 'despots'. Its writers described the destruction of 'the spirit of free institutions', with working people reduced to a 'state of servitude' in which they 'see a moneyed aristocracy hanging over us like a mighty avalanche threatening annihilation to every man who dares to question their right to enslave and oppress the poor and unfortunate'. 'They who work in the mills ought to own them' and thus overcome 'the blasting influence of monarchical principles on democratic soil', workers in New England industries declared well before radical intellectuals entered the fray, recognizing that in the new 'manufacturing population' that is being created, the 'tendency in the scale of civilization, health, morals, and intellectuality, is manifestly downwards'. Such sentiments did not pass unnoticed by southern slave-owners, who used them in defense of the paternalistic practices of masters for whom people were at least considered capital to be preserved.

Reviewing such material seventy years ago in his classic study of mid-nineteenth-century American labor, Norman Ware observes that the imposition of industrial capitalism and its values 'was repugnant to an astonishingly large section of the earlier American community'. The primary reason was 'the decline of the industrial worker as a person', the 'degradation' and 'psychological change' that followed from the 'loss of dignity and independence' and of democratic rights and freedoms. These reactions were vividly expressed in the working-class literature, often by women, who played a prominent role despite their subordination in the general society.

'For working people', labor historian David Montgomery observes, 'the most important part of the Jeffersonian legacy was the shelter it provided to free association, diversity of beliefs and behavior, and defiance of alleged social superiors in society'. The structures of civil society 'obstructed bourgeois control of American life at every turn', and therefore had to be destroyed. Hence the unremitting efforts to demolish the independent press and effective forms of community solidarity, from trade unions to political clubs and organizations. US labor history is unusually violent in comparison with other industrial societies, and it was not until the Great Depression that elementary rights were won, soon to be lost, in part as a result of the huge propaganda campaigns that Carey describes. These continue to the present, with the 'concerted efforts' of corporate America, described by the *Wall Street Journal* with much enthusiasm, 'to change the attitudes and values of workers' with a variety of devices of indoctrination and stupefaction designed to convert 'worker apathy into corporate allegiance'.

As for unions, the favored device of recent years has been corporate crime. Reviewing some of the methods encouraged by Reaganite 'conservatives', *Business Week* reports in 1994 that 'Over the past dozen years, in fact, U.S. industry has conducted one of the most successful antiunion wars ever, illegally firing thousands of workers for exercising their rights to organize'. 'Unlawful firings occurred in one-third of all representation elections in the late '80s, vs. 8% in the late '60s.' Crime does pay, particularly when state power stands firmly behind it. The independent press, which retained its vigor until the Second World War in the United States and for another thirty years in Britain, succumbed finally to concentration of capital resources in the 'free market', removing a significant support for the vibrant working-class culture that had survived considerable repression, notably under the progressive Wilson Administration.

In Third World domains, more direct means have been used to 'domesticate the expectations' of people tainted by the hope for freedom, with considerable success even where a democratic culture had once flourished. Chile is an important case. The US-backed military dictatorship and the subsequent 'fragmentation of opposition communities', Latin Americanist Cathy Schneider observes, 'has transformed Chile, both culturally and politically, from a country of active participatory grassroots communities, to a land of disconnected, apolitical individuals' — just the outcome to which the huge resources of the ideological institutions have been devoted where violence is not so readily available.

The effects of the vast campaigns of ideological warfare are sometimes rather complex. The late 1993 debate over NAFTA, one of the mislabelled 'free trade agreements', was instructive in this regard. It had been anticipated that the accord would sail through unnoticed, but public opposition developed. Much of it was organized by the usually quiescent labor movement, which proposed constructive alternatives, as did the Congressional Office of Technology Assessment and others — all ignored in favor of the executive version of NAFTA, carefully crafted as an investor rights agreement. The unanticipated popular reaction elicited a propaganda campaign of quite unusual fanaticism. The media — which, like the corporate world in general, were close to 100 percent in support of NAFTA — followed the President's lead as he denounced the 'real roughshod, muscle-bound tactics' of organized labor, 'the raw muscle, the sort of naked pressure that the labor forces have put on', even going so far as to resort to 'pleading ... based on friendship' and 'threatening ... based on money and work in the campaign' when they approached their elected representatives, a shocking interference with the democratic process. Front-page stories featured the President's call to Congress 'to resist the hardball politics' of the 'powerful labor interests'. At the far left of the permissible spectrum, *New York Times* columnist Anthony Lewis berated the 'backward, unenlightened' labor movement for the 'crude threatening tactics' it employed to influence Congress. The attempts of working people to approach their elected representatives aroused particular hysteria, across the spectrum. Corporate lobbying, which overwhelmed the meager capacities of labor, passed virtually unnoticed; that is only reasonable, on the understanding that the role of the state is to serve the masters. The facts were so dramatically obvious that the *New York Times*, after the vote, even permitted itself the usually forbidden phrase 'class lines' in describing the 'nasty' and 'divisive battle' over NAFTA, now happily concluded.

The passionate denunciations of labor had a curious impact on public attitudes. Surprisingly, most people continued to oppose the executive version of NAFTA to which consideration was restricted by the ideological institutions, but later polls showed that about two-thirds criticized unions as unreasonably opposed to change and 'too involved in politics', particularly on the NAFTA issue. The propaganda barrage seems to have left opinions on NAFTA relatively unchanged, while causing people to oppose the major popular forces that represented those opinions and sought to protect them in the political arena. A closer analysis suggests further modifications of Hume's maxim. As in 'the most despotic and military governments', control of opinion is not all that important, as long as other means are available to ensure that people have 'humility enough to submit' to the rule of the masters.

Changes in world order provide new ways to contain the 'crisis of democracy' that liberal elites perceive when the public seeks to escape its assigned spectator role. Of particular significance is the accelerated globalization of the economy, which places unprecedented power in the hands of increasingly concentrated and virtually unaccountable institutions of private power, transnational in scale, carrying out centrally managed planning and transactions (much of it mislabelled 'trade') beyond public scrutiny or interference. As in earlier eras, structures of governance are coalescing around the centers of real power, giving rise to what the international business press has called a 'de facto world government': the IMF, World Bank, GATT and the new World Trade Organization, G-7 and European Union executive power, and so on. These processes have many welcome effects. They protect wealth and privilege from both market discipline and public interference. And they tend naturally to increase the polarization of global society, as the sharply two-tiered Third World model, with sectors of great wealth amidst increasing poverty and despair, extends increasingly to the richer societies as well, the United States and Britain leading the way.

But these developments have their problems too. It may be no easy task to control growing masses of people who are superfluous for profit-making, and therefore lack rights in accord with the value systems that must be implanted. The problems are variations of familiar ones, and the means available to 'the masters of mankind' are adaptations of the old as well. Equally venerable is the need for people to draw aside the veil of deceit and imposed ignorance, and to persist in the unending struggle for freedom and justice. To this end, Alex Carey's work has made a distinctive and powerful contribution.

Noam Chomsky, 17 August 1994

ACKNOWLEDGEMENTS

I would like to thank Alex Carey's wife, Joan Carey, and his daughters, Cathy Carey and Gabrielle Carey, for their encouragement and support on this project.

I would also like to thank Lyn Trantor for her generous advice, Julia Collingwood and the UNSW Press for having the confidence to support this venture and Venetia Nelson for her diligent assistance in editing this book.

ORIGINAL ARTICLES BY ALEX CAREY*

Note: all essays, published or unpublished previously, have been edited to a consistent style for this book.

* Appearing in this Book

ABBREVIATIONS

ACC	Australian Chamber of Commerce
AEF	American Economic Foundation
AEI	American Enterprise Institute for Public Policy Research
AFL	American Federation of Labor
AIDA	Australian Industries Development Association
AIPR	Australian Institute for Policy Research
AMA	American Management Association
AmCham	American Chamber of Commerce in Australia
CED	Committee for Economic Development (US)
CEDA	Committee for Economic Development in Australia
CEO	Chief executive officer
CIA	Committee for Immigrants in America
CICC	Committee on Immigration of the (US) Chamber of Commerce
CIG	Commonwealth Industrial Gasses
CIO	Congress of Industrial Organizations
CIS	Centre for Independent Studies
CPA	Consumer Protection Agency
CPI	Committee on Public Information
EA	Enterprise Australia
FBI	Federal Bureau of Investigation
FTC	Federal Trade Commission
GKN	Guest, Keen & Nettlefold
GNP	Gross National Product
GRS	Great Red Scare
IBM	International Business Machines
IEA	Institute of Economic Affairs
IPA	Institute of Public Affairs
IWM	Interchurch World Movement
IWW	Industrial Workers of the World
NAC	National Americanization Committee

NACLI	North American Civic League for Immigrants
NADC	National Americanization Day Committee
NAM	National Association of Manufacturers
NCOH	National Committee of One Hundred
NJ	New Jersey
NML	National Mutual Life
n.d.	no date
n.p.	no pagination
NSW	New South Wales
NY	New York
OPA	Office of Price Administration
PR	public relations
TNEC	Temporary National Economic Committee (US)
TPC	The Psychological Corporation
UN	United Nations
US	United States
USA	United States of America
USIC	United States Industrial Council
YAA	Young Achievement Australia
YMCA	Young Men's Christian Association

INTRODUCTION

The development of a theory of persuasion began as long ago as 500 BC in the Greek city-states. At that time philosophers compiled a set of rules for the use of rhetoric and persuasion. So compelling were these systems that only small changes in theory took place until the Industrial Revolution opened the way for mass persuasion through mass marketing. After 1900 marketing studies began to be made of consumers' wants and habits and their susceptibility to alternative kinds of salesmanship. It was, however, the advent of World War I which provided mass propaganda with its central place in twentieth-century political thinking. For the first time propaganda was used as a systematic weapon of war.

Two men on either side of the Atlantic were deeply affected by this development. They were the democrat Harold D. Lasswell, the first modern analyst of propaganda, and Adolf Hitler, arguably its most perverse practitioner. Lasswell wrote his doctoral dissertation on the subject and called it 'Propaganda Techniques in the World War'. Several years earlier Hitler had written *Mein Kampf*, in which he described how effective the Allied propaganda was in contrast to German attempts at persuasion, the incompetence of which he believed had contributed to the demoralization of German soldiers and civilians and hence to Germany's defeat.

Lasswell's overall conclusions on the importance of propaganda and on who won the propaganda war in World War I were not markedly different from Hitler's. Later the fascist Hitler was to turn his attention to managing public opinion in totalitarian Germany, while the democrat Lasswell studied the need for managing public opinion in democratic America. While totalitarian propaganda is universally condemned in the West as the loss of personal and democratic freedom, the management of public opinion in a democracy is generally considered to be good business. Why the discrepancy?

Lasswell always seemed too mesmerized by the power of propaganda to propose a pluralistic defence against the management of public opinion in democracies like Australia and the United States. In this century many academics like Lasswell, as well as many members of the 'free' press, have tacitly assumed the need to take the risk out of democracy by assisting in the management of public opinion—a management which has been in the interests of business. This imprudent academic and media conformity has helped to close the American mind to the kind of critical thought needed for a healthy, culturally diverse and pluralistic democracy. That this management of democracy should seem necessary and go unchallenged for so long in what is often hailed as the leading democracy in the world is a situation which reflects on the intellectual character of political and academic leaders in the United States.

Unlike most of his academic colleagues, Alex Carey rejected this undemocratic tradition of managing public opinion within democracies. He did this by empirically analysing the propaganda strategies and programs which were put in place this century in the United States and Australia, programs designed to take the 'risk' out of these democracies. The essays appearing in this book represent a major challenge to the continuing effects of this covert and widely orchestrated series of campaigns. Alex Carey has traced how the 'risk' to democracy has been constructed out of a perceived risk to business interests and how business interests are not sold to the public overtly as sectional interests protecting their wealth but instead are linked to national interests. National interests therefore come to be seen as identical with business interests and so together are represented by such emotive words as 'freedom', 'freedom of the individual', 'free enterprise' and 'the free market'.

The identification of business interests with national interests in patriotic strategies 'for or against' the nation has been stunningly successful over a long period. These propaganda programs construct the 'risk' to democracy as coming from the unions and from such government initiatives as welfare and environmental policies, as well as from any government intervention in the economy directed at redistributing wealth. These community and public policies and programs are never attacked as a 'risk' to democracy because they may involve some redistribution of wealth. Propaganda does not work in such straightforward ways. Rather, community policies and activities are characterized as a 'risk' because they reduce the 'freedom' of the individual, restrict 'initiative', or hamper 'free' enterprise. The identification of patriotism with the 'freedom' of business interests is the simplest of covert messages. That this simple regime of thought-control should prove to have been so triumphant, with so little public resistance, must be put down to its persistent, repetitive orchestration.

One effect of these propaganda programs has been to generate public cynicism in the capacity of governments to protect, represent and enhance the public interest. As the nature of representative government is about politicians seeking large numbers of votes, almost every politician in the United States and Australia must become and has become, to some degree, an advocate for business. Those who resist are denied money, media space and business backing. Governments of whatever political persuasion are therefore held captive to business interests and so have largely failed to take the necessary action to protect the interests of the wider community. As an Australian politician for almost fourteen years I have had direct experience of the methods by which governments reactively and continually place business interests before public interests. Witness the difficulties of environmental legislation and enforcement in the United States and Australia over the last two decades, or the difficulties the Clinton administration has encountered in introducing universal health insurance. The failure of governments to protect the interests of the wider community has probably produced more widespread disillusionment with democratic institutions in the United States than in Australia, for Australia has tended to lag behind America in reproducing democratic propaganda campaigns.

Not only does there seem to be widespread social fragmentation and disillusionment with democracy in the United States, but the possibility of reversing this sense of alienation appears to many of us to be already lost. Any Democrat president who wants to institute the desperately needed reforms in health, welfare and the environment faces one of two options. He can stick by his reform program and suffer a loss of public confidence through orchestrated campaigns to publicly portray him as 'too liberal' and ineffectual (the Carter image) or too indecisive or sexually indiscreet (the Clinton image). Alternatively, a reforming Democrat president can move further to the Right, forget his promises and become part of the propaganda campaign. Given the history of democratic propaganda in the United States, some of us doubt that another Roosevelt or New Deal is possible. The political system is now so attuned to business interests that this kind of reformer could no longer institute the substantial health, welfare, education, environmental and employment reforms the country needs.

These are the conclusions to be drawn from Alex Carey's scholarly research into democratic propaganda. In this book he documents the Americanization programs which began before World War I, which have continued through the McCarthy era until today, and which have been exported to Australia. He takes us back to when business started the Americanization movement, ostensibly to Americanize the immigrant worker, who was perceived as being under threat from the subversive forces of the Industrial Workers of the World. What started as a method of controlling the political opinion of immigrant workers quickly turned into a massive program for controlling the thinking of an entire population. One of the most startling examples of the escalation of the whole population in the processes of propaganda was how the Americanization program (a word which conjures up the 'thought police') came to be transformed into a national celebration day for the fourth of July. To many of us it comes as a shock to discover that American Independence Day had its beginnings in a business-led program to control public opinion, rather than as the direct expression of a nation celebrating its historical birth (see p. 60).

Through his careful and sometimes exhaustive work in detailing the processes, rituals, celebrations, symbols and propagation methods of these crusades, Alex Carey provides us with a historical context to much of the string-pulling behind our thinking.

When he died in 1988 Alex Carey left behind a mountain of papers and articles, many of which had never been sent to any publisher. *Taking the Risk out of Democracy* represents a selection of those papers and articles which, taken together, add up to a history of democratic propaganda in the United States and Australia. If there are gaps in this history it is because the material was written as individual articles and was not originally designed to constitute chapters in a larger corpus. This particular selection of papers may not have been made by Alex, particularly Chapter 3 with its heavy indebtedness to Hartman, but I have included this essay because it covers a significant period in the American history of propaganda, and without it the rest of the book would be less intelligible.

Like most politically active people in Australia in the 1970s and 1980s I knew of Carey's anti-Vietnam writing and speeches, but it was not until I met him in the early 1980s that I became aware of his interests in industrial psychology and propaganda. In a chance meeting with his daughter Cathy in 1988 I was surprised to learn that the bulk of her father's work remained unpublished. In 1992, with the support of Carey's family, I began work on editing this book.

Alex Carey was a rare kind of academic. He was a public intellectual passionately committed to social justice issues. Perhaps one of the reasons for that commitment was that he came to university late.

His parents owned a sheep property near Geraldton in Western Australia and, as the only son, he was required by his father to stay at home and work the farm. Carey's headmaster travelled all the way from Perth to persuade his parents to let him go to university after he finished secondary school, but to no avail. Carey then turned his energies to improving the family property, which had become run down. Though there was much about the life that he liked, it ran against his natural inclinations, yet despite this he became a competent farmer and was known as a good judge of sheep. (This capacity may well have foreshadowed his later work in propaganda.) Eventually the Korean War brought high wool prices and after eleven years Carey was able to sell the family property, which he had managed successfully, and enrol at London University.

Appointed as a lecturer in psychology in 1958 at the University of New South Wales, Carey continued in that position until his death. Over the years he lectured in industrial psychology, industrial relations and the psychology of nationalism and propaganda. Each of these subjects he took outside the classroom as the theoretical basis for his own political activism. Consequently he became very well known to the Australian public on a range of issues. He is best remembered for his outspoken opposition to the Vietnam War, but he was also involved in less public enterprises, for example his influential reports and evidence to government committees and industrial inquiries.

Like everything he did, Alex Carey took his liberal humanism seriously. He was one of the founding members of the Australian Humanist Society in 1960, and one of the society's most public spokesmen. In those days the Humanist Society produced a series of influential reports. One of these was the Sex, Marriage and Divorce Report; when in the mid-1970s the federal Attorney-General, Lionel Murphy, radically rewrote the Family Law Act, the ensuing legislative changes were based almost entirely on that report. Alex Carey also helped to provide the initial stimulus for the formation of the Australian Council for Civil Liberties, an organization which has now largely taken over from the Humanist Society.

Two things about Alex Carey impress. He was a very courageous man and he had tremendous political integrity. On the first count, he never shrank from the personal attacks of the 'mainstream' as represented by business interests and many of his colleagues. A long-time union official who had seen the inside of many industrial disputes told me that he had never witnessed anything to equal the range and ferocity of vilification directed at Carey by several of his colleagues during the course of his work in the industrial area. As for integrity, Carey was held in high regard by the union officials he worked with, both for his applied skills and for his commitment to progressive 'interactive' reforms. More generally, he was an outspoken public intellectual in a country that has a cultural cringe about intellectualism. He said and did what he believed in. One of his strongest convictions was that the material he was studying would provide truths which could change society for the better. He was one of the few academics who understood the complexities of industrial relations because he was willing to 'mix it' with those involved, but he was never willing to forgo, for the sake of fraternal interests, his commitment to new research and rigorous analysis.

This last point is pertinent to this book. If it has any impact on its readers it will come not from its polemics but from the enormous amount of empirical evidence Carey presents. Slowly the reader is overwhelmed by the sheer amount of detail.

Carey's interest in propaganda in democracies grew out of his study of industrial psychology in the 1960s. This interest was fortified in 1978 when he spent twelve months at the Massachusetts Institute of Technology studying with Noam Chomsky. Some of the articles published here were written at that time. Australia has been the recipient of much of the democratic propaganda produced in the United States, and the nature of this 'colonial' relationship is documented in the second part of this book.

What is startling about *Taking the Risk out of Democracy* is how it undermines our commonsense opinions about freedom, liberty and civil rights. We do not have to engage with theories of propaganda, because the nature of this history does not demand that kind of reading. We have only to be able to follow the story of how a minority set of business interests sold their values and perspectives to the rest of society. The selling of these values has been so successful that most of us have taken them on board without any sense of having been brainwashed. Take, for example, the current case of the Young Achievers program where Australian high school students spend twelve months learning how to make a profit by starting up a company. Most of us tend to view this activity as unproblematic. Yet imagine for a moment that we change the subject so that the students spend twelve months learning how to establish and run a trade union. Such an educational activity is likely to be widely denounced as biased, one-sided and 'inappropriate'. Yet what has changed? In both cases a set of economic interests seek to have their values inculcated in the young. That profit over community appears more acceptable is only one indication of the nature and effects of propaganda in our democracies.

Since Alex Carey's death in 1988 the world has changed dramatically with the collapse of communism in Eastern Europe. No longer are the Cold War and the communist bogy available as symbols for mobilizing public opinion in favour of business. Yet while the McCarthy era has passed, the overall effect of such a long history of intolerance and social engineering continues on in many forms. It continues in the declining membership of unions and the 'bad' press unionism generally receives. It is seen in the way environmental policies are automatically inhibited and marginalized as anti-business, anti-progress and therefore anti-social. It is seen in the way the 'free' press of the United States and Australia reacts against proposals to democratize the media. It is seen in the ease with which individuals who seek policies for the betterment of their community are labelled 'Left liberals'. It is apparent in the alienation, racial prejudice and social fragmentation evident in the United States and Australia today.

In Australia the effects of this history of democratic propaganda can be seen in the pervasive idolatry of the 'free market'. In the last decade in almost every sphere of government of all partisan persuasions, the 'free market' has taken precedence over public and community interests. The notion of community interest has lost its traditional central, democratic place and is now referred to as 'non-market' benefits: a marginalized element within a market focus. In this climate it is possible to talk of community health only in terms of the costs to employers of lost production. In this climate it is possible for education to be reformed into a training reform agenda. In the Australian training reform agenda a slippage has occurred between education and training, so that those in charge cannot distinguish between the two. In this agenda successful reform is referred to as 'Competitive Skills for Australians and Australian Enterprises' by the Allen Consulting Group, who in 1994 were asked to review the progress of the agenda. To speed it up we are urged to develop a training 'market' which is centred on direct client-to-trainer providers, to 'customize' courses for industry and to focus on the competitive needs of industry. This is the language of the 'free market' applied to education, which has traditionally been seen as having non-market benefit.

In a climate where there is an almost religious worship of the 'free market' it is possible for a federal Labor government (traditionally representing unions and workers) to set up an Inquiry into a National Competitive Policy. This Hilmer Inquiry has equated 'anti-competitive potentials' with the public interest and seeks to institute measures so that non-market benefits have to prove their worth. This position reverses the democratic 'onus of proof', in that it is democracy which now has to prove its worth to the market, rather than the market proving its worth to the democratic community.

The effects of this history are also to be seen in Australian government policies of privatization and the widespread uncritical acceptance of these policies. Australian governments have always controlled more of the social resources than administrations in the United States. But now in this country there is an assumed, almost habitual, policy of selling off government instrumentalities to private enterprise. The reason? It is now simply accepted that government organizations are always and by definition inefficient. Thus to increase their efficiency it is necessary to sell them off to the private sector. This is the established wisdom that comes from the long heritage of democratic propaganda. Never mind that this wisdom is empirically wrong, as instanced by Telecom Australia, which is one of the most efficient large organizations in the world. The policy assumes that to break it up and sell it off is automatically a progressive move.

The policy of privatization is usually justified by common sense and by 'value-free' words like 'initiative', 'efficiency' and 'competition'. Recently added to this vocabulary are several newly created verbs of business. These are designer words intended to reinvest the old concepts of sacking employees and reducing overheads with new technological meanings that also entail the benefits of a 'free market'. To continue the business program of privatization we are now told of the benefits arising from 'downsizing' and 'outsourcing'. These are new verbs for sacking employees and reducing public bureaucracy by contracting work out to the private sector. The established wisdom is that these words will improve efficiency and competitiveness and will lead to privatization. No one has yet calculated the social cost, the quality of work performed or the overall public benefit of these policies, and no government is likely to be interested while it is taken for granted that the nation's future lies with business interests.

These are the continuing undemocratic effects of nearly a hundred years of democratic propaganda in this country and the United States. This is a history which is important to read and know about so that its gestures and programs of intolerance, alienation and social divisiveness, which will continue on in different forms in the future, can be resisted and changed.

Andrew Lohrey

PART I

CLOSING THE AMERICAN MIND

CHAPTER 1

THE ORIGINS OF AMERICAN PROPAGANDA

In 1942 Henry Wallace coined the phrase 'the century of the common man' to epitomize his belief that American (and world) society would come under the influence of the needs and aspirations of the great mass of ordinary people. He foresaw a society where education, science, technology, corporate power and natural resources would, to an unprecedented extent, be controlled and used in the service of large humane ends rather than in the service of individual power and class privilege (Blum 1973:635–40).

In the United States, which is often seen as the epitome of a modern democracy, the outcome has been very different from Wallace's expectations. The 'common man', instead of emerging triumphant, has never been so confused, mystified and baffled; his most intimate conceptions of himself, of his needs, and indeed of the very nature of human nature, have been subject to skilled manipulation and construction in the interests of corporate efficiency and profit.

It is a central thesis of this chapter that the failure to move significantly towards the 'people's revolution' and the 'century of the common man' foreseen by Wallace is due in important measure to the power of propaganda. For sixty years in the United States propaganda techniques have been developed and deployed to ensure that, though the common man escape the coercive control of political despotism, he will remain manageably in the service of interests other than his own. Domestic propaganda is propaganda directed, not outwards to control or deflect the purposes of some external enemy in wartime, but inwards to control and deflect the purposes of the domestic electorate in a democratic country in the interests of privileged segments of that society.

Academic and practising experts are agreed on what propaganda consists of:

> Propaganda is the management of collective attitudes by the manipulation of significant symbols ... Collective attitudes are amenable to many modes of alteration ... intimidation ... economic coercion ... drill. But their arrangement and rearrangement occurs principally under the impetus of significant symbols; and the technique of using significant symbols for this purpose is propaganda. (Lasswell, Bardson and Janowitz 1953:776–80)

Thus the successful use of propaganda as a means of social control requires a number of conditions: the will to use it; the skills to produce propaganda; the means of dissemination; and the use of 'significant symbols', symbols with real power over emotional reactions — ideally, symbols of the Sacred and the Satanic.

The United States has, for a long time, provided all of these conditions in greater abundance than any other Western country. I shall consider each of these conditions in turn.

The will

Contrary to common assumptions, propaganda plays an important role — and certainly a more covert and sophisticated role — in technologically advanced democratic societies, where the maintenance of the existing power and privileges are vulnerable to popular opinion. In contrast, under authoritarian regimes power and privilege are not open and vulnerable to dissenting public opinion. This was the point made by Robert Brady after an extensive study of business and corporate public relations — a term he uses to cover domestic propaganda. Brady (1943:288–9) concluded that in the United States, Britain, France, Germany, Italy and Japan during the half-century to 1940, 'broadly speaking the importance of public relations ... decreases as one moves away from countries with long and deep-seated liberal, democratic and parliamentary institutions'. Brady argues that Italy and Japan had the least experience of democratic institutions and therefore produced the least competent propaganda. In Germany, where there had been greater, though still limited experience of democratic institutions, 'Nationalist Socialist propaganda was by all means better organised ... more vociferous and more versatile than the propaganda of either Italy or Japan'. At the other end of the scale, that is among countries with the longest experience of liberal, democratic institutions, 'public relations propaganda ... in the United States ... is more highly coloured and ambidextrous than it has ever become, even in England'.

Professor Raymond Bauer (1958:126) comes to a similarly unexpected conclusion from his study of social science in the Soviet Union:

> One area of social science that is ordinarily assumed to be useful to a totalitarian regime is research on social and political attitudes ... Ironically, psychology and the other social sciences have been employed *least* in the Soviet Union for precisely those purposes for which Americans popularly think psychology would be used in a totalitarian state — political propaganda and the control of human behaviour.

It is interesting to contrast these results with the situation in America as described by Harold Lasswell in 1927 when he wrote *Propaganda Techniques in World War I*. Lasswell unjustifiably believed that, in the after-knowledge of the Allied propaganda used during World War I, 'familiarity with the behaviour of the ruling public has bred contempt'. As a consequence he assumed that 'despondent democrats' turned elitist, no longer trusting intelligent public opinion, and therefore should themselves determine how to make up the public mind, 'how to bamboozle and seduce in the name of the public good. Preserve the majority convention but dictate to the majority!' (Lasswell 1971:4–5). Moreover, Lasswell's justification for 'democratic propaganda' indicates a complacency wholly at variance with democratic values but in tune with the interests of private enterprise. Such a view tends to reinforce the legitimate role of propaganda in a democracy. Thus Lasswell can report, uncritically, that within recent years propaganda has become a profession. 'The modern world is busy developing a corps of men who do nothing but study the ways and means of changing minds or binding minds to their convictions. Propaganda ... is developing its practitioners, its teachers and its theories. It is to be expected that governments will rely increasingly upon the professional propagandists for advice and aid.'

Such control through propaganda is, Lasswell concludes, a response to 'the immensity, the rationality, the wilfulness of the modern world. It is the new dynamic of [a] society ... [where] more can be won by illusion than by coercion' (ibid.:34).

Finally, an illustration of democratic propaganda practice in the United States in the 1920s. In 1928–29 the Federal Trade Commission conducted investigations into the multi-million dollar propaganda activities of the private utilities. Mr B. J. Mullaney, director of the utility interests' Illinois 'information committee', produced in testimony a statement that Robert Dahl has described as the 'classic formulation of the importance of indirect techniques' of political influence. Mullaney observed:

When a destructive bill is pending in the legislature it has to be dealt with in a way to get results. I am not debating that. But to depend year after year on the usual political expedients for stopping hostile legislation is short-sightedness. In the long run isn't it better and surer to lay a ground-work with people back home who have the votes, so that proposals of this character are not popular with them, rather than depend upon stopping such proposals when they get up to the legislature or commission. (Dahl 1959:30)

We could agree with Professor Harwood Childs when he contends that 'Americans are the most propagandised people of any nation' (Meier 1950:162).

The skill

Commercial advertising and public relations are the forms of propaganda activity common to a democracy. In the United States over a very long time now these methods have been honed by incomparably more skill and research than in any other country. In the 1940s Drew Dudley, then chief of the Media Programming Division of the Office of War Mobilization and Reconversion, not only observed with satisfaction that 'advertising is peculiarly American', but added on a note of (perhaps rather less well founded) pride that 'Hitler ... employ[ed] the technique of advertising during the pre-war and war years, frequently referring to America's advertising in glowing and admiring terms in *Mein Kampf*, and later utilising advertising's powerful repetitive force to the utmost' (Dudley 1947:106, 108).

The means

United States pre-eminence in the means of communication through which to disseminate propaganda — the scale and reach of the mass media from TV, radio and films to comic strips, nationally and internationally — has long been beyond serious challenge. However, it is the fourth condition, the creation and maintenance of emotionally 'significant symbols', that has given propaganda its extraordinary power and particular role in American culture.

The symbols

The propagandist in the United States starts with advantages deriving from independent features of American society which predispose its members to adopt — or accept — a dualistic, Manichean world-view. This is a world-view dominated by the powerful symbols of the Satanic and the Sacred (darkness and light). A society or culture which is disposed to view the world in Manichean terms will be more vulnerable to control by propaganda. Conversely, a society where propaganda is extensively employed as a means of social control will tend to retain a Manichean world-view, a world-view dominated by symbols and visions of the Sacred and the Satanic.

In addition, US society has a pragmatic orientation. This is a preference for action over reflection. If the truth of a belief is to be sought in the consequences of acting on the belief, rather than through a preliminary examination of the grounds for holding it, there will be a tendency to act first and question later (if at all — for once a belief is acted upon the actor becomes involved in responsibility for the consequences and will be disposed to interpret the consequences so that they justify his belief and hence his action). If it is that American culture, compared with most others, values action above reflection, one may expect that condition to favour a Manichean world-view. For acknowledgement of ambiguity, that is, a non-Manichean world where agencies or events may comprise or express any complex amalgam of Good and Evil — demands continual reflection, continual questioning of premises. Reflection inhibits action, while a Manichean world-view facilitates action. On that account action and a Manichean world-view are likely to be more congenial to and to resonate with the cultural preference found in the United States.

Moreover the kind of evangelical religious belief to which American culture has always been held hostage provides habits of thought already formed to accommodate the Manichean world-view. Some indication of the Manichean distinctiveness of American culture is provided by an International Gallup Poll about religious belief conducted in America and ten European countries in 1968. The poll yielded the following results. More people in America claimed to believe in God (98 percent) and in Heaven (85 percent) than in any other country polled (cf. Britain, 77 percent and 54 percent; France, 73 percent and 39 percent). Similarly 60 percent of Americans claimed to believe in the Devil and 65 percent in Hell (Britain, 21 percent, 23 percent; France, 17 percent, 22 percent). Here too Americans led all the rest, with the single exception that they lost to Greece by 7 points with respect to the Devil. These are surely surprising results in a country characterized by more advanced technological development and a more extended educational process than any other.

The Manichean dichotomy that has been most powerful — as a means of social control — in respect of both domestic issues and foreign policy issues is not God/Heaven versus Devil/Hell but the secular equivalent of these. Thus on the one hand an extravagant idealization of the Spirit of America, the Purpose of America, the Meaning of America, the American Way of Life — the transcendent values by which the United States is represented to the world as the Manifest Destiny of the world in Piety and Virtue (see Morgenthau 1960). On the other hand the extravagant negative idealization of Evil secularized in communism/socialism as *sui generis*, in all places and at all times, malevolent, evil, oppressive, deceitful and destructive of all civilized and humane values.

The most cursory acquaintance with American political propaganda will suggest that the psychological power of almost all such propaganda derives from a calculated exacerbation of American national sentiments. Notions like the American Way of Life, the Meaning of America, the Spirit of America, become symbols with the irrational power of the Sacred, and from an equally calculated exacerbation of American apprehension about the 'alien ideology' of communism and all its allegedly un-American characteristics, communism/socialism, etc., become symbols of the Satanic. So long as these symbol-identifications can be maintained in popular sentiment it is a simple matter to curb popular demand and support for significant reform of the institutions and conditions of American society. By associating welfare provisions and other (selected) government interventions with Socialism/Communism and conversely the Free Enterprise System with Loyalty, Patriotism, Freedom, the American Dream, the American Way of Life, propagandists are doing no more than manipulating appropriate Satanic and Sacred symbols.

The manipulation of patriotic and nationalist sentiments has, above all else, given American anti-communism its remarkable psychological force as a means of social control. Peacetime 'patriotic' hysteria such as characterized the McCarthy period is a phenomenon largely peculiar to the United States among Western countries which have any extended experience with democratic forms of government. Fear of communism as Satanic is largely derived from hypersensitive nationalism. In popular consciousness it comes largely from the representation of communism as threatening the cherished, the secular-sacred idealized 'American Way': threatening, in a word, 'national security' — a term conceived of as broadly as the Middle Ages conceived of defence of the faith against threats and seductions from heretical ideas and agencies.

It is no new notion, of course, that American anti-communism during the postwar decade took on a medieval temper (see Miller 1964; Parenti 1970; Trevor-Roper 1967:53, 93). Nonetheless some illustration in passing may be useful to remind us just how regression toward a superstitious, magical world-view may be induced under the influence of aggravated nationalist faith. In the nineteenth century those who refused to accept the diabolism of old women were pilloried as 'patrons of witches' (Trevor-Roper 1967:48). In the decades after 1946 anyone who argued against the diabolical view of communism was likely to be pilloried as 'soft on communism' or as a 'communist fellow-traveller'.

In the sixteenth century witches were regarded as possessed by (that is, as obedient to remote and magical control by) the Devil. In 1955 a reputable American journal that catered to intellectuals editorialized: 'that [Ho Chi Minh] is our enemy is obvious. He belongs to that particularly dangerous species of men whose nervous system has been rewired to make it obedient to remote control from Moscow' ('Who-What-Why' 1955:8).

During the past sixty years this form of crass stereotyping was made tolerable because of the defeat of a culture of critical consciousness.

CHAPTER 2

THE
EARLY YEARS

The twentieth century has been characterized by three developments of great political importance: the growth of democracy, the growth of corporate power, and the growth of corporate propaganda as a means of protecting corporate power against democracy.

There have been two principal aspects to the growth of democracy in this century: the extension of popular franchise (i.e. the right to vote) and the growth of the union movement. These developments have presented corporations with potential threats to their power from the people at large (i.e. from public opinion) and from organized labour. American corporations have met this threat by learning to use propaganda, both inside and outside the corporation, as an effective weapon for managing governments and public opinion. They have thereby been able to subordinate the expression of democratic aspirations and the interests of larger public purposes to their own narrow corporate purposes.

Corporate propaganda directed outwards, that is, to the public at large, has two main objectives: to identify the free-enterprise system in popular consciousness with every cherished value, and to identify interventionist governments and strong unions (the only agencies capable of checking the complete domination of society by the corporations) with tyranny, oppression and even subversion. The techniques used to achieve these results are variously called 'public relations', 'corporate communications' and 'economic education'.

Corporate propaganda directed inwards, that is, to employees of the corporation itself, has the purpose of weakening the links between union members and their unions. Techniques employed in the United States for this purpose come under the broad disguise of 'human relations', 'employee participation' and 'employee communications'. From the beginning of the century large-scale, professionally organized propaganda campaigns have been a key feature of the political activities of American business.

The use of these tactics to defend business interests against the mass-based power of popular governments and of the labour movement has had large institutional — hence enduring — consequences for American society. Their long-continued use has brought into being a vast complex of institutions which specialize in propaganda and related social science research. This complex of institutions has been created expressly for the purpose of monitoring public opinion and managing it within ideological confines acceptable to American business.

For fifty years US business, alone in the world, made great progress towards the ideal of a propaganda-managed democracy. Since about 1970 business in other countries has begun to adopt the American model. Currently a rapid transfer to Australia of almost all aspects of the American system of ideological control is taking place. This transfer carries a profound threat to the traditionally egalitarian values of Australian society at large, and to its democratic institutions and its union movement in particular.

As already indicated, there are two principal publics to which corporate proselytizing is directed: one within the corporation, one without. American business recognized long ago the political potential of the fact that it has a large proportion of the voting public within its own walls, as a captive audience for 'corporate communications', on every working day of the year. In consequence the present analysis distinguishes between 'external propaganda', which is directed to the general public, and 'internal propaganda' directed to a corporation's own employees and commonly constituting a kind of battle with unions for the minds of the workforce.

Two limitations should be recognized which affect the argument and evidence of this study. The first concerns the paucity of earlier work in the field on which to build, the second the nature of the evidence available.

Despite the likely importance for American society of business propaganda on the vast scale that has developed, the subject has been largely ignored by the relevant scholarly disciplines over some seventy years. The neglect includes, moreover, the role of corporate propaganda in the drastic decline of the American labour movement in recent decades.

In the 1930s and 1940s there was a widely recognized shift in the focus of battle between American corporations and unions from direct violence and picket-line confrontation to a competition for public opinion via the mass media. The change in battleground gave immense advantage to the corporations, whose overwhelming resources, both in funds and in public relations talent, were thereafter targeted on degrading the public standing of unions, and hence the vital legislative support available to them. Yet American students of industrial relations have given scant attention to the importance for the American labour movement of the shift by American business to the conduct of industrial relations via public relations and propaganda.

The subject of the present enquiry also limits the form of relevant evidence. For the subject embraces a 75-year-long multi-billion dollar project in social engineering on a national scale. It is the nature of such an enquiry that it has more the nature of historical research than of a controlled experiment in social science. In consequence evidence surveyed has chiefly the character of correlations between the establishment of nationwide programs of propaganda and dramatic shifts in public opinion of a kind the programs were designed to bring about.

Readers will vary in their judgement about how far the evidence produced justifies a firm conclusion that Western societies face a serious threat from business propaganda to the integrity of their democratic systems. However I believe most people will recognize, at least, the profound importance of the questions raised and the urgency of the need for an end to their long neglect.

Finally, since the concept of propaganda is central to my argument, I should provide some indication of the meaning I attach to it. By 'propaganda' I refer to communications where the form and content is selected with the single-minded purpose of bringing some target audience to adopt attitudes and beliefs chosen in advance by the sponsors of the communications. 'Propaganda' so defined is to be contrasted with 'education'. Here, at least ideally, the purpose is to encourage critical enquiry and to open minds to arguments for and against any particular conclusion, rather than close them to the possibility of any conclusion but one. Of course, in daily life, mixed or 'impure' cases predominate. But when dealing, as in the present study, with the work of public relations and propaganda professionals it is usually possible to apply the distinction without difficulty.

Ironically, even while corporate propaganda overwhelms democracy, it is able to create an ever-strengthening popular belief that the free-enterprise system which sponsors it is some kind of bulwark and guarantor of a democratic society: that is, a society where official policies and values are realistically within the free choice of a majority of ordinary citizens. Indeed it remains, as ever, an axiom of conventional wisdom that the use of propaganda as a means of social and ideological control is distinctive of totalitarian regimes. Yet the most minimal exercise of common sense would suggest a different view: that propaganda is likely to play at least as important a part in democratic societies (where the existing distribution of power and privilege is vulnerable to quite limited changes in popular opinion) as in authoritarian societies (where it is not). It is arguable that the success of business propaganda in persuading us, for so long, that we are free from propaganda is one of the most significant propaganda achievements of the twentieth century.

The first popular challenge

Between 1880 and 1920 in the United Kingdom and the United States the franchise was extended from around 10–15 percent of the populace to 40 or 50 percent (Lippman 1955:39–40). Graham Wallas and A. L. Lowell, leading students of democracy in Britain and the United States, warned as early as 1909 of the likely consequences of this development. Popular election, they agreed, 'may work fairly well as long as those questions are not raised which cause the holders of wealth and power' to make the full use of their resources. But should they do so, 'there is so much skill to be bought, and the art of using skill for production of emotion and opinion has so advanced that the whole condition of political contests would be changed for the future' (Lowell 1926:43).

Four years later, in 1913, a committee of the US Congress was established to investigate the mass dissemination of propaganda by the National Association of Manufacturers (NAM), the leading business organization of the time, for the purpose of influencing legislation by influencing public opinion. The committee appears to have been no little awed by the apparent ambitions of the NAM for meeting the challenge to its interests from popular democracy by controlling public opinion. It reported that the 'aspirations' of the NAM were 'so vast and far-reaching as to excite at once admiration and fear — admiration for the genius that conceived them and fear for the effects which the … accomplishment of all these ambitions might have in a government such as ours' (Lane 1950:58).

The committee's report coincided with the beginning of World War I, during which the Allied governments expended unprecedented resources on the development and dissemination of propaganda to heighten patriotism and hatred. Propaganda became a science and a profession. A campaign launched by President Wilson on America's entry into the war in 1917 filled every home, workplace and leisure activity with its messages. The campaign produced within six months so intense an anti-German hysteria as to permanently impress American business (and Adolf Hitler, among others) with the potential of large-scale propaganda to control public opinion.

Walter Lippman, the eminent journalist, and Edward Bernays, a nephew of Sigmund Freud, served with Wilson's propaganda organization. Bernays led the transfer of wartime propaganda skills to business's peacetime problems of coping with democracy. When the war ended, Bernays (1952:87) later wrote, business 'realized that the great public could now be harnessed to their cause as it had been harnessed during the war to the national cause, and the same methods could do the job'.

The test of this expectation was not long in coming. When the war ended there was a confrontation between American business and labour. Business was determined to roll back the limited union gains made under wartime conditions. The confrontation culminated in the Great Steel Strike of 1919. The central issue of the strike was, in the words of Samuel Gompers, 'the right of wage earners ... to bargain collectively' (Murray 1955:149). At the outset public opinion favoured the strikers, who worked an 84-hour week under notoriously bad conditions.

Five days after the strike began the Steel Corporation launched a campaign of full-page advertisements which urged the strikers to return to work, denounced their leaders as 'trying to establish the red rule of anarchy and bolshevism' and the strike as 'un-American', and even suggested that 'the Huns had a hand in fomenting the strike' (Commission of Inquiry 1921:97, 99). The strike was monitored by a remarkable body called the Interchurch World Movement (IWM) which comprised twenty-six Protestant churches. The IWM produced a two-volume report which concluded that the strike was defeated by 'the strike breaking methods of the Steel companies and their effective mobilisation of public opinion against the strikers through the charges of radicalism, bolshevism and the closed shop. None of which were justified by the facts' and through 'the hostility of the press giving biased and coloured news' (Commission of Inquiry 1920:248). Under the influence of the steel companies the press built up false Red charges to make the public lose sight of the real issues. Historian Robert Murray (1955:152) sums up the consequences:

When the strike ended in 1920 the men had gained not a single conces-
sion ... twenty lives had been sacrificed and ... $112,000,000 ... lost in
wages. Backed by a favourable public opinion which was based on an exaggerated fear of bolshevism, this corporation proved that not even 350,000
striking workers could prevail against it.

The Secretary of Labor of the period, Louis Post (1970), has
described how, supported by corporate interests, the propaganda
assault on public opinion was widened and extended until it produced an anti-Red hysteria about an invented plan by workers and
their leaders to overthrow the government. A McCarthyist period
ensued from 1919 to 1921, more severe, though shorter in duration, than the McCarthy period after World War II. Murray
(1955:17) sums up the consequences for the entire American
society: 'the Great Red Scare soon subsided, but not before the
forces of reaction ... achieved their goal. Civil liberties were left
prostrate, the labour movement was badly mauled, the position of
capital was greatly enhanced, and complete antipathy towards
reform was enthroned'.

Meantime in Europe, where a similar progressive period was not
cut off by a propaganda assault on public opinion, a different result
ensued. Charles Forcey (1961:306) observes that 'after [World War
I] in Great Britain and elsewhere liberal parties gave way to labour
or social democratic groups'. In the United States by contrast politics moved in the opposite direction and 'the socialists during the
twenties virtually disappeared while liberals were reduced to an ineffective few'.

During the 1920s American intellectuals, reflecting on wartime
and postwar experience, believed that democracy had reached a crisis.
'The manufacture of consent ... was supposed to have died out with
the appearance of democracy', Walter Lippman (1932:248–9) wrote.
'But it has not died out. It has, in fact, improved enormously in technique ... Under the impact of propaganda, it is no longer possible ...
to believe in the original dogma of democracy', that is, that it necessarily reflects the popular will in any significant way. Reviewing the
experience of World War I, Professor Harold Lasswell, the leading
American student of propaganda for the next fifty years, reached similar conclusions. In 1927 he warned that with the decline of the
authority of crown, church and social class, and the rise of egalitarian-
ism generally, propaganda had become the principal method of social
control. 'If the mass will be free of chains of iron', he concluded mor-
dantly, 'it must accept chains of silver. If it will not love, honour and
obey, it must not expect to escape seduction' (Lasswell 1971:222).

The second popular challenge

Throughout the 1920s American business had no more problems with democracy or trade unions. However, the onset of the Great Depression changed that situation dramatically. With tens of millions of jobless and hungry, business was initially stunned by the intensity of public hostility. For the first time American business's ideological hegemony over American society was temporarily broken. It became politically and morally respectable to advocate government owner-ship, socialism and even communism, as alternatives to the free-enterprise system (a development which provided a multitude of vic-tims for the second McCarthy period of the 1950s).

By 1934 American business, led by the NAM, had oriented itself for a massive campaign to recapture public opinion. 'Public policies in our democracy are eventually a reflection of public opinion', the NAM warned its members, so public opinion must be reshaped 'if we are to avoid disaster' (Cleveland 1947:323–4). A nationwide assault on public opinion was rapidly co-ordinated. By 1935 the president of the NAM could report to a meeting of business leaders: 'You will note especially that this is not a hit or miss program. It is skilfully coordinated so as to blanket every media … and then … it pounds its message home with relentless determination' (Rippa 1958:60). But while the Depression lasted, even the resources of business and its Red scare tactics could not rapidly prevail. As late as 1938 the NAM's board of directors, in a curiously Marxist for-mulation, still found the 'hazard facing industrialists' to be 'the newly realized political power of the masses'. It warned that unless their thinking was directed, 'we are headed for adversity' (ibid.:62).

The following year the La Follette Committee, a committee of the US Senate which had been established to investigate violations of the rights of labour, incidentally exposed the extraordinary scale of business's assault on public opinion. Of the NAM in particular, the committee reported that it

> blanketed the country with a propaganda which in technique has relied upon indirection of meaning, and in presentation of secrecy and deception. Radio speeches, public meetings, news, cartoons, editorials, advertising, motion pictures and many other artifices of propaganda have not, in most instances, disclosed to the public their origin within the Association. (US Congress 1939:218)

In the same year Lasswell (1939:357), referring to the 'tremendous campaign' that had been conducted by business, concluded that 'for better or for worse' the future of business 'is bound up with propaganda'. Meantime public relations techniques for combating unions had also made progress.

Until the passage of the Wagner Act in 1935, which required management to bargain with representatives of labour, unions had few rights, and attempts to organize workers were commonly met with violence and intimidation. After the Wagner Act the industrialists sought, in the words of the La Follette Committee, 'a new alignment of forces'. That is, they sought, through propaganda and other means, to arouse and organize the public at large 'to do to labour on industry's behalf what the individual employer himself could no longer do legally' (Auerbach 1966:136–7). This tactic, it was reported at the time, 'envisages a public opinion aroused to the point where it will tolerate the often outrageous use of force by police or vigilantes to break a strike' (Chapman 1939:43–7).

The Remington Rand Corporation is credited with having 'perfected' this tactic, whereafter it became known as the 'Mohawk Valley Formula'. The NAM distributed details of the formula to all members in a special release in July 1936. 'In essence the Formula consists', an academic who observed it in action later reported, 'in employer mobilisation of the public ... in a labour dispute' (Sward 1939:66–7). Some excerpts from an account of its use will indicate its more significant features. These features foreshadow the general *subordination of industrial relations to public relations* that developed in the decades after World War II.

The dispute in the steel strike of 1919 was between the CIO and the Bethlehem plant at Johnstown, Pennsylvania, which refused to recognize the steel union. Bethlehem Steel was aided in the dispute

> by the national publicity of the Iron and Steel Institute and the National Association of Manufacturers. Radio programs, outdoor advertising, news services, films, and speakers bureaus deluged the country with anti-CIO propaganda. A full page advertisement in 375 papers at the outset of the CIO steel campaign had cost as much as $314,000. (ibid.:85)

Before the strike began, Bethlehem Steel, the NAM and the local Chamber of Commerce authorized two advertisements. 'One dealt with "Americanism". The other was a standard NAM "harmony" appeal.' During the strike a '"National Citizens' Committee"', which purported to be a spontaneous expression of community sentiment, was launched by local businessmen. The committee engaged an advertising agency and a public relations counsel. More than $62000 in donations was collected. 'The Committee twice broadcast its messages over a national network. Two full page advertisements ... appeared in thirty newspapers in thirteen states at a cost of $64,000.'

After the strike was broken a labor bulletin of the NAM epitomized the rationale of the Mohawk Valley Formula. 'If there ever was a strike that was broken by public opinion and the determination of employees to work, it was the one [at Johnstown]' (ibid.:85, 84, 90, 87).

After the strike James Rand addressed the 'Citizens' Committee' and jubilantly declared: 'Two million businessmen have been looking for a formula like this and business has hoped for, dreamed of, and prayed for such an example as you have set' — an example that, he concluded, would 'go down in history as the Mohawk Valley Formula'. Fourteen years later, in 1950, John Streuben (1950:231) wrote: 'Since then these "scientific" methods of strike-breaking have been applied in every major strike in the country'.

The La Follette Committee summed up the propaganda tactics of the NAM in the 1930s as follows:

> The leaders of the association resorted to 'education' as they had in ... 1912–1921 ... They asked not what the weaknesses and abuse of the economic structure had been and how they could be corrected, but instead paid millions to tell the public that nothing was wrong and that grave dangers lurked in the proposed remedies ... The association also considered its propaganda material an effective weapon in the fight against labour unions. (cited in Tedlow 1976:42)

Tedlow elaborates on the industrial relations methods of the corporations in the 1930s and the shift that occurred between the prewar and postwar periods. In the 1930s 'the corporate public relations apparatus had indeed sought to quell labour unionism'. Wherever the 'most vicious anti-union tactics' had been employed, the public relations apparatus 'had been used in tandem ... to protect the public opinion flank of the conservative corporation'. Thus Republic Steel hired the PR firm of Hill & Knowlton to look after its reputation while it was 'equipping a private army, employing an extensive espionage network, and locking workers out of plants'. Moreover, public relations had aided in the formation of citizens' committees, which acted as a 'vehicle of employee intimidation of workers after direct communication for this purpose was prohibited by the Wagner Act' (ibid.:43). Auerbach concludes in this connection that during the 1930s:

> While none of the steel companies eschewed traditional anti-union practises, they all added a modern refinement, the organisation and manipulation

of public opinion. As one executive explained to the La Follette Committee, 'strike breakers and violence and things of that kind [are] things of the past. The way to win or combat a strike was to organize community sentiment'. (Auerbach 1966:133; emphasis added)

In the 1930s industrial relations were first conducted through campaigns of direct violence and intimidation, with a protective screen of public relations activities; then, after the Wagner Act, by popular hostility and violence calculatedly aroused as a consequence of the company's public relations activities. In the final stage, after the war, the emphasis was shifted almost wholly to public relations. 'Symbolic of this shift', Tedlow (1976:44) observes, 'was a March 1937 *Printers Ink* article which the NAM public relations staff believed to be sufficiently important to merit circulation to Association members'. The article held that, although many manufacturers seemed to think that advertising was of no account as an anti-strike weapon, if they would just invest 'one tenth of the money in advertising preparation that they are apparently quite willing to invest in labour spies, tear gas and other methods, which have proved worse than useless, they will stand a far better chance of winning public support than is possible under present circumstances'. Tedlow concludes that 'most major employers have abandoned strong arm tactics while increasing their investment in public relations'.

During World War II it was necessary for American business to curb its 1930s campaigns, which sought to arouse public anxiety about the Roosevelt administration carrying the country towards communism or fascism. In the last year of the war, however, American business, and the NAM in particular, geared up, as it had after World War I, to beat back both government intervention and the growing power of unions. Beginning in 1945, the postwar conservative assault on public opinion revived the two dominant themes of the 1930s campaigns: identification of the traditional American free-enterprise system with social harmony, freedom, democracy, the family, the church, and patriotism; and identification of all government regulation of the affairs of business, and all liberals who supported such 'interference', with communism and subversion.

The postwar triumph of corporate propaganda

It is impossible, at less than book length, to describe adequately the propaganda onslaught by which, at the cost of the McCarthy period, business first beat back the unions with the Taft-Hartley Act and then secured a shift to conservatism in American politics similar to the shift which followed its campaigns of 1919–20. I shall, however, provide an indicative sampling.

In December 1945 the NAM summarized its use of newspapers and radio during 1945:

> Every day one or more news stories about the NAM appears in newspapers in some part of the country and often in all newspapers in all parts of the country ... On the airlines [this year] NAM members, officers and committees spoke directly with the public for a total of 1,350 hours of time, or 56 full 24-hour days. Their words reached into the homes of Americans and into barracks of Americans stationed in all parts of the world. ('NAM Gets the Story Across' 1945:29)

A Harvard University thesis describes the NAM's propaganda activities during 1946:

> All available media were used to arouse the general public to insist that the country replace bureaucratic control with free competition. A series of four full page advertisements in more than 400 daily and 2,000 weekly newspapers carried the opening message ... For each advertisement a corresponding booklet was printed and distributed by the hundreds of thousands. Special articles were written for magazines, business periodicals and farm papers; the Association's Industrial Press Service carried a steady stream of statements and answers to 4,200 editions of weekly papers, 500 editors of metropolitan dailies and 2,700 editors of trade publications and employee magazines; 'Brief for Broadcasters' told the story to 700 radio commentators, and 'Industry's Views' channelled the Association's beliefs to more than 1,300 editorial writers and columnists. (Cleveland 1947:341)

In the four years from 1946 to 1950 the NAM distributed 18 640 270 pamphlets. Of this number 41 percent went to employees, 53 percent to high school and college students and 6 percent (i.e. still more than one million) to community leaders, including ministers of religion and women's club leaders throughout the entire nation. The NAM reported that the most popular propaganda weapon 'to reach masses of people in both the employee and student market with broad messages' was the full-colour 'comic type' booklet ('NAM Propaganda' 1951:9). Dramatizing the scale of its activities, the NAM reported:

> If all NAM-produced pamphlets ordered for distribution to employees, students and community leaders in 1950 had been stacked one on top of the other they would have reached nearly four miles into the sky — the height of sixteen Empire State Buildings ... a record ... distribution [of] 7,839,039 copies. (ibid.:9)

By 1946 the NAM was only one of a great number of business-sponsored organizations that were co-operating to drench the country with anti-communist, anti-socialist, anti-union and anti-New Deal propaganda. An annual report of the US Chamber of Commerce summarizes one very specific part of its proselytizing activities during 1946–47 — the distribution of large pamphlets of about fifty pages each:

> 1946. More than a million copies of the Chamber pamphlet 'Communist Infiltration in the United States', were distributed — and received with shocked surprise in many quarters.
>
> 1947. 'Communists Within the Government', a Chamber publication, brought screams of anguish not only from known Communists, but from others. A cabinet officer sought its withdrawal. However the government's loyalty program — inadequate but still a loyalty program — was begun. (Chamber of Commerce of the US 1952:31)

In the pamphlet about communists in the government, published in January 1947, the chamber offers an estimate that about 400 communists 'hold positions of importance' in government service in Washington alone. In particular, 'Soviet sympathisers' have, the chamber reports, infiltrated the State Department 'in important numbers'. The chamber specifically recommends a program for dealing with the alleged situation that foreshadowed the worst of the tactics adopted by Senator Joseph McCarthy's committee three years later, after McCarthy claimed to possess a list of 150 communists employed in the State Department (ibid. 1947:13–14).

Pamphlets of the above character were classified as part of the chamber's 'Economic Education' and 'Economic Research' programs. These publications were 'reported to Congress, to the public via radio and television, and widely circulated among writers, speakers, students and teachers' (ibid. 1952:5).

Corporations realized they could use captive audiences of employees for proselytizing purposes. 'Many of the countries [*sic*] largest firms', *Fortune* magazine observed in 1950, 'have started extensive programs to indoctrinate employees'. These programs consisted of so-called 'Courses in Economic Education'. They were given to employees during working hours, in groups of ten to twenty, with tests to measure increase in commitment to the free-enterprise system (Viteles 1954:424–36; Williams and Peterfreund 1954). Sears Roebuck, for example, took three years to produce its own economic education program, which included a series of films and the training of 2600 'meeting leaders'. In 1952 these leaders conducted 71 000 meetings to put Sears's 200000 employees through the course at a total cost of $6 million (Cellier 1953:29–40). The two leading economic education programs, both 'evangelistic' in temper, were produced by Dupont and Inland Steel. By 1953 they had been used with about nine million employees (Cooke 1954:105).

A survey of corporations by the American Management Association (AMA) found 'a good number of respondents actually stated that "propaganda" and "economic education" are synonymous in their companies. 'We want our people to think right.' Communism, socialism and particular political parties and unions, the AMA reported, 'are often common targets of such campaigns', which 'some employers view ... as a sort of "battle of loyalties" with the unions' (Williams and Peterfreund 1954:31, 14, 29).

The American Advertising Council represents large corporations and large advertising agencies. In April 1947 the council announced a $100 million advertising program which, over the next twelve months, would use all media 'to "sell" the American economic system' to the American people. The program was officially described as a 'major project of educating the American people about the economic facts of life' (MacDougall 1952:568–9).

Daniel Bell, then an editor of *Fortune*, provides a perspective on both the scale and the anti-union and anti-New Deal purposes of these campaigns:

> It has been industry's prime concern, in the post war years, to change the climate of opinion ushered in by ... the depression. This 'free enterprise' campaign has two essential aims: to re-win the loyalty of the worker which now goes to the union and to halt creeping socialism [i.e. the New Deal] ... In short the campaign has had the definite aim of seeking to shift the Democratic majority of the last 20 years into the Republican camp ...

Bell sketches some of the resources, created to sell goods but now used in an overwhelming campaign to sell ideas. 'The apparatus itself is prodigious: 1,600 business periodicals, 577 commercial and financial digests, 2,500 advertising agencies, 500 public relations counsellors, 4,000 corporate public relations departments and more than 6,500 "house organs" with a combined circulation of more than 70 million.' Of the opinion-shaping product Bell observes: 'The output is staggering. The Advertising Council alone, in 1950, inspired 7 million lines of newspaper advertising stressing free enterprise, 400,000 car cards, 2,500,000,000 radio impressions ... By all odds it adds up to the most intensive "sales" campaign in the history of industry' (Bell 1954:254).

American business's pre- and postwar assaults on public opinion had a double objective: to turn the public against the Democratic administration of Roosevelt and Truman and their liberal supporters, and to turn it against the growing power of the trade union movement that resulted from the Wagner Act of 1935. The first objective was achieved with the McCarthy period and the election of Eisenhower in 1952. Progress towards the second objective began in 1937. There was in that year an unprecedented number of strikes, chiefly over demands for the recognition of unions provided by the Wagner Act. From 1937 onwards the high level of strikes, suspicion of union power and internal union problems 'all contributed to a shift in public attitudes', as did corporate propagandists, who 'using all the devices of modern communication did everything they could to encourage this shift' (Wilcock 1961:308).

During the war business made unprecedented profits while wages remained controlled. When the war ended business had, in addition to its long-term objective of weakening the union movement, two immediate concerns: to minimize wage rises and maximize price rises. It will be instructive to consider the methods by which all of these results were sought. Daniel Bell (1954:250–1) has described the circumstances:

> Wage rates during the war had been tethered by The Little Steel Formula, although income had risen because of extra overtime work. Now, as the work week fell, labour opened a drive to maintain take-home pay. Industry decided to sit tight. The result [in 1946] was the greatest strike year in American history ... In none of [the strikes] ... did industry attempt the violence and back-to-work measures of the late thirties. The counter action came through the legislator ... The fact that labour was powerful enough to shut down a whole industry lent colour to middle class fears that Big Labour was running the country. Each national strike ... with the attendant publicity about the economic effects, had given rise to outcries for action.

At the 1946 elections 'labour problems' was one of the chief political issues on which the Republicans won control of Congress. Shortly afterwards the NAM drafted a new labour law and arranged for its submission to the new Congress. 'Except for a ban on industry-wide bargaining', Bell observes, 'the Taft-Hartley Act passed [in 1947] embodied [the NAM's proposals] completely'. Not surprisingly, 'it placed tremendous obstacles in the way of new organisation' of workers (Brandeis 1957:232). 'Public opinion, however muddled', Bell (1954:250–1) concludes, 'was the force which backed the new curbs on unions enacted in the post-war years'. Bell's judgement is supported by Jack Barbash (1948:198), who observes that 'the General Motors strikes, like most of the other important strikes in the 1945–6 upsurge, were fought not on the picket line … but in Washington and in the press and over the radio'. The outcome was that while the unions won the strikes business won the public relations battle — with the Taft-Hartley Act as its prize.

Apart from the years affected by the Korean War, the American labour movement was never again able to increase the (low) proportion of the workforce it had organized. Thirty years later, in the face of a renewed public relations propaganda onslaught by business in the 1970s, organized labour in the United States went into a steep and possibly terminal decline. It will therefore be worthwhile to look more closely at the public relations aspects of the 1945–46 strikes.

Business, which had bred and trained a public relations profession for thirty years, conducted detailed opinion polls to monitor the impact of the strikes on public opinion. The following excerpts are from a report of polls conducted for business during December 1945 and February 1946:

> Strikes have held the limelight … for the better part of the year … Now, with the culmination of major strikes in the manufacturing industry, management has asked for a checkup on the after-effects. The resulting survey is directed to two questions: How well did the struck companies play their hand? Did the unions gain or lose in public favour? In short, what have we learned from the strike? Here is a report of public thinking during the last half of February, nearing the close of the auto and steel disputes …

The present survey, the authors observe, permits 'a direct comparison' with a similar survey in December 1945. In both cases the public's reactions 'yield guide posts for handling strikes in the future'. For 'a strike is not only a test of economic strength, it is a public relations problem of primary importance … Smart managements give as much attention to public relations aspects of strikes as to economic and legal aspects'. For 'people don't like strikes. Strikes stir up public emotion — leave lasting impressions … People pay close attention to strikes. Therefore a strike is a potent public relations vehicle' (Opinion Research Corporation 1946:i–ii).

The public relations aspects of the strikes were found to be very satisfactory to business. Both the December 1945 and February 1946 surveys show that 'unions came off worse with public relations than companies … The unions show a large net loss, the companies a small net gain'. About 80 percent of respondents found no fault with the way companies handled the strikes, and in comparing companies and unions, many more respondents considered the companies to have shown a greater regard for the public interest than the unions. It was a tribute to the public relations expertise of business that respondents made these judgements. Yet at the same time respondents believed the profits of companies were enough to meet pay rises without raising prices. One explanation for this apparently contradictory view is that profits were not the subject of a public relations campaign, whereas unions and strikes were.

Perhaps most significantly of all, one-third of union members among respondents became less favourably disposed to the unions, and one-quarter more favourably disposed to the companies over the period of the strikes. In addition, most union members considered that the unions displayed no more regard for the public interest than the companies. No wonder Truman could not block the Taft-Hartley Act twelve months later. The principal concrete criticism of unions is found to derive from their association in the public mind with mass picketing and related violence (ibid.:2, A10, A21, A7, A18, A15).

This was truly a propaganda victory. For there was, Barbash (1948:140) reports, 'practically no violence in the strike wave of 1945-7'. But that did not lessen the seriousness of the political consequences. The mid-term elections of 1946 'marked labour's worst defeats since Hoover's day'. In the words of the CIO it was 'a signal defeat for the liberal and labour voters of America' (Vale 1971:101).

So much for American business's tactics for dealing with the industrial relations of wage rises and union power via public relations. It remains to consider the use of the same tactics to secure uncontrolled price rises. The propaganda campaign to be described is of particular interest in that it provides in microcosm a picture of the techniques that are periodically employed on a much vaster scale to manage democracy more generally in the interests of American business.

Prices

After World War II, President Truman sought to continue price controls while civilian goods remained in short supply by extending the life of the Office of Price Administration (OPA). Business, as represented by the NAM and the Chamber of Commerce, launched a massive campaign against OPA, which ranged from full-page ads to leaflets stuffed in housewives' shopping bags. They tried to convince the public 'that price controls themselves were the cause of shortages and inflation; they argued that removal of controls would bring a vast increase in production and reasonable prices' (Rayback 1966:392).

Two agencies integral to business's mind-managing apparatus monitored public opinion on this issue: the Opinion Research Corporation and the Psychological Corporation. A poll conducted in February 1946 found that most people believed prices had been held down 'pretty well' so far and gave 'much credit' to OPA. Eighty-one percent favoured OPA's continuation (Opinion Research Corporation 1946:8, A32). A year later the Psychological Corporation reported: 'One of the most sweeping reversals of public opinion we have encountered since our first poll in 1932 is that toward the OPA'. In spring 1946, the report continues, 'several polling organisations showed substantial majorities in favour of OPA'. Yet by October 1946 only 26 percent were in favour of OPA (Link 1947b:134–5).

The operation of OPA was first curtailed in July 1946 and then terminated in November. President Truman subsequently described the events which intervened between the earlier and the later polls:

> Right after the end of the war, big business in this country set out to destroy the laws that were protecting the consumer against exploitation. This drive was spear-headed by the National Association of Manufacturers, the most powerful organisation of big business in the country ...
>
> We know how the NAM organised its conspiracy against the American consumer. One of its own officers ... spilled the story ... after price control was killed ... [He] told how his organisation spent $3,000,000 in 1946 to kill OPA. The NAM spent a million and a half on newspaper advertising. They sent their own speakers to make a thousand talks before women's clubs, civic organisations and college students. A specially designed publication went to 37,000 school teachers, another one to 15,000 clergymen, another one to 35,000 farm leaders, and still another to 40,000 leaders of women's clubs. A special slipsheet with NAM propaganda went to 7,500 weekly newspapers and to 2,500 columnists and editorial writers ...
>
> This is what the NAM had to say about the result of their three-million-dollar propaganda campaign ... [When] NAM started the campaign against OPA, a survey showed that 85 percent of the people believed OPA was absolutely necessary. In November, 1946, after the campaign ... only 26 percent of the people believed that OPA was vital. (Schnapper 1948:84–5)

During 1946 Congress first diminished, then destroyed, the Office of Price Administration. As a consequence, between June and December 1946, consumer prices rose by 15 percent, with food prices rising 28 percent. The rise more than cancelled the wage increases labour had secured from the 1946 strikes and so real wages dropped from $32.50 a week to less than $30.00. This was the lowest figure since American entry into the war. 'In the meantime corporate net profits soared to the highest point in history, reaching $12,500,000,000 — 20 percent higher than in the best war year' (Rayback 1966:393).

And so the conduct of industrial relations became a subordinate aspect of public relations which once again left management triumphant and the unions nowhere.

After World War II, as after World War I, the United States turned politically Right while Europe turned Left. Each of these shifts of opinion in the United States coincided with a large-scale assault on public opinion. In January 1947 Melton Davis, public relations officer with the State Department's European service, observed the contrast and suggested a cause.

> Smart public relations [has] paid off as it has before and will again ... [and] it wasn't labour's public relations. The public opinion climate, the thing that makes social change easy or difficult, has changed completely in America. While the rest of the world has moved to the left, has admitted labour into government, has passed liberalized legislation, the United States has become anti-social change, anti-economic change, anti-labour. It is not moving to the right, it has been moved — cleverly — to the right. In France, England, Italy there have also been shortages, difficulties in controlling prices, labour troubles, strikes. Yet in each, labour and the left have continued winning elections. In America ... labour and liberals are fair game today ... [They] find themselves grouped with anarchists ... with the defunct IWW ... with communists. (Davis 1947:24)

Propaganda within the corporation

I have sketched some of the main aspects of business's propaganda and public relations activities external to the corporation. The parallel developments within corporations extended this propaganda in ever more subtle ways. The Wagner Act, as we have seen, led to a shift in external tactics from direct intimidation of unions to (indirect) stimulation of public hostility against unions. An analogous development occurred within corporations. The Wagner Act made company unions illegal as a means of guaranteeing independent unions. It led to a search by corporations for less formal systems of management–worker communication that could be used to preempt independent unions without breaking the letter of the Wagner Act.

This search was known officially as the 'human relations'

movement and is described in more detail in Chapter 9. It embraced notions such as 'employee participation', 'employee communication' and 'democratic decision-taking'. The movement did not exist in 1937. Yet by 1942 Robert Brady reported that the Hawthorn studies, the symbol and supposedly scientific foundation of the human relations movement, had achieved 'an extraordinary influence in the American personnel literature' (Brady 1943:284).

When, at the end of the war, American business returned to an all-out onslaught on public opinion and on unions, vast amounts of money suddenly became available for the study of 'human relations' in industry — research on techniques of communication between management and workers, on techniques of small-group leadership, on ways of influencing worker attitudes (Carey 1976a:240–2). In four years from 1947, Will Herberg (1951:590) observes, 'perhaps more new books and studies have been published on [the subject of human relations in industry] than in all the preceding years'.

The flood of corporate funding for research on communication, attitudes and behaviour in work groups that began in the late 1940s continued to swell. During the decade of the 1950s there were four times as many studies of small groups published in social science journals as in all previous history (Deutsch 1968:265). By contrast social and political scientists gave virtually no attention to the import for democracy of management's vast new ventures in attitude and opinion control. In 1959 Professor Robert Dahl of Columbia University documented the remarkable extent of this neglect and sharply defined the issue at stake. How much of the generally favourable attitudes of Americans toward business, he asked, 'can be attributed to deliberate efforts to manipulate attitudes?' He continued:

> Much in the way of political theory ... depends on the assumptions one makes about the sources of political attitudes ... If one assumes that political preferences are simply plugged into the system by leaders (business or other) in order to extract what they want from the system, then the model of plebiscitory democracy is substantially equivalent to the model of totalitarian rule. (Dahl 1959:37–8)

There could scarcely be a more profoundly important question for a democratic society to confront. Yet the refusal to face it by intellectuals and social scientists has become a special characteristic of social science in the United States.

CHAPTER 3

THE FIRST AMERICANIZATION MOVEMENT

Popular economic proselytizing is common practice in the United States. American corporate capitalism has, since shortly after the turn of the century, directly intervened with vast, popular propaganda programs on behalf of its values and institutions whenever and wherever popular sentiment within the nation was judged to be taking uncongenial forms. These programs have had much of the temper of secular Billy Graham crusades, though with a greater reach and pervasiveness. The first among them was the pre-World War I Americanization program launched in 1912. Its most active sponsors were chambers of commerce and associated business interests. The crusade later merged with the fervour of the war, and then emerged after the war's end as a distinct nationalistic program pursued by industrial interests.

The broad political background and the immediate industrial context of the original crusade are of special interest because they form part of a pattern that is substantially repeated with each further Americanization crusade of subsequent decades. The pattern has three principal components. (1) A threat (real or imagined) from outside the United States achieves a dramatic impact on popular consciousness. (2) This effect occurs at a time when liberal reforms and popular hostility to the large corporations and the power they exercise are perceived by conservative interests as a profound threat from inside the US social and political system. (The reforms generally have to do with some improvement in the legal and political position of organized labour and with a parallel check, through increased regulation, to the position of organized capital.) Finally (3), the two perceived threats merge, to the discredit of the internal reforms and of any political party, persons or policies associated with them.

In respect of external developments: from 1890 to 1910 a vast influx of immigrants aroused popular fears that traditional American social values and institutions were threatened by alien influences.

In respect of internal developments: the period of Theodore Roosevelt's presidency (1901–12) saw legislative action aimed at curtailing the power of trusts and combines and providing some legal protection to unions. The large, elitist and ideologically conservative American Federation of Labor tripled its membership from 600 000 to 1 800 000 over this period. The small radical anarcho-syndicalist Industrial Workers of the World (IWW) was founded in 1905. Its leaders loudly proclaimed to millions of impoverished immigrants and others a path of violent revolution as the only solution to labour's condition. From the founding of the IWW the federal government saw internal security problems largely in terms of this body. The significance of this reaction was that it set a pattern for all subsequent ideological crusades in the United States. Each one has been portrayed in terms of an internal security problem which has been seen as a communist threat.

Two developments were of particular importance for the response of the public and of industrial interests to the IWW. Between 1909 and 1912 the IWW — with extensive liberal support — won a series of free-speech fights against suppression of their proselytizing and propaganda activities that caused great consternation. In February 1912 the IWW won a dramatically successful strike among foreign-born workers at Lawrence, Massachussets, which brought it to the peak of its membership (60 000), influence and fame.

By 1912 these developments contributed to arouse business interests to energetically promote the need for an Americanization campaign for the foreign-born — in modern terms, a campaign for cultural cleansing. The development which galvanized business into action in this connection was the active liaison in the Lawrence strike between the IWW, with its radical message, and dissatisfied foreign workers. This liaison would lend itself to the creation in the public's mind of images depicting a violent alliance between a foreign immigrant threat to American culture and a radical labour threat to American institutions. As in the later McCarthy period, liberals and unions would be caught up by association (real or fancied) with one or another aspect of the radical-alien-subversive bogey. All significant sources of criticism of the status quo (i.e. liberals and unions) could then be discredited and reaction entrenched.

The nationwide crusade on behalf of an Americanization program by chambers of commerce and associated interests from 1912 largely achieved the required dramatization of a combined foreign and domestic threat in the form of an alien workforce captured by a radical union movement. However, developments thereafter were complicated by the interruption of the war years, so that full-scale popular retreat into conservatism and suppression was not achieved until 1919–20.

This chapter traces in some detail the rise of the Americanization movement before the war; its blurred continuation during the war as an integral part of an extravagantly nationalistic propaganda campaign launched to unite all Americans, native and foreign-born, behind the war effort; and finally the revival in 1919–20 of the distinct apprehensions and goals of the original Americanization campaign, again in the context of confrontations between organized business interests and organized labour.

Beginnings

From 1880 to 1910 there was a large growth in immigration to the United States. But there was an even more rapid change in the principal sources of immigrants, from north-west Europe to areas of eastern and southern Europe that were relatively depressed both economically and culturally. By 1890 some popular concern had developed about the impact of so many (often illiterate) newcomers, with their foreign languages and foreign customs, on American society.

During the 1890s and until about 1904 the considerable agitation that developed was primarily (and unsuccessfully) directed to obtaining some restriction on the annual intake of immigrants. Organized labour, religious groups and racist groups (but not employer interests) were prominent in this agitation. Unlike the other groups, labour's objections to the newcomers were chiefly of an economic nature.

Labour, in particular, reacted in a very hostile manner to immigrants from southern and eastern Europe because of their comparatively lower standards of living, their docility in the face of the most trying labour situation and their use by the industrialists to break strikes and destroy collective bargaining. American labour leaders naturally viewed the immigrants as a definite menace to the struggle to raise wages and reduce hours, at that time in its infancy.

After 1900 an alternative and more generous movement developed that actively assisted in immigrant assimilation. Some patriotic and religious organizations undertook to provide instruction in English and in citizenship rights and duties, as well as other practical assistance, to substantial numbers of immigrants. Most notable among these was the YMCA, which by 1912 had helped 55 000 immigrants learn English and was offering training in English and

rudimentary education about American society at about 300 branch-
es throughout the United States (Hartman 1948:23–9).

When the YMCA began this work, in 1907, the annual intake
of immigrants from southern and eastern Europe alone approached
one million. Moreover, in many industrial centres of the north-east
and middle west, where the immigrants mainly congregated, their
working and living conditions were appallingly depressed. Hence
the educational and material assistance provided by the YMCA and
others remained wholly inadequate to the scale of the problem.

Against this background, support for a national program to assim-
ilate the immigrant developed. A substantial pressure group was not
long in forming and as a result of its efforts the movement was inaugurated which culminated eventually in the Americanization crusade
of the years immediately preceding, accompanying and following
World War I. This movement, Hartman observes, 'offered a program
which would solve the problem of the immigrant with the least dis-
turbance to the economic and political life of the nation; a program
which would not result in the loss of an exceedingly valuable labour
supply to America' (ibid.:8).

In February 1907 the YMCA sponsored a conference in New
York of interested persons to form an organization to accomplish the
civic betterment of the immigrant. Thus was born the first of the
active Americanization groups, the North American Civic League
for Immigrants (NACLI). The league was composed of the more conservative economic interests. Its president was W. Chauncy Brewer,
lawyer and later executive head of the Boston Chamber of
Commerce; its vice-president was Bernard J. Rothwell, industrialist
and president of the Boston Chamber of Commerce. 'The organisation of the League reflected that fear for the continued safety of
American institutions which was so current during the first decade
of the 20th century ... The League ... can be said to have inaugurated the movement to Americanize the immigrant' (ibid.:38–41).

The first work of the league was to conduct an investigation into
conditions among the immigrants. It found them to be generally
deplorable and that, perhaps in consequence, immigrants frequently
came under the influence of 'mischievous radicals'. In the two years
to 1909 the league did much to direct the attention of civic and
charitable bodies to the needs of immigrants.

A separate branch of the NACLI known as the New York (later
New York-New Jersey) Committee of the NACLI was established in
December 1909. Comprised almost wholly of corporate executives,
the NY–NJ Committee rapidly assumed leadership in its region, as

had the parent body in New England. The committee undertook many activities of benefit to immigrants including preparation of a course in citizenship for use in night schools.

In March 1910 the league organized a conference of New England industrial leaders. Not surprisingly the conference unanimously endorsed the work of the league and recommended heartily continued support of the league's program both as a means of 'self-preservation' from the menace of the immigrant and because of its economic value. In December 1910 a similar conference of industrial leaders heard a report from the Federal Immigration Commission, which had been set up four years earlier to investigate the whole question of immigration. The commission's chairman fully endorsed the work of the league and its concerns about the social and political circumstances of immigrants. Its official report attracted wide attention for the remedial action of the kind proposed by the league (ibid.:88–90, 68).

The 1910 conference generated considerable enthusiasm over the possibility of co-operation between the league and the industrial interests in bringing the immigrants into the 'right relations' with the American people and institutions. A New England Industrial Committee was formed, consisting of fifteen men prominent in the New England industrial world, to devise ways and means of aiding the league in its work.

This committee worked out a plan to rally industrial opinion behind the league. It also undertook an investigation into industrial conditions in the New England textile cities of Lawrence, Lowell, Haverhill and Manchester, all of which had been marked by unrest and agitation among crowded colonies full of non-Americanized foreigners. Hartman observed that 'the recent IWW outbreaks in the New England section ... had aroused fear of an increase in radicalism among the immigrant working-class population of that area'. The investigation, based at Lawrence, 'confirmed the worst fears of the Committee in regard to the increasing radicalism of the immigrant worker'. In reaction the league called for financial aid to support work in the area, and distributed widely among the workers a pamphlet entitled 'Respect the Law and Preserve Order' which cautioned foreigners about 'the desirability of allying themselves with the orderly part of the communities in which they lived' (ibid.:90–1).

The influence of the IWW

From the IWW's founding in 1905 until 1909 it was of little significance, politically or industrially. From 1909, however, a series of confrontations over free speech gained the IWW a national reputation for 'unbeatable militancy'. The revolutionary propaganda of the IWW enraged the average American citizen. But locking the IWW speaker up simply called forth a succession of soapbox orators who jammed the city jails until town fathers were willing to give in. According to Preston, in the free-speech fights the IWW fought the propertied classes and civil authorities to a standstill and won. With the Bill of Rights supporting the IWW, there seemed no legal way to silence them.

> From Spokane in 1909 to San Diego in 1912, through Washington, Montana, South Dakota, Minnesota, Wisconsin, Pennsylvania, Massachusetts, Missouri and Colorado the IWW['s] … defence of the First Amendment had somehow become subversive and seditious, while the non-violent resistance of IWW speakers left Americans scared and perplexed. Citizens felt themselves being dragged into the deep water of anarchy by an uncontrollable current of protest. (Preston 1963:44)

The next major activity of the IWW, the textile strike at Lawrence, was even more important for the growth of the Americanization movement. Harris (1938:313–28), describing the background and course of the strike, tells us that by 1900 from 70 to 90 percent of all operatives in the New England textile mills were foreign-born. The Lawrence workers earned 'destitution' wages. They had for years been forced 'to live in slums … with as many as 17 people to five rooms'. One in six children died before their first birthday. Those who survived had rickets and the diseases of malnutrition. On 11 January 1912 about 25 000 foreign-born workers 'rebelled against the Woolen Trust as represented chiefly by the American Woolen Company'. Because their appeals had been long rejected by the American Federation of Labor, the textile workers invited Joseph Ettor of the IWW (to which only about 4 percent of their members belonged) to come to Lawrence and take charge of the strike (ibid.:313–15).

Following Ettor's arrival hundreds of militiamen were called out to patrol the mills; stocks of dynamite were planted to discredit Ettor and the strikers ('a local undertaker confessed that he had planted it at the behest of company and police officials'); a Citizens Committee of company officials and local notables was formed to denounce the strike as an anarchist plot; and 'thugs were hired to derail street cars and smash their windows in order to accuse the strikers of "un-American violence"' (ibid.:319–21).

On 29 January a woman weaver among the strikers was killed by a bullet 'presumably fired by a police officer'. Ettor and another IWW official were arrested and charged with being accessories to the murder and imprisoned. They were later acquitted amid strong international protests. Martial law was declared, picket lines overrun and workers arrested (ibid.:321–2).

In order to ease human problems associated with the strike, the unionist Strike Committee made arrangements to board children of strikers with friends and sympathizers away from Lawrence. After one shipment of 119 children had been welcomed at Grand Central Station, New York, on 10 February by cheering crowds of workers, the marshal of Lawrence and the head of the militia (Colonel Sweatser), banned further trainloads of such 'ambassadors for the strikers' cause'. When on 24 February the Strike Committee tried to send a further forty children to Philadelphia, children, mothers and guardians gathered at the Lawrence station were clubbed by the police with a ferocity usually reserved for criminals. A pregnant woman was beaten unconscious and her unborn child died. These actions had disastrous political consequences.

> The nation was horrified, and its editors outraged, by the vision of defenceless women and children battered and bruised by officers of the law … The protests of a nationally aroused social conscience whipped about the heads of the mill operators until they were frightened by the repercussions of the barbarity they themselves had fostered … Early in March [1912] they retreated step by step … until on March 12 the American Woolen Company granted all of the strikers' demands. (ibid.:323–5)

After nine and a half weeks the strikers had gained one of the few unequivocal victories in the history of American labour to that date. Yet although the victory was dramatic and apparently complete it was also short-lived. The IWW and its revolutionary-minded leaders were organizationally and temperamentally equipped for hard-fought battles with employers, not for maintaining day-by-day defence of workers' interests against erosion. In a short time managements at Lawrence introduced programs which offset the gains that had been won.

The Americanization movement after Lawrence

The early apprehension on the part of the conservative Industrial Committee (of the NACLI) about the circumstances in the New England textile mills had proved prescient enough. The league moved quickly to counter the success of the strike at Lawrence. On

29 February, five days after the battering of women and children that led to the public outcry, the Boston Chamber of Commerce and the league held a joint meeting about immigration. The meeting, which comprised a large gathering of business and industrial representatives, was addressed by Brewer (president of the league and executive head of the chamber), Rothwell (vice-president of both league and chamber) and Colonel Sweatser, who was in charge of the militia at Lawrence during the current strike. The meeting stressed the need for an increase in vigilance in regard to the immigrant situation.

Shortly after the Lawrence strike, in the spring of 1912, the league instituted a campaign to awaken the various chambers of commerce and boards of trade to a realization of their duties as the conservators of the 'best interests' of their communities. These duties required recognition that the industrial future of the country depended largely upon the education of the adult alien workers in industry. Chambers of commerce and other business organizations over a wide area responded to the call to arms, so that in a short time, Hartman (1948:92–6) observes,

> the Americanizers had succeeded in arousing an interest in their campaign among the various commercial and industrial bodies of the New England area; they had inaugurated a movement which was to spread to the Middle Atlantic States and the middle west until practically every chamber of commerce or similar organisation of every municipality of significance containing an alien population had a special immigration committee taking a vigorous and active part on behalf of the Americanization of the immigrant.

Through the prewar years the league continued to push its program with chambers of commerce, church organizations, boards of trade and manufacturing groups throughout New England. In consequence, when the Americanization drive reached its height in the war years it found a population receptive to propaganda and ideological control.

While the parent organization continued its concerted drive to rally the industrial interests behind its program of Americanization, the NY–NJ Committee of the league decided, early in 1914, to extend its program to the entire nation. It therefore changed its name to the 'Committee for Immigrants in America' (CIA). Thereafter its activities were enlarged on a national scale until it became, as Hartman (ibid.:96–7) reports, 'the spearhead and guiding genius of the attack upon the unassimilated status of the immigrant' and 'the general consulting headquarters for immigrant and Americanization work throughout the country'.

In April 1914 the CIA proposed that the Federal Bureau of Education should sponsor the Americanization program. This was the first step in extending the campaign nationwide and also in giving it an official and legitimate stamp of approval. Such legitimacy is important if propaganda is to be widely and uncritically accepted. The bureau proved sympathetic but had no funds available. Undeterred, the CIA provided both the necessary money and a complete staff of investigators and other experienced personnel to run the program from the Federal Bureau of Education.

As a consequence of this 'generosity' a special Division of Immigrant Education was established within the Federal Bureau of Education. It was of course headed and run by CIA staff. Late in 1914 this new division set to work to develop a comprehensive program of re-education for the foreign-born. This campaign of Americanization continued for five years, until the division closed in July 1919, when the federal government finally decided that it could no longer accept financial aid from private organizations. (Coincidentally this was at a time when business began to view the Americanization program as less important.)

As the division was unable to obtain public funding for its activities it focused largely on publicity and promotion of the 'Americanization problem'. This was done through bulletins, circular letters and press releases. However, extra federal government assistance was close at hand. Late in 1913 the Federal Bureau of Naturalisation held conferences with the Secretary of Labour, school principals, government officials and of course business organizations about a 'nation-wide plan for citizenship preparedness through the Americanization of the resident alien body'. In this way the Bureau of Naturalisation joined the Americanization movement. Its plan was to work with public schools to sponsor a publicly funded system of citizenship classes throughout the nation. The bureau's plan for the betterment of citizenship would be extended to every hamlet in the United States. Schools were to be involved with the programs for 'assembling' candidates for naturalization and to conduct patriotic classes and exercises. This was a plan that the special Division of Immigrant Education had itself hoped to operate.

Summing up developments in the period 1910–14, Hartman says that it had 'witnessed a marked heightening of interest in the Americanization of the immigrant largely due to the industrial strikes and disorders of the period'. The NACLI had begun the process of lining up the industrial interests in support of the movement, while its daughter organization, the NY–NJ Committee, had undertaken to push the movement on a national scale. Both federal bureaus, of Education and Naturalisation, had entered the lists and had begun plans for the sponsoring and strengthening of the movement. *'The stage was set for a grand campaign of action in support of Americanization when the opportune moment should arrive'* (ibid.:103–4; emphasis added).

The pursuit of state legislative support and funding

From 1910 to 1914 the NACLI directed much effort to obtaining both state and federal legislative support and funding for the Americanization program. In these four years six of the states had taken action of one sort or another in support of the program outlined by the NACLI and its affiliated groups. To this extent the Americanizers had been successful in their efforts to obtain government support for their pet project. Henceforth they could depend upon the legitimacy provided by the new state agencies in their further efforts to arouse the country to a fuller appreciation of the magnitude of the problem of the 'resident alien body'.

During 1910 the NACLI was chiefly responsible for legislation by the State of New York, which created a special Bureau of Industries and Immigration. The new bureau was given responsibility for bringing about the rapid assimilation and Americanization of the resident immigrants. It was required to investigate the conditions of immigrants in New York State and recommend measures for their protection, assistance and assimilation. Miss Frances Kellor, secretary of the NY–NJ Committee, was appointed as the bureau's chief investigator.

Following NACLI'S success in New York State the NY–NJ Committee drew up a special bill to provide for a State Immigration Commission in New Jersey. The bill was passed in 1911 but no state funds were provided for it, with the result that the commission's work had to be funded by the NY–NJ Committee and private donations. At the same time the NACLI drafted a similar bill for a Massachusetts Commission which was passed in May 1913. The Massachusetts Commission was headed by Bernard J. Rothwell, vice-president of the NACLI and president of the Boston Chamber of Commerce.

In 1913 California and Pennsylvania, and in 1914 Rhode Island, established similar agencies to investigate the problem of the immigrant and recommend remedial action. In the case of Rhode Island the agency's activities were again handicapped because no funds were made available to it.

Americanization becomes patriotic

Up to 1914 the Americanization movement had not succeeded in capturing the mind of the American public and had made limited progress in obtaining the support of public funds. Despite the active propaganda of the North American Civic League for Immigrants, the Committee for Immigrants in America, and the two federal bureaus of Education and Naturalisation, the public remained largely indifferent. However, this situation changed in 1915, mainly as a consequence of the war in Europe. The war stimulated intense nationalist feelings and a growing suspicion of all things alien as certainly 'un-American' and possibly subversive. Many Americans began to suspect that the prior allegiance of immigrants and national minorities might be to their old rather than their new country.

Thus in 1915 an atmosphere of suspicion and distrust of the immigrant provided a much more receptive audience for the Americanizers than they had ever found before. 'The time was ripe', says Hartman (1948:105–9), 'for a campaign of crusading proportions'. In the summer of 1915 plans carefully laid by the Federal Bureau of Naturalisation six months earlier blossomed into the full crusade.

At the suggestion of the bureau arrangements were made for President Wilson to speak at a highly dramatized 'patriotic' reception for 5000 newly naturalized citizens at Philadelphia on 10 May 1915. Immediately before the reception the bureau had publicized the campaign widely throughout the entire school system. Wilson's address affirmed his dislike and suspicion of what he called 'hyphenated Americans' and stressed the idea 'that those who thought of themselves as belonging to a particular national group in America had not yet become Americans'. As a result of the President's widely publicized address 'a wave of patriotic sentiment was aroused' and Americanization committees were 'formed in cities throughout the country to promote and celebrate naturalisation of immigrants' (ibid.:109–11).

Meanwhile the CIA saw this newly aroused public interest as a means to strengthen and legitimize the Americanization program. With Frances Kellor as editor, it launched a quarterly periodical entitled *The Immigrants in America Review*, which set about influencing public opinion towards adopting a national policy for this poor creature the 'alien immigrant' and on the provisions for their final assimilation.

The CIA also produced a brilliant propaganda strategy to involve every American in an annual ritual of national identification. This ritual would embed the cultural intolerance of the Americanization program within an identification that was formally and officially sanctified. The CIA thereby launched its campaign for the fourth of July 1915 to be made a national Americanization Day, a day for 'a great nationalistic expression of unity and faith in America'. To ensure the success of this proposal it established a National Americanization Day Committee (NADC) comprised mainly of leading corporate executives and their wives. The chairman of the CIA, Frank Trumbull (who was also chairman of the Chesapeake and Ohio Railroad, vice-chairman of the NY–NJ Committee of the NACLI and, later, chairman of the Immigration Committee of the Chamber of Commerce), chaired the new committee. The executive committee of the NADC comprised Mrs Vincent Astor, Frances Kellor, Peter Roberts of the YMCA, Mrs Cornelius Vanderbilt, and Felix Warburg, banker and financier.

This new committee issued a pamphlet written by Kellor which argued the need for a domestic policy on the immigrant and 'stressed in particular the great role which American industrial organisations could assume in working out this policy'. The pamphlet welded together the various interests of the campaign into a single message. It emphasized that however well government, business and philanthropy might conceive and launch a national policy for the Americanization of the immigrant, the ultimate success of that policy would depend on how effectively the 'average American citizen' could be induced to bring the influence of his conservative views to bear on the immigrant. For 'such a citizen is the natural foe of the IWW and of the destructive forces that seek to direct unwisely the expressions of the immigrant in his new country and upon him rest the hope and defence of the country's ideals and institutions' (ibid.:115). Here we have a blatant industrial and partisan view fused with an intolerance of the immigrant and the values of national security, in a submission which would cement these interests and intolerances within the paraphernalia of the annual ritual of what became Independence Day. Such was the breadth and scope of this propaganda campaign.

For the fourth of July program the NADC managed to obtained the support of the Federal Commissioner of Immigration, who sent letters to the mayors of every city in the nation asking for support in observing the fourth of July as Americanization Day. A similar request was sent to school authorities nationwide. A vast amount of promotional material was widely distributed and displayed. This included a supporting article by ex-President Theodore Roosevelt, a message from President Wilson, suggestions for speech content for hundreds of speakers and 52 000 Americanization Day posters. On 4 July Americanization ceremonies covered the country:

> At Pittsburg, more than 10,000 adults heard almost 1,000 school children sing patriotic airs as they formed a huge American flag. In Indianapolis, speeches in eleven different languages on the duties of American citizenship were given by newly made American citizens ... In many of the churches special Americanization Day sermons were preached. (ibid.:121)

The Americanization Day campaign generated so much new activity and interest that the NADC decided to continue in operation to guide and direct this development. Changing its name to the National Americanization Committee (NAC), it set to work on a permanent campaign for the Americanization of the immigrant. In October 1915 the NAC launched an 'America First' campaign at the home of Vincent Astor in New York. The official objectives of the campaign were to establish standardized citizenship courses in all normal schools and night schools and by this and other means to promote the Americanization and naturalization of immigrants. It was apparent that the NAC was making a strong bid to have its Americanization program made a part of the general war preparedness campaign which had seized the country as a result of America's increasing diplomatic difficulties with Germany. The NAC therefore expected that by linking the Americanization program to growing public anxieties about national security it would gain popular support and public funding, which the industrial leaders of the movement had long sought for a program against radicalism among immigrant workers.

As part of its campaign the NAC prepared and issued a syllabus on civics for 'public school work' (which was printed by the Federal Bureau of Education) and prepared a course to train men and women to become leaders in Americanization work. It also produced a series of simple Americanization lessons, stressing the traditional American ideals, which were designed for inclusion in pay envelopes and for use in communities (such as mining and lumber camps) where normal educational facilities were unavailable.

The NAC also organized, late in 1915, an experiment in fully fledged Americanization among the workers of Detroit, where 75 percent of the population was foreign-born. Notices in pay envelopes and posters in almost every shop and factory in the city urged foreign workers to attend night school and learn English. Supported by pressure on employees from their employers, attendance at night school soared and the experiment was judged dramatically successful; as a result of the Detroit experiment NAC members felt that 'industrial Americanization' was a great success, even more it was the 'work of the future'. The NAC, in co-operation with the US Chamber of Commerce, thereafter set about on a national scale to interest employers of immigrant labour in the benefits of Americanization.

As an example of this industrial promotion in December 1915, John Fahey, a member of the NAC and also president of the US Chamber of Commerce, organized the chamber's own Immigration Committee to encourage 'Industrial Americanization'. The chamber's Immigration Committee was funded mainly by the CIA and the NAC. Its chairman was Frank Trumbull (who was also chairman of the CIA and the NAC and vice-chairman of the NY–NJ Committee of the NACLI). From these connections we can appreciate the incestuous and unrepresentative nature of those in control of the whole campaign.

At the beginning of 1916 the Chamber's Immigration Committee set itself up as a centre for Americanization activities for local chambers of commerce, trade associations and industrial plants, and made plans for carrying the crusade to the attention of these groups. While the chamber's committee assumed responsibility for industrial Americanization, the NAC continued its drive to win over the general public by using the services and prestige of the Federal Bureau of Education — within which, of course, the CIA maintained its own Division of Immigrant Education. As part of this drive the bureau distributed 150 000 'America First' posters as a means of publicizing the night school movement.

Summing up these activities, Hartman observed:

> The Americanizers had used the year 1915 very well indeed. Benefiting from the general uneasiness and suspicion engendered by the European War and the rise of a spirit of American patriotism and nationalism, the advocates of a strong domestic policy for the Americanization of the foreign-born were able, through excellent publicity and well-thought-out campaigns, to convince a substantial portion of the American populace of the urgent need for action along the lines first advocated as early as 1908. (ibid.:131–3)

Developments in 1916

During 1916 the NAC continued to propagandize and to lead the drive for the Americanization of the immigrant. In addition, the newly appointed Committee on Immigration of the Chamber of

Commerce of the United States (CICC) also began to play an active role in the campaign and rapidly became one of the most powerful forces in support of the Americanization drive.

As an agency of the Federal Department of Labor, the Bureau of Naturalisation largely confined its activities to dealing directly with the school authorities through its field representatives and steadily aroused the interest of high schools and school boards around the country in Americanization activities. By contrast the Bureau of Education, through its Division of Immigrant Education, actively propagandized on behalf of the Americanization movement through the publication of literature and posters. The division continued to be financed by the CIA so that for all practical purposes its activities formed a very valuable and influential supplement to the work which the CIA and its affiliate the NAC had undertaken under their own names.

The NAC opened the year with a national conference on Americanization in Philadelphia. The stated purpose of this was to unify the Americanization movement at the national level and to obtain some standardization of content and procedures with respect to instruction on citizenship and Americanization activities generally. In explaining the need for a national commitment to Americanization the conference organizers stressed the important role which Americanization could play in the national preparedness effort. The country would not be prepared, the committee warned, if 'only military necessities' were considered. A social and economic preparedness was essential for maintaining 'good industrial relations', general prosperity and 'a strong national spirit'.

For the first time, the Philadelphia conference brought together, at a national level, representatives of almost all important community organizations and interests: business, government, education, the churches, women's clubs and patriotic bodies. The single major exception was organized labour. The NAC reported that, as a result of the conference, 'for the first time, government and private organisations of all kinds and creeds had pledged themselves to cooperate in carrying out Americanization as a national endeavour' (ibid.:135).

Speakers at the conference included Frank Trumbull of the Chamber of Commerce, P. P. Claxton, Commissioner of Education, Louis F. Post, Assistant Secretary of Labor, and former President Theodore Roosevelt. Following up the impetus of the conference, the NAC secured the vigorous and nationwide participation in the Americanization drive by a very influential group, the rapidly growing women's clubs and organizations.

The principal contribution of the women's clubs consisted in lobbying for and then organizing (under the guidance of the NAC) special classes in civics and citizenship in schools, night schools and elsewhere throughout the country. Meanwhile the NAC continued its work of promoting Americanization through the distribution of pamphlets and other literature. Taking advantage of the experience of the previous year, it produced a pamphlet for distribution in local communities (*Americanization Day — Fourth of July*) which set out guidelines 'on how to carry through a successful Americanization program for the coming Fourth of July'. The guidelines described such problems as finance, publicity, the press, the churches and many other factors like the correct procedure for flag ceremonies, pledges of allegiance, pageants, parades and citizenship receptions. The NAC also published *A Call to National Service,* rallying support for Americanization, and distributed a CIA pamphlet, *Citizen Syllabus,* for use in night schools.

The CICC began its activities in January 1916 with a survey (presumably among Chamber of Commerce membership) about immigration and associated problems. It claimed to find 'an insistent demand' for 'practical Americanization to strengthen the country's unity'. From April 1916 the CICC published a monthly *Bulletin* for the purpose of reaching each of the local chambers with the need for Americanization and industrial Americanization in particular. Jointly with the NAC and the CIA it conducted surveys relevant to Americanization which covered the material and social conditions of immigrants in 244 industrial towns. Summaries of the information collected were sent to local chambers of commerce, other commercial bodies, industries and local organizations, along with recommendations to work for 'practical Americanization'.

In order to further stimulate local chambers the CICC arranged a series of 'Industrial Americanization Conferences' in fourteen cities. The conferences led to new Americanization activities in many cities throughout the nation. The CICC also sponsored a special industrial Americanization conference in New York for industrial leaders, another for engineers and a third for publishers and editors. In addition it acted as a national service department and information bureau which sought to keep control over the principles of Americanization.

During 1915–16 the Federal Bureau of Naturalisation also distributed a vast amount of material on citizenship for the use of teachers in connection with 'their Americanization work'. Somewhat defensively, it would appear, the bureau pointed out that 'it was not attempting to assume the role of educator, but was merely serving as an aid to the public schools of the entire country in their citizenship programs'. Despite an immense amount of publicity for the efforts to enrol immigrants in citizenship classes, however, a great many immigrants did not respond.

The bureau decided that a more 'personal touch' was needed. It therefore sent letters to each candidate for naturalization requesting attendance at a public school for instruction. It then sent each candidate's name to the local school superintendent, similar but separate letters to the wives of all candidates and the names of all wives to local public schools, and requested teachers in citizenship classes to press students to prevail on their friends to enrol. Even so it proved difficult to secure regular attendance at such classes. Believing some material inducement might help, the bureau advocated that prizes be offered for papers and debates on different aspects of Americanization by students.

Although the immigrants themselves appeared less than enthusiastic about the process of cultural assimilation, the bureau's proposals did receive a large measure of support from the various Americanization agencies. Moreover, while in July 1915 only thirty-eight towns and cities had responded to the appeal by the Secretary of Labor for support of the bureau's program, by the end of 1916 the number of towns and cities that had agreed to co-operate with the bureau in carrying on citizenship classes increased to more than a thousand.

During 1916 the Federal Bureau of Education continued to lend its authority and influence to Americanization work through the industry-run and industry-financed Division of Immigrant Education. During the year the division distributed a vast amount of promotional material, including almost 100000 circulars, newsletters schedules of standards and syllabuses and 29400 news releases. It made progress towards establishing itself as the national clearing-house for all types of information on the Americanization movement. The Federal Bureau of Education happily reported that during 1916 'much progress had been made toward the Americanization of the immigrant and that healthy tendencies toward centralisation were underway', that is, tendencies toward standardization and control of citizenship courses through a general acceptance of recommendations for content and method largely developed by industry-sponsored bodies such as the CIA, the NAC, the CICC and the Division of Immigrant Education (ibid.:158–61).

There was only one adverse development of consequence for the

Americanization program during 1916: the activities of the Americanizers had, until this time, aroused no opposition. Now, however, some suspicion of the motives of the propagandists, and of the NAC in particular, was expressed by organized labour. Samuel Gompers, the profoundly conservative head of the American Federation of Labor (AFL) suggested that perhaps industrialists should be Americanized as well. He wrote in the *American Federationist*:

> It is not reasonable to expect an intelligent understanding of American ideals or patriotism among those whose daily lives are filled with industrial injustice and who meet with nothing but abuse and exploitation. Any serious attempt to Americanize the foreign workers who have been crowded into our industrial centres and our mining districts must concern itself also with the problem of Americanizing employers, trusts and corporations ... So long as [the United States Steel Corporation] hires armed thugs to beat into submission workers who have the manhood to make a fight for their rights, that corporation will remain ... an obstacle to the work of Americanizing aliens within our country. (ibid.:141)

In addition Frank Walsh of the United Mineworkers Union wrote to Frank Trumbull, chairman of the NAC, and told him that

> you are attempting to set up a paternalism that will bring the workers of this country even more absolutely under the control of the employers ... Among the active members of your Committee are many large employers who are relentlessly resisting any movement ... to free their employees from industrial tyranny and gross economic exploitation.

Walsh listed a number of such large employers on the committee who used spies, armed guards, wretched working conditions or in other ways had treated labour unfairly. The list included Elbert Gary, president of the United Steel Corporation, and Trumbull himself, as executive head of the Illinois Central Railroad. Walsh continued:

> I find much positive evidence that your efforts are primarily directed to strengthening the chain of industrial tyranny in this country. You propose to sanctify and confirm oppression by waving the American flag in the face of its victims and by insidiously stigmatizing as unpatriotic any attempts they may make to throw off the yoke of the exploiting interests you represent. (ibid.:142–3)

In general, however, labour's attitude was ambivalent in that it recognized from the outset that teaching English to immigrants (which was part of Americanization) could benefit everyone. As the Americanization movement (and patriotic fervour) gained momentum after 1916, criticism ceased from this quarter. Indeed, once state and federal agencies began to play an ever more important role in legitimizing the Americanization campaign the dominant union attitude, like the rest of the country, unfortunately became one of positive support.

Developments during 1917

At the time of American entry into the war (April 1917) the various Americanization groups had for years been carrying on a campaign of agitation and propaganda. They had thereby developed a broad foundation of private, municipal, state and federal support. On this basis the leadership of the movement (a leadership comprising a small group of businessmen who controlled the NACL, CIA, NAC and CICC) hoped to build an even larger movement. This was a golden opportunity, the Americanizers realized, for pushing their crusade to the limit.

> This they accomplished by having their movement accepted by the various governmental war agencies as a definite part of the national war program. It was to be expected that as a result ... the Americanization movement should wax increasingly stronger ... until practically every hamlet in the United States which contained an immigrant populace felt the full impact of the crusade. (ibid.:164)

During 1917 the CIA was at the forefront of the movement and continually hammered away at its industrial Americanization drive. It established a Committee on Industrial Engineering (under the ubiquitous chairmanship of Frank Trumbull) to promote what was called 'human engineering work'. Such a title gives us a flavour of the CIA's systematic application to the problems of shaping the minds and behaviour, not only of immigrants, but of the public at large.

The CIA recorded several significant achievements during 1917. It organized the foreign-language division of the Committee on Public Information and provided a special assistant to the division; it drafted and submitted a bill for the registration of enemy aliens; and it investigated production delays in war-related industries. These efforts did much, the CIA believed, both to assist the war effort and to forestall 'subversive' activities by the IWW.

In April 1917 the CIA appointed a National Committee on Patriotic Literature (chairman, Frank Trumbull) which thereafter produced about two million copies of patriotic booklets and flag posters for distribution in immigrant communities. The CIA also organized and extensively financed Americanization activities by a wide range of wartime agencies at national, state and municipal levels. Such agencies included military and security organizations, defence leagues, committees of public safety and patriotic societies.

Through its offshoot the NAC, the CIA published a pamphlet entitled *War Americanization for States,* in a continued attempt to identify Americanization with the war effort. Together these two committees presented a memorandum to the Council of National Defence in an effort to get official recognition of Americanization as part of the official war program. The memorandum recommended a war policy for aliens which would take account of the following conditions: the presence of about three million unassimilated immigrants who could not speak English and whose attitudes toward the US were unknown; industrial conditions which 'enable pacifists, agitators and other anti-American groups' to foment unrest, dissatisfaction and disloyalty; an alleged prevalence of industrial subversion by German agents; IWW progress in gaining support among aliens; and a claimed general increase in industrial unrest, sabotage and strikes. It was contended that these conditions, combined with alien and anti-American influences (read anti-business) and in particular with the influence of some of the foreign-language press, had produced important delays in war production.

Overall a policy was called for which, although formally acknowledging the importance of 'industrial injustice and unfavourable living conditions', generally attributed industrial unrest and war-production delays to the control of industries by aliens and anti-American influences, notably the IWW.

The CIA's general recommendations included the removal of conditions which tended to render men and women susceptible to anti-American (anti-business) influences and to provide for increased opportunities to become Americanized, that is, patriotically business-minded. However, its more specific recommendations were also more punitive: 'the prevention of anti-American propaganda activities and schemes through the surveillance of all aliens', both allied and enemy, the drafting of 'enemy' aliens into internment camps or non-war industries and of 'friendly' aliens into the armed forces.

The purging of the workforce of radical or un-American, anti-business influence had been, of course, a long-sought objective of the industrial leadership of the Americanization movement. Under the new proposals from this leadership the purge would be carried out by the federal government in the name of patriotism and wartime security — as would an increased provision of Americanization courses for aliens. The endless emphasis on the threat to the war effort from 'un-American' influences among immigrant workers made it possible for business leaders now to advocate a publicly funded program for Americanization of the immigrant workforce without inviting the plausible objection (from trade unions, for example) that business was taking advantage of wartime conditions to promote partisan political and ideological interests at public expense.

In December 1916 a National Committee of One Hundred (NCOH) had been appointed by the Commissioner of Education to mobilize federal departments as well as state and local groups active in Americanization. NCOH attempted to make all state and local groups co-ordinate their programs so that they could work effectively with the bureau, and propagandized ardently on behalf of Americanization for the remainder of the war. Early in February 1917 the NCOH held a conference at which industrial leaders and officials were present to lay plans for the Americanization campaign for the coming year. Throughout 1917 the bureau continued an active campaign for extension and standardization of Americanization courses, chiefly through general publicity and provision of materials and instruction to teachers throughout the country.

During 1917 two more agencies (in addition to the NACLI, CIA, NAC, Federal Bureau of Education and NCOH) played substantial roles in advancing Americanization and in influencing public opinion to support an overall War Americanization Plan. These agencies were the Committee on Immigration of the Chamber of Commerce and the Federal Bureau of Immigration. Thus in 1917 (as in 1916) the campaign for Americanization was, with the exception of the Bureau of Immigration's work with schools, led and dominated by the business-based CIA and the NAC.

Through publicity and promotion by the US Chamber of Commerce, local chambers in 104 cities were, by the end of 1917, engaged in extensive local campaigns and Americanization programs, while in certain larger immigrant centres the chambers became the nuclei around which the Americanizers rallied. Hartman reports that factory Americanization activities increased and Americanization classes were inaugurated at work in at least twenty-seven industries.

During that same year, the Bureau of Naturalisation continued to push its citizenship training campaign in co-operation with the public schools until it spread to virtually every section of the country with an immigrant population. In this connection the bureau reported an 'astonishing advance' which it acknowledged had been stimulated by the actions and propaganda of the various

Americanization groups. The year also saw an almost threefold increase (from 610 to 1754) in the localities which had joined the movement. In all these localities great emphasis had been placed on attendance by unassimilated foreign-born at thousands of night schools that were opening for this purpose throughout the country. The bureau concluded happily that 'the spirit of "alienage" cannot hope to survive in the presence of this intense Americanizing force that is being built up in the public school-houses of the land' (ibid.:180–1). Commercial organizations played a major role in achieving this result.

Thus during 1917 the Americanization movement had seen progress on two fronts. It had achieved a steadily widening support for the Americanization of the immigrant and for the Americanization program in general. In one important particular, however, success had so far eluded them. Although interest had been whipped up as the result of America's entry into war and the consequent heightening of patriotism, the Americanization drive had not, so far, been made a definite, official part of the war program.

1918 – Americanization gains full federal support

During 1918 the leaders of the Americanization movement completely achieved two objectives they had long pursued: the movement was officially accepted as one of the fundamental parts of the war program, and it obtained the full benefit and prestige of two new federal agencies, the Council of National Defence (CND) and the Committee on Public Information (CPI). Achieving this government support meant that business propaganda received an enormous increase in its power of persuasion.

These advances were obtained chiefly by the efforts of the Federal Bureau of Education, which, through its Division of Immigrant Education, took the lead in publicizing and promoting the Americanization movement as a fundamental part of the war effort. To achieve this end, the bureau had taken steps to secure a resolution from the Council of National Defence endorsing the federal program of Americanization. The official approval by the Council of National Defence was a distinct compliment to the CIA and the NAC. As for the business of propaganda, it meant a complete identification of business interests with patriotic endeavour. From this point on business interests became patriotic.

After this the Council of National Defence requested all state councils of defence to form Americanization committees to assist the bureau in carrying out its national Americanization program according to the plans it had outlined. The bureau supplied every state council of defence and a large number of local and community councils with its national plan for Americanization — and with a great deal more detailed guidance as well. As a result, in every state that had any significant immigrant population the work of state and local agencies was controlled and co-ordinated under the Americanization committees of the state and local councils of defence.

Not content with these measures, in April 1918 the Federal Bureau of Education took a further step to establish Americanization as a war measure. It arranged a national conference on Americanization to be attended by every state governor, the chairmen of the state defence councils and the presidents of industrial corporations and chambers of commerce. The conference adopted resolutions calling on Congress to provide funds for Americanization work throughout the country. A committee representing the conference was later appointed to lobby Congress, and the Federal Bureau of Education drew up bills that would provide the desired federal funds.

Until 1918 state councils of defence had been primarily occupied with registration and surveillance of the foreign-born, 'to prevent sedition'. Their main occupation now became 'War Americanization', a version of Americanization which integrated preparation for citizenship with promotion of patriotic support for the war and surveillance of all the foreign-born. In addition, Americanization work was also carried out by the Women's Division of the Council of National Defence, which proselytized widely through its state councils. At the state level tens of thousands of women were recruited to help with War Americanization activities.

To enable the Bureau of Education to accomplish this enlarged role (for which no federal funds were available) the NAC completely funded a great expansion of the bureau's Americanization staff and facilities. Special offices with a staff of thirty-six people were opened in New York and Washington, headed respectively by Joseph Mayper and Frances Kellor. In addition, more than a hundred other people were employed throughout the country at NAC expense. This enlarged body of workers was combined, in May 1918, with the earlier Division of Immigrant Education to form a new Americanization Division of the bureau.

The NAC also provided funds for work for a thousand Americanization committees which had been set up throughout industry at the request of the Department of the Interior (whose chief responsibility was security). The NAC continued a pervasive program of propaganda directed to the foreign-born through conferences, lectures, articles and active participation in local activities; it published 'civic lessons' in foreign-language newspapers, conducted home visits to the foreign-born and distributed an abundance of vigilante and other War Americanization material to thousands of plants employing the foreign-born.

On behalf of the Committee on Public Information, the NAC's staff conducted a comprehensive survey of Americanization activities. The survey covered 50000 national state and local agencies having any connection with the foreign-born. On the basis of the survey results the CPI was able to plan a strategy in support of the Americanization movement. From the results of the survey conducted by the NAC, the CPI decided that it should recruit group leaders from the various national groups to act as the spearhead of its Americanization campaign. Group leaders were therefore sought out within the ethnic communities, to undertake the kind of evangelism demanded by the Americanization program.

During 1918 the CPI set up fourteen foreign-language bureaus and made them responsible for developing, among their people, Americanization sentiment and support for the war. These bureaus were so successful that 745 foreign-language newspapers co-operated out of a total of 865. In addition, it was the foreign-language bureaus which were largely responsible for the petition presented to President Wilson on 21 May 1918, asking that the fourth of July be especially recognized as a day for the foreign-born to demonstrate their loyalty to their adopted country. Wilson agreed. With the President's stamp of approval the CPI set to work to plan an enthusiastic celebration for what was to be called Independence Day.

The amendment to 'Independence Day' rather than the 'Americanization Day' as originally proposed in 1915 by the NAC is an interesting change. It could be argued that the cultural and ethnic intolerances inherent in the term 'Americanization' were too obvious in 1918 to engender overwhelming public support for a national celebration. 'Independence Day', while less obviously ethnocentric, does, however, suffer from a certain ambiguity. Within its historical context 'Independence Day' refers to both an immigrant's separation from old cultural ties and their alienation from the new business-oriented American culture. Current Independence Day celebrations still contain the residual power and meaning of these historically dislocating circumstances, even though most people would think of the day as a celebration for national rather than ethnic independence.

The Bureau of Naturalisation also continued its Americanization efforts during 1918, especially with respect to schools. It reported that Americanization committees had been organized in virtually all US communities, that chambers of commerce were widely active and that scarcely a commercial or business organization in the nation was not represented in some way in support of the bureau's efforts. Churches in many areas had also organized programs for Americanization. The bureau continued to sponsor Americanization classes in industrial plants and influenced the city of Chicago to provide a thousand teachers for such work. Overall the bureau did all in its power to preach the gospel for a full red-blooded American campaign of Americanization.

The postwar Americanization drive

After the end of the war in November 1918 both business and labour prepared for a major confrontation. Between 1900 and 1918 the union movement had greatly expanded. During the war years organized labour — or at least the vastly predominant conservative component of it represented by the AFL — had benefited from the novelty of government administrations which were at least neutral and occasionally favourably disposed towards it. Nonetheless, while industry's wartime profits soared, wage increases scarcely kept pace with the cost of living. Once peace had been achieved labour mobilized to use its new strength and improved relationship with government to wrest formal recognition and improved conditions from powerful employers.

For more than a decade before the war, big business had been continually on the defensive against muckrakers, hostile public opinion and related efforts by government to check, through various forms of regulation, the worst abuses of financial and industrial power. The wartime atmosphere of relentlessly drilled patriotism had made it a requirement of citizenship to believe well of the free-enterprise business system — indeed Sedition Acts and universal surveillance made it highly dangerous not so to believe. This circumstance, coupled with business's wartime production role, substantially restored the dominance of representatives of big business within the administration and the political parties (Murray 1955:8–9).

These factors largely restored the standing of business in public opinion — the point of this whole Americanization exercise. In spite of this favourable stance, at the war's end big business was still paranoid. It was determined to end what it saw as two decades of retreat before hostile public opinion, legal harassment by 'progressive' administrations and the growing strength of organized labour. Further still, business was determined to regain what it regarded as the traditional and 'moral' condition of business leadership and general dominance in politics and society. So far as any demands from organized labour were concerned, business was spoiling for a fight. The result, in 1919, was a year during which more time was lost through strikes than in any previous year in American history, a year in which organized labour suffered a general and crushing defeat.

During 1918 business's most effective weapon for the ensuing confrontation with the unions was public apprehension about the threat to American society and institutions from 'un-American' sentiment and 'un-American' radicalism among the foreign-born. This useful public anxiety had been nurtured by ceaseless propaganda ever since the successful Lawrence strike by foreign-born textile workers under IWW leadership in 1912. After the armistice in November 1918 there was initially a continuation of public interest in Americanization of the foreign-born. Within a year this interest had began to subside. But the Great Steel Strike of 1919 gave the campaign new life. The strike, begun in late September, was to be the decisive confrontation between corporate power and organized labour. In its war to gain control over public opinion, business was again assisted by government, this time by the Federal Department of Justice. Under the leadership of Attorney-General Mitchell Palmer, the Department of Justice alerted public opinion to the necessity of Americanizing, once again, the nation's foreign-born.

This revival of an intense (indeed, on this occasion hysterical) public interest and concern about the foreign-born resulted from the Great Red Scare. The scare was set in train by a series of highly public and dramatic actions of the Department of Justice between October 1918 and February 1919. These actions had the proclaimed purpose of ridding America of the malevolent influence of the so-called 'alien radical'. In response to these exciting developments there was a heightened spurt of Americanization activity from the old agencies and groups that had sponsored Americanization activities — groups still led and dominated by business. In January 1920 the Great Steel Strike collapsed, with disastrous consequences for the entire labour movement. It had predictably been represented by government and business interests as a Bolshevist revolutionary challenge to American society by un-American foreign-born workers.

By late 1920 the Great Red Scare had largely subsided. Its rapid decline followed a quarrel which broke out between the departments of Justice and Labour and largely discredited the Red-hunting activities of the former. As a consequence a saner attitude was assumed by the agents of the Department of Justice and gradually the mass hysteria ran itself out. By 1921 a Republican president completely identified with business interests ('the business of America is business') occupied the White House. Thereafter the business leaders of the Americanization movement could permit a level of public indifference, for they had gained control over the presidency as well as public opinion and had begun the long process of closing the American mind to critical thought.

CHAPTER 4

THE
McCARTHY CRUSADE

There is little popular comprehension in Australia of the extraordinary, Orwellian/Kafkaesque control McCarthy exercised over American domestic politics and foreign policy during a crucial five years in the early 1950s. But to understand McCarthy's influence we should not regard his form of paranoia as unique in American history. It represented an extreme but nonetheless typical form of propaganda and mind-control which the US public had been subject to since before World War I; there was nothing in the intolerance of the McCarthy crusade which had not already been served up to the public many times before. By the early 1950s corporate campaigns of persuasion, replete with their anti-American scapegoats, had become so common that there were few who saw McCarthy's anti-communist crusade as anything but a normal part of the political scene. That this campaign was able to influence such trivia as the Girl Scouts handbook[1] while also affecting domestic and foreign policy speaks volumes for the degree of conformity imprinted on the American mind over the previous forty years of conditioning.

From 1945 to 1950 the Republican Party, representing American conservatism, gained greatly increased support. (In November 1946 the Republicans had won the Congressional elections for the first time since 1928.) These were years of incipient Cold War. Much of the growing Republican support was won on the charge that 'failures' in Democratic foreign policy had allowed, and even assisted, enlargement of communist power and influence throughout the world. In particular, it was alleged that inadequate security measures had permitted the Russians to 'steal' the secret of the atom bomb, and that a 'soft' foreign policy had 'lost' China to communism. All this had happened, it was claimed, because the

Democratic administration was full of New Dealers, liberal intellectuals and such-like 'fellow-travellers' who were secretly sympathetic to communism.

To blunt the Republican attack, Truman introduced, in 1947–48, new security checks ('loyalty' tests) for two and a half million government employees, a provision shortly extended to cover eight million wage and salary earners (Horowitz 1967:95–7, 104). So began a preoccupation with anti-communism which was to produce, for about twenty years, a near paralysis of liberal/imaginative political thought in the countries most affected by it.

Truman's decision to try to beat the Republican game by joining it rather than confronting it led to a frenzied vote-catching competition between Democrats and Republicans for anti-communist honours — a frenzied exaggeration of the 'Red menace'. With some poetic justice the Republican madness which Truman helped promote in 1947–48 eventually caught up with him. 'In November. 1953, the Attorney General of the United States ... charged Truman himself with having knowingly harboured a Russian spy' (ibid.:97).

At first the main line of Republican argument was that the Democratic Party inherited Roosevelt's New Deal traditions (which showed some regard for social planning and social welfare) and that it was, in consequence, 'socialistic'. With Roosevelt dead (1945) and a postwar confrontation between Russia and the West developing, a whole new range of possibilities opened up for Republicans, who believed that US society had been under continuous subversion by the Democrats ever since Roosevelt introduced his New Deal Policy in 1933.

From merely charging the Democrats with being socialistic and therefore subversive of the 'real' and 'best' American traditions, the indictment could be made larger and much more ominous (see Ginsburg 1954:10–14). The Democrats' long-impugned (though non-existent) 'socialistic' tendencies made them sensitive to charges that they were 'soft on communism'. Every advance of communism in the world, every political, scientific or military success achieved by a communist regime, was construed to be a consequence of Democratic policies that were 'soft on', or 'sympathetic to', the 'red menace'. The drastic shift in position — from Roosevelt's determination in 1944–45 to work for a co-operative settlement with the Russians, to Truman's and Eisenhower's refusal for nearly ten years (1946–55) even to meet with Russia's top leaders (Horowitz 1967:13–14) — was occasioned more by the Democrats' need to defend themselves against the Republicans than by any realities of the international world. The same point holds for the changes in US Asian policy in the years after 1945: from a policy of opposition to France's return to Vietnam and a more benevolent, impartial mediation between Mao and Chiang in pursuit of a compromise settlement of China's civil war, in 1945, to a total repudiation of any such objective by 1948 (see 'US Relations with China' 1949).

It was against this background that Senator Joseph McCarthy came on stage. In January 1950 McCarthy had been for three years an inconsequential senator from Wisconsin. He was looking for an issue to assist his re-election in 1952. His biographer Richard Rovere (1959:9)[2] informs us that McCarthy 'discovered Communism — almost by inadvertence as Columbus discovered America, as James Marshall discovered Californian gold'.

On 9 February 1950 McCarthy made a speech in Wheeling, West Virginia, in which he said that the State Department was full of communists and that he and the Secretary of State (Acheson) knew their names. Through March, April and May life in Washington seemed largely a matter of determining whether American diplomacy was in the hands of traitors (ibid.:11). Quoting the London *Times*, Rovere reports that 'the fears and suspicions which centre around ... Senator McCarthy ... now ... count as an essential factor in policy making for the West', and concludes, 'McCarthy has become the direct concern of the United States' allies' (ibid.:14).

McCarthy's single and potent weapon was the communist smear. From the very beginning he used it to devastating effect.

In 1950, just a few weeks after McCarthy's Wheeling speech, Millard Tydings of Maryland had accepted the chairmanship of a committee that was to inquire into McCarthy's charges against the State Department. Tydings was a titan in the Senate; no man seemed better established there than he, a Maryland patrician, a man of enormous wealth and a member of the inner circle of the Senate. In 1938 Franklin D. Roosevelt, then at the very apex of his career, had tried to get Tydings, a reactionary as Roosevelt saw it, defeated. Roosevelt failed wretchedly. But McCarthy, a nobody in 1949, threw his weight against Tydings in 1950, and what happened? Tydings lost. (Of course the methods were somewhat different. Roosevelt went into Maryland and tried to persuade the voters to choose another man; McCarthy stayed in Washington and sent agents into Maryland spreading the word that Tydings was pro-communist.) That same year (1950) McCarthy went gunning for Scott Lucas of Illinois, the Democratic floor leader. Lucas was also defeated. Rovere notes that Tydings's role as McCarthy's chief adversary passed to

William Benton, who had placed before the Senate a resolution calling for McCarthy's expulsion. McCarthy was not expelled; Benton was, though, by the voters. With Lucas also gone, Ernest MacFarland of Arizona became the Democratic floor leader. McCarthy campaigned against him. MacFarland was also defeated. In 1951 McCarthy attacked the Secretary of State, General George Marshall, forced his resignation and altogether 'destroyed' his career.

McCarthy accused Truman's Democratic administration in general of 'conniving with and being supported by communists'. 'It tends now to be forgotten', Rovere comments, 'that McCarthy was almost as successful in obelising the Truman administration [1950–53] as he later was in demoralising [Eisenhower's] government' (ibid.:16). Dean Acheson, Truman's Secretary of State, spent a large part of those years explaining to service organizations like Elks, Moose, Women Voters, Legionnaires that he was not corrupt, that he was opposed to communism, and that he did not hire traitors. To prove its virtue, the State Department hired John Foster Dulles and fired a number of career officers McCarthy had been attacking.

If the appointment of Dulles had been McCarthy's only influence on the State Department it would have been a lasting one. From 1953 almost until his death in 1959 Dulles ran US foreign policy virtually as his private property, and with an unflagging anti-communist zeal (Roberts 1954:13; see Holsti 1965). It will be recalled that Dulles's repeated attempts to disrupt the Geneva Conference led the British Prime Minister, Anthony Eden, to conclude despairingly that 'the Americans seemed deeply apprehensive of reaching any agreement, however innocuous, with the communists' (Eden 1960:127).

General Bedell Smith and Walter Robertson, who deputized for Dulles throughout most of the Geneva Conference, were both under personal attack by McCarthy as 'soft' on communism (Hale 1954:14, 16). At McCarthy's whim they were both liable to be hauled before his Senate Committee as 'security risks'. McCarthy thus decimated the State Department of its more experienced and liberal-minded personnel. For example, of twenty-two members of the State Department's China Service with more than ten years' service, only two remained with it a year or so after McCarthy's rise to power. During 1952 alone McCarthy secured the removal of 534 people from the State Department on alleged 'security' grounds — without producing any evidence whatever of subversion or disloyalty (Horowitz 1967:104; Hale 1954:16). It was later widely believed that an 'abused' and demoralized foreign service resulted, one in which 'diplomats abroad were ... reluctant to present objective reports for fear that Security [i.e. McCarthy's disloyalty hunters] might hold something against them' (Hale 1954:17, 22–4; Fullbright 1954:10).

The State Department's White Paper of 1949, *United States Relations with China*, was reprinted in 1967. The Introduction contains the following passages:

> McCarthy's charges [of Communist influence in the State Department] finally proved baseless, but in the meantime lives and careers were ruined and lasting harm was done to the conduct of American foreign policy. The reception of the White Paper instructed many government officials on the value of caution ... Some of America's most able and best qualified China specialists were dismissed from the State Department ... Others were transferred to less sensitive positions ... Some were persuaded to accept early retirement. In any case, their long experience and intimate knowledge of China were lost. Among the best known of these men were John Carter Vincent, John Stewart Service and John Paton Davies. Their reports on China in the 1940s stood the test of time ... Many of the reports for which they were condemned were penetrating insights into the Chinese political realities. They saw clearly, and warned their superiors, of the dangers of tying the US irrevocably to a regime that was rapidly discrediting itself and might well be unable to survive. For telling unpleasant truths about the nationalists they were later called Communists. Professor John K. Fairbanks' tribute to them is no more than just: 'These men were true China specialists and we have no one like them today [1967]. In our lifetime we shall never again get this much grasp of the Chinese scene'. (China White Paper 1967)

For four years McCarthy silenced the most liberal and courageous politicians. The Democratic administration was driven to ridiculous demonstrations of anti-communism. For example, in the course of Senate hearings on Far Eastern policy, Dean Acheson and his immediate predecessor, General George Marshall — both of them under savage attack by McCarthy — testified that they would never so much as consider the recognition of communist China or support its admission to the United Nations. They assured the Senate that the very idea of recognition was so abhorrent to them and to other American diplomats that it was never even discussed in the Department of State (Rovere 1959:17–18). Deception, stupidity, stubbornness and a commitment to perpetuity — these were the lengths to which McCarthy and McCarthyism drove these intelligent men.

In November 1952 a Republican administration under

Eisenhower and Nixon was elected. In 1953 this administration negotiated an armistice in Korea that the Democrats would almost certainly have been unable to accept — because it would have given McCarthy additional grounds for impugning their loyalty. 'I would have been crucified for that Armistice', Harry Truman said (ibid.:18).

The Korean War, with its frustrations, its high toll of death and destruction, its eventual involvement of Chinese forces in long and bitter battles with American forces, unquestionably set and fixed US attitudes and policies towards Asia in the rigid mould that has shaped them for so long since. As Professor Bernard Fall (1967:219) has noted, it was the Korean War which 'put the French struggle in Vietnam in a new light, transforming it from a colonial war into an anti-communist crusade'.

Consider, for a moment, the likely import of the fact that Truman was captive to McCarthy's forces in his handling of the Korean War. The Korean War began on 25 June 1950. About twelve weeks later the invaders had been driven back to the boundary of North Korea. Up to this date, casualties and destruction had been relatively light. Until the invasion of North Korea by US troops came in question (mid-August) there had been no sign or suggestion that China might enter the war (see Whiting 1960).[3] If Truman had wanted he could have moved to end the war after twelve weeks, at the 38th parallel. But, because of McCarthy's dominance of the domestic scene, Truman had to reject repeated moves for a truce and negotiations from Russia, India and China; he had to ignore the explicit warnings given by China, as the US forces approached the 38th parallel, that if US troops (as distinct from South Korean troops) entered North Korea, China would come into the war.

Instead, on 17 August 1950, Warren Austin, US Ambassador to the United Nations, argued that the war should be carried into North Korea. On 25 August Navy Secretary Francis Matthews (whom McCarthy had threatened to impeach for communist sympathies) anticipated the McCarthyist zeal within the formal US decision to invade North Korea. Matthews concluded that the American 'peace seeking policy, though it cast us in a character new to a true democracy — an initiator of a war of aggression — it would earn for us a proud and popular title — we would become the first aggressors for peace' (Horowitz 1967:119; Whiting 1960:96). US troops invaded North Korea on 8 October. After a final warning, and a finally rebuffed appeal to the United Nations for a truce and negotiations, Chinese troops crossed the Yalu River into North Korea on 16 October.

The Korean War continued for a further two and a half years, laid waste to the entire peninsula, increased US casualties fivefold and brought death and desolation to millions of civilians. An armistice was finally agreed near the 38th parallel, almost exactly where Truman could (and on every consideration of rationality and legality should) have ended the war only twelve weeks (rather than three years) after it began.

McCarthy and the Republican Party promoted an atmosphere of fear: fear of subversion within and of threat without. Posing, against this background, as the patriotic scourge of the 'pro-communist' democrat, and of 'disloyal', 'fellow-travelling' liberals, intellectuals, etc., McCarthy won great popular support both within his own party and in the country at large. He was able to get his own candidates — often ex-FBI men — into various key positions in the State Department and elsewhere, and under them he built up an elaborate 'security' organization. The explicit objective of this organization was to search out 'derogatory information' on staff and employees. Allegedly on the basis of such 'information' he brought charges, which made the headlines, against anyone who opposed him. By 1951 'he was a pure delight ... to the [Republican] campaign committees, and the Republican organisations were in hot competition to have him come in with a load of documents on anyone who was giving them trouble' (Rovere 1959:144). He was the highlight of the Republican Convention in 1952 and received a 'wild and sickening demonstration of support'. As late as January 1954, four years after his rise to power, Gallup Poll results showed 50 percent of the American people to have a 'favourable opinion of him; only 29 percent an unfavourable opinion' (ibid.:24).

In January 1953 Eisenhower replaced Truman. The paralysis Truman suffered was as nothing to that which overcame President Eisenhower, at least during his first two years in office (a period embracing the Geneva Conference in 1954). Eisenhower had been forced into a large surrender even before he was elected. He had planned a small gesture of defiance. He would go into McCarthy's Wisconsin and speak a few affectionate words about his old chief and patron, General Marshall (ex-Secretary of State, ex-Chairman Joint Chiefs of Staff), whom McCarthy had all but called a traitor. (McCarthy had said of Marshall that he was 'one in whose activities can be seen a pattern which finds his decisions ... always and invariably serving the world policy of the Kremlin' [ibid.:17]).

Concerned at the prospects of McCarthy's fury at such an action, the party leaders in Wisconsin pleaded with Eisenhower to omit that part of his speech, which, according to Rovere, he did. McCarthy's victory was made sweeter by the fact that he himself had played no part in gaining it. He had let it be known that Eisenhower could say whatever he pleased about Marshall and that he, McCarthy, couldn't care less. He had even offered to remove himself from the campaign train at Wisconsin if that would make the general feel any better. But so great was the fear of him that Eisenhowever gave in, even though McCarthy had magnanimously said that this would not be necessary. In 1953 the very thought of Joe McCarthy could 'shiver the White House timbers and send panic through the whole executive branch' (ibid.:18).

When the Eisenhower administration took over, in January 1953, McCarthy largely controlled appointments and dismissals at home and abroad. When the President appointed John Foster Dulles as Secretary of State, McCarthy appointed Scott McLeod as the State Department's personnel and security officer; and in the early days it was pretty much a toss-up whether Dulles or McLeod, who had prepared for a diplomatic career as an FBI agent in Manchester, had more influence in departmental affairs. When it came to appointing ambassadors and hiring and firing departmental officers Dulles cleared everything with McLeod, who cleared everything with McCarthy.

In the *New York Times* of 28 February 1954, Hanson Baldwin commented that 'whether President Eisenhower realises it or not, Senator McCarthy is now sharing with him command of the Army'. In February 1954 only one man (Fullbright) in a Senate of eighty -six members found it possible to vote against an appropriation of $214 000 to support McCarthy's activities. Top-level Democrats vied with McCarthy for the honour of being the toughest communist-fighter and they competed with the Republicans in a kind of 'slavering praise of the FBI, an agency deeply involved in some of the worst of McCarthy's offences' (ibid.:176).

McCarthy's influence was all-pervasive. A few examples show this.

In 1953 McCarthy secured the burning of all books in American Information Service libraries throughout the world that were offensive to him; from books suspected of being 'soft' on communism to detective stories by pro-communist authors. He secured the removal of the Chief of Intelligence, Major General Partridge, for including in the bibliography of a study course on Russia a book by a writer sympathetic to communism in which the author (Corliss Lamont) said that the Siberian masses were not likely to become anti-communist soon. He decimated the Voice of America organization of anyone suspected of liberal (i.e. anti-McCarthy) views. By the time McCarthy was through he had toppled most of the Voice leadership, forced the administration to disown it and sown despair and confusion through its ranks.

In February 1953, Eisenhower called in a millionaire business man (R. L. Johnson) to rescue the situation, and put him in charge of the International Information Administration — covering all US information agencies abroad, including Voice of America broadcasts and 201 libraries in 89 countries. McCarthy at once told Johnson whom he must sack as 'pro-communist liberals'; told him he must ban 418 authors including such people as Arthur Schlesinger, John Dewey, Auden Louis Bromfield, Theodor Dreiser, Edmund Wilson — and Foster Rhea Dulles, cousin to the Secretary of State!

Johnson bucked and appealed to Eisenhower. The only stand the President would take was to say that he thought 'we should not ban the detective-story writer Dashiell Hammett'. Johnson appealed to Dulles — to even less effect: 'When I went to see him on June 15 [Dulles] ... remarked plaintively "Why have they got my cousin on that list?"' Johnson was abandoned to McCarthy, who told him that unless he apologised and played ball there'd be no funds for his organization. Johnson resigned. McCarthy had won (Merson 1954).

The scientific and university communities suffered similarly. Asked to comment on the situation in November 1954, almost five years after McCarthy's rise to power, Albert Einstein wrote:

> Instead of trying to analyse the problem I may express my feelings in a short remark: If I would be a young man again and had to decide how to make my living, I would not try to become a scientist or scholar or teacher. I would rather choose to be a plumber or peddler in the hope to find that modest degree of independence still available under present circumstances. (*Reporter* 18 November 1954:8)

In the hysterically patriotic atmosphere McCarthy fostered, any sentiment or organization (especially the United Nations) directed towards international peace and goodwill was 'subversive' and 'Un-American'. So extreme was the paranoia that even fluoridation was widely opposed throughout the US on the grounds that it was a form of 'socialized medicine' and that it was a communist plot to break down the wills of the people. Opposition on these grounds was usually successful (*Reporter* 16 June 1955:28–30).

Finally, the flavour of the time can be gleaned from a few excerpts from a case history of a Bell Aircraft workman declared a 'security risk' because of his 'past associations'.

[Mike] had no idea of the specific charges levelled against him or of who had requested the government investigation ... The company fired Mike the moment it received word of the screening board's decision, and three detectives hustled him bodily out of the plant.

During the days of the Truman loyalty program [1948–53] Bell Aircraft used a system in which workers without clearance wore an identifying label, a sort of security version of the Star of David. Bell now follows the general pattern, firing the 'risks' and then waiting to see if he wants to fight the case.

The chances are good that employees discharged in this way will give up rather than face the time expense and anguish of fighting against the heavy odds inherent in the present system ...

Although a general effort to protect the individual's job rights is taking shape [i.e. in July 1954] it has a long way to go. The firings continue. There remains the minority among the rank and file who favour anything that will get the Reds. In some shops ... members take personal reprisal against 'lefties' identified by investigating committees or clearance boards.

The consequences of being fired as a security risk are always very great ... [The worker] loses the precious seniority that is the key to well-paying jobs. His home, his family, his relationship with his friends are all affected.

Mike, tough and confident as he is, finds it almost incomprehensible. 'You know,' he said, 'there are kids around here that won't talk to my sixteen-year-old daughter since this has happened ... I didn't think things like this were supposed to happen in America.

Even the man who is cleared and returns to work often finds his place on the job more difficult. There are always those who thrive on suspicion. And the cleared man must live with the threat over him that his file may be 're-activated' and the whole process begun again. (*Reporter* 6 July 1954:14–18)

Four and a half years after McCarthy's emergence the *Reporter* reflected on the just-concluded Oppenheimer case and assessed the overall situation:

Is there any citizen not exposed to the decisions of loyalty boards, or the reprisals of informers? Certainly not the millions of employees in industrial concerns with government contracts — and the government happens to be by far the largest customer of private business. Certainly not the hundreds of thousands of teachers from university to kindergarten who are exposed to the raids of disloyalty hunters all over the country ... There is no sphere of activity, private or public, that can ultimately remain exempt. (6 July 1954)

McCarthy's personal power came to an end late in 1954, but he retained a vast popular following. Even to the very end he was never repudiated by a majority of his own party. Drink and ill health brought his death two years later. But the intolerance and paranoia his crusade embodied continued largely unabated. Building on the propaganda programs of previous years, his purges reinforced the imprinting of earlier times so that the McCarthy sentiment continued long after his death. The whole period of the Vietnam War has been little more than the working out of the overheated temper which McCarthy gave US politics during a crucial five years. It is a measure, I believe, of the unconscious depth and the all-pervasiveness of McCarthy's irrationally anti-communist legacy that, incredible as it may seem, most reputable studies of American foreign policy and the Vietnam War do not even mention McCarthy and his influence.

CHAPTER 5

RESHAPING
THE TRUTH

At the end of World War II the United States of America enjoyed an international pre-eminence in power, prestige and moral regard that is perhaps unprecedented in the history of human societies. Now, a mere thirty years later, American prestige and moral authority have, for ten years, suffered an almost ceaseless sequence of damaging revelations. Cumulatively these revelations have produced an immense gulf between the claims expressed in popular images and official rhetoric and the increasingly visible and increasingly ugly reality behind the images and rhetoric. Hence the new euphemism for telling lies and being found out — the credibility gap.

Consider for a moment the symbols by which Americans defined their dream and pictured social reality: the Statue of Liberty with its Christlike promise of succour and compassion to the poor and wretched of the earth; the Declaration of Independence with its noble proclamation of respect for the equal and inalienable rights of all men and women; the unending public litany of adulation for American freedom, American individualism and American democracy; a near religious commitment to the American form of free-enterprise economic system, with its supposed almost immaculate joining of private interest to public well-being.

Consider some of the harsh lines of the reality that has broken through the dreamtime image so long cherished:

◆ the elitist contempt of high American officials for the ordinary people they are supposed to serve that is implicit in the decades of sophisticated deceit and urbane barbarity revealed by the Pentagon Papers, deceit and urbanity that enabled those officials to wrest from the American people 'democratic' authority to desolate three inoffensive peasant societies;

◆   the very nadir of systematic abuse of minds and bodies by American institutions and policies that is revealed in Lieutenant Calley's trial plea after the My Lai massacre: 'nobody ever told us they were human';

◆   the discovery that General Motors, Standard Oil and Firestone Tyres, publicly among the most patriotic and self-righteous of American corporations, had privately conspired together to destroy much of America's public transport system in order to boost the sale of their products (Snell 1974); and that ITT had not only continued during the war to operate factories in Germany that built bombers for the German Airforce, but subsequently collected $27 million indemnity from the American people because the American Airforce bombed ITT's German factories (Sampson 1974:45).

◆   finally, the most crushing blow of all — the corruption that enveloped an American president and in no small measure the American presidency also, when it was cynically traded for a lawless pardon.

Moreover Nixon was, in 1972, no mistrusted or unwanted president. Since his fall it is common to hear people recall Nixon's history of deceit, ruthlessness and corruption running back twenty years. But in 1972 he was still the new, warm, almost lovable Nixon who (as responsible commentators observed in their role of official image-makers to his presidency) had grown, had gained a new stature, almost a new personality, under the sanctifying influence of the responsibilities of presidential office.

While the image-makers thus re-created and projected Nixon so that he won more popular votes than any previous presidential candidate in American history — in this very period, the presidential tapes reveal, the President and his highest aides and ministers were plotting, in the diction and the moral temper of a clique of Mafia thugs, how they might use the powers of the presidency even further to corrupt and deceive. Nor is there any longer, unfortunately, substantial reason to believe that, if Kennedy or Johnson had been reckless enough to put the reality behind their public images on as many spools of tape as Nixon, their credibility gaps would have been notably less.

The corruption of American ideals and American power which the past decade has revealed are an American tragedy. But, given the scale of American power, they constitute also a world problem of a quite different order of magnitude: an unpredictable source of exacerbation to the risk of nuclear annihilation. For this reason it is of the first importance to try to understand how the tragic deterioration in the American democratic system has come about — and whether and how it might be remediable.

In so far as cultural history is continuous, any starting date for an explanation of the contemporary American malaise must be arbitrary. That point acknowledged, I shall, for reasons I hope to make clear, start at the beginning of this century.

The most influential social thinkers in the recent history of American society have been William James and John Dewey. Both were men of exemplary character and generous humane intent. But just as Marx did not intend Stalin, so the intentions of James and Dewey have not determined the consequences of their theories. Both were pragmatists; that is to say, they made the truth of a belief depend not on the evidence which leads to its adoption but on the consequences which follow that adoption.

Because they were also popular evangelists for pragmatism, it is convenient to refer to James and Dewey for a summary characterization of the pragmatic outlook. (American culture has, of course, a much longer history of pragmatic preoccupation with appearances and consequences). As Boorstin (1961:212) succinctly observes: 'The whole American tradition of pragmatism, from Benjamin Franklin, who insisted that it was less important whether any religious belief was true than whether the consequences of the belief were wholesome, down to William James ... has expressed a consuming interest in the appearance of things'. James (1907:75, 222, 299) held that 'an idea is true so long as to believe it is profitable to our lives' and that '"the true" ... is only the expedient in the way of our thinking, just as "the right" is only the expedient in the way of our behaving'. He maintained, for example, that if the belief that God exists works satisfactorily in the widest sense of the word, it is true; and added, 'experience shows that it certainly does work'.

Dewey (1920:128–30) similarly held that beliefs should be distinguished as 'good' and 'bad', not as 'true' and 'false'. Beliefs are good if believing them has beneficial consequences. 'Facts' do not exist for Dewey, Bertrand Russell (1945:825–6) observes, 'in the sense that "facts" are stubborn and cannot be manipulated'. Dewey (1938:7–11, 118, 546) proposed to replace the notion of truth with the notion of 'warranted assertibility'. Any belief which can be claimed to bring useful consequences may acquire 'warranted assertibility' on that ground alone.

The notion of 'warranted assertibility' already has an air of Watergate about it. For the moment we shall not follow that particular lead, expect to cite Russell's warning about any philosophy which, by making the consequences of a belief the test of its truth, delivers to powerful individuals and nations the right to say what beliefs shall be called 'good' or 'true'.

> In all this I feel a grave danger ... The concept of 'truth' as something dependent on facts largely outside human control has been one of the ways in which philosophy hitherto has inculcated the necessary element of humility. When this check upon pride is removed, a further step is taken on the road toward a certain kind of madness — the intoxication of power ... I am persuaded that ... any philosophy which, however unintentionally, contributes to [this intoxication] is increasing the danger of vast social disaster. (Russell 1945:828)

For twenty years from about 1900 there was, in the American press, a 'flood of articles on pragmatism'. This flood was started by James and Dewey. James employed much vivid rhetoric such as 'truth is what works', 'the true is the expedient' and 'faith in a fact helps create the fact' (Weisner 1958:180).

James and Dewey's evangelism *coincided* with the growth of a 'problem' for business corporations, for which their pragmatic viewpoint authorized a congenial 'solution'; it was closely *followed* by the development of a mass communications technology (especially radio and television) which greatly assisted the implementation of that solution.

The pragmatic viewpoint — denying the existence of a world independent of human belief — advocated that human beings should resolve their problems and frustrations by adopting and promulgating any belief which 'works' to that effect. The following observations by V. O. Key, professor of government at Harvard University, indicate the congeniality of this viewpoint to American corporations in the political context that developed after 1900:

> Businessmen are a small minority highly vulnerable to political attack ... They ... have to depend on something other than their votes. They have to use their wits — and their money — to generate a public opinion that acquiesces in the enjoyment by business of its status in the economic order ... To gain public favour business associations employ in large numbers public relations experts, those masters of the verbal magic that transmutes private advantage into the public good ... [and] continuing propaganda calculated to shape public attitudes favourably toward the business system. (Key 1958:103)

Thus as industrial power grew after 1900 a conscious policy of managing public attitudes to retain that power came to be adopted. From about 1920 an increasing number of corporations appointed public relations executives whose function was to deal in and with words, words designed to influence the public without necessarily involving any basic change of attitude or action on the part of the company (Bernays 1952:87).

By the mid-1930s a well-organized, nationwide business propaganda system had developed, a campaign concerned with selling the ideas and values of the free-enterprise system to the American people. The selling of these almost hallowed ideas also became an exercise in promoting pragmatic values, and this was done with slogans such as 'all the traffic will bear', 'repetition is reputation' and 'truth is believability' (Brady 1943:292–3; Bursk 1948:372–84). After World War II business interests more and more used their public relations resources for the 'dissemination of political ideology ... [until they produced] an almost overwhelming propaganda of doctrine ... [and] saturation of the media with advertising calculated to sell ideas rather than merchandise' (Key 1958:106–7).

By 1948 American business's anti-New Deal/socialist/communist propaganda campaign was costing $100 million a year for such advertising alone (MacDougall 1952:568; *Fortune* September 1950:78). The year 1950 brought an unplanned bonus in Senator Joe McCarthy; and that profit, duly cultivated, brought in 1952 the final dividend to which the campaign was ultimately directed (*Fortune* September 1950:79; Moulton and McKee 1951:126): an end to twenty years of Democratic administrations (an unbroken period equal to the sum of *all* Democratic administrations in the ninety years before 1933).

One general point should not escape notice. There is a remarkable correspondence in attitude to truth between pragmatists and propagandists. Both justify the promotion of false beliefs wherever it is supposed that false beliefs have socially useful consequences. Indeed the principal difference between them consists perhaps in this: the ordinary propagandist may know that he is telling lies, but the pragmatist-propagandist, having redefined truth to make it indistinguishable from propaganda, is likely to become inescapably trapped in the supposedly 'useful' deceptions and illusions he approves as 'warranted assertibilities'.

I wish now to trace the growing accommodation of intellectuals associated with American industry to the partisan and pragmatic values of business, and the convenient rationales by which (as true pragmatists in their own right) they preserved their pretensions to integrity without handicap to their career chances.

Until 1900 American business corporations took a contemptuous attitude to public opinion. But from 1900 to 1910 Upton Sinclair and others so effectively exposed the exploitation and brutality of American industry that, as *Fortune* magazine wrote later, 'business did not discover ... until its reputation had been all but destroyed ... that in a democracy nothing is more important than [public opinion]' ('Business is still ...' 1949:198). This discovery led rapidly to the development of a profession of specialists in 'public relations' whose task it was to ensure that public beliefs about industry were such as to keep both industry and the public happy. (It should perhaps be recalled that, according to James and Dewey, any public belief that has such consequences is true.) Ivy Lee was the first great PR man. He taught business to use the press. But his 'best known feat', as *Fortune* observes, 'was to convert John D. Rockefeller, in the public mind, from an ogre to a benefactor' (ibid.:70).

After Ivy Lee, Edward L. Bernays was the next major figure in the new propaganda–public relations field, a field he developed and dominated for the next thirty years. By 1937 *Business Week*, after noting that Bernays was 'a nephew of Sigmund Freud, the great Viennese psychoanalyst', observed that 'Mr Bernays has attained corresponding stature in his own sphere of psychology', which *Business Week* described as the motivation and control of the 'mass mind' (23 January 1937:34).

A major application of the pragmatic conception of truth came in 1917. With American entry into World War I, a Committee on Public Information (better known as the Creel Committee) was formed. Bernays, who worked with the committee, reports that 'every known device of persuasion and suggestion [was employed] to sell our war aims to the American people', who were initially unenthusiastic. Bernays (1952:71, 75, 74) observed that the Creel Committee's 'reports that the Germans were beasts and Huns were generally accepted. The most fantastic atrocity stories were believed'. The Creel Committee was generally credited with producing 'a revolutionary change in the sentiments of the nation'. Bernays considered that at the end of the war businessmen realized that the public could be harnessed to their cause in the same way that they were harnessed during the war to the national cause. Not surprisingly, when Bernays and others associated with the Creel Committee 'returned to civilian life [they] applied (on behalf of business) the publicity methods they had learned during the war' (ibid.:78).

The use of propaganda by corporations and industries to control public opinion grew, and Bernays prospered. *Fortune* magazine later wrote that 'the 1920's ... were notable for the rise of E. L. Bernays [who] ... became known for what he called "the engineering of consent", and for "creating news"' ('Business is still ... ' 1949:200). By 1923 Bernays was giving courses in public relations and propaganda at New York University. In 1928 the *American Journal of Sociology* published a how-to-do-it article by Bernays (1928) entitled 'Manipulating Public Opinion', in which Bernays paid tribute to sociologists for the help he obtained from their work.

From 1930 to 1960 Professor Harold Lasswell held a position of academic leadership in the field of propaganda and communication comparable with Bernays's leading role as a practitioner in the business world (see Crick 1959:176). In 1933, in an article for the *Encyclopedia of the Social Sciences*, Lasswell cynically observes that since the 'masses are still captive to ignorance and superstition', the arrival of democracy, in America and elsewhere, has 'compelled the development of a whole new technique of control, largely through propaganda'. For propaganda, Lasswell continues, is 'the one means of mass mobilisation which is cheaper than violence, bribery or other possible control techniques'. Moreover he held (in conformity with the corporate view) that propaganda was essential in a democracy because 'men are often poor judges of their own interests' and must therefore be swayed by propaganda to make choices they would otherwise not make (Lasswell 1930–35:523, 524, 527).

Until the mid-1930s conscientious objection to the engineering of consent had been quite widely evident. But by 1947 the war for control over the American mind had all but been won. Objection to democratic propaganda on ethical grounds had almost completely disappeared by this time. One of the reasons for this silence was that by 1947 large numbers of social scientists and university departments were actively engaged in promoting the practices of consent-engineering — largely because they worked on behalf of corporations.

In 1947 an article by Bernays entitled 'The Engineering of Consent' was published in the prestigious *Annals of the American Academy of Political and Social Sciences*. In this article Bernays offers a rationale for the use of propaganda in a democracy which *Fortune* magazine and others later adopted. The logic of this rationale consists in equating 'propaganda' with 'persuasion', and then with 'democracy'. 'The engineering of consent', Bernays firmly and deceitfully asserted, 'is the very essence of the democratic process, the freedom to persuade and suggest'. There would be many business-men today who would agree with these disingenuous sentiments.

By this date Bernays displayed the same elitist contempt for the ordinary citizen and for democracy that we saw in Lasswell in 1933. Bernays (1947:114–15) observed that the average American adult 'has only six years of schooling ... [Therefore] democratic leaders must play their part in ... engineering consent ... Today it is impossible to overestimate the importance of engineering consent; it affects almost every aspect of our daily lives'.

In 1949 Bernays was honoured by the American Psychological Association for his contributions to science and society ('Edward L. Bernays ... ' 1949:265). In the same year *Fortune* magazine, following Bernays's lead, observed that 'it is as impossible to imagine a genuine democracy without the science of persuasion [i.e. propaganda] as it is to think of a totalitarian state without coercion'. Such a paucity of imagination is unusual. *Fortune* continued: 'The daily tonnage output of propaganda and publicity ... has become an important force in American life. Nearly half of the contents of the best newspapers is derived from publicity releases; nearly all the contents of the lesser papers ... are directly or indirectly the work of PR departments' ('Business is still ... ' 1949:69).

In 1950 a particularly mordant description by Lasswell (1950:180) of the role of propaganda in (American) democracy was republished in a set of readings 'representative of the best work in the field':

> Conventions have arisen which favour the ventilation of opinion and the taking of votes. Most of that which formerly could be done by violence and intimidation must now be done by argument and persuasion. Democracy has proclaimed the dictatorship of [debate], and the technique of dictating to the dictator is named propaganda.

One voice in opposition to these cynical rationalizations was Professor William Albig of Illinois University. In 1956 Albig (1957:14) reviewed the work of the previous twenty years on public opinion and related subjects. He observed that in that time 'there has been more organised study of public opinion in the U.S .... and more special pleading and propaganda ... than in all previous cultural history'. Albig found that whereas before 1936 there had been continuous concern 'with questions of ethics in relation to the formation and effects of public opinion', this concern had largely disappeared from later writing and research. By contrast he found in the later work evidence of the intense excitement of professionals at the vision of the possibility of increased psychological control of their fellow men, and evidence also of 'further degeneration of respect for their target, the common man'. Albig concluded his review with the warning that 'many of the younger social scientists' had not 'adequately pondered' the likely political results of the values and assumptions expressed in their work (ibid.:21–2). Such pondering of course would have usually led to them losing their contracts with business.

In 1961 an American historian, Daniel Boorstin, published a book entitled *The Image; or What Happened to the American Dream*. Boorstin, who is now librarian of the Library of Congress, was much concerned about the effects of the huge growth in advertising and associated propaganda. One major effect, in his view, had been a popular shift from concern with 'ideals' to concern with 'images'. It is instructive to compare Boorstin's description of American society in 1960 with the ideas about truth promoted by James and Dewey fifty years earlier. Boorstin (1961:84, 205) wrote that 'the "corporate image" ... is, of course, the most elaborately and expensively contrived of the images of our age', and that 'the momentous sign of the rise of image-thinking and its displacement of ideals is, of course, the rise of advertising'. Boorstin considered that Americans have underestimated the effect of the rise of advertising. 'We think it has meant an increase of untruthfulness. In fact it has meant a reshaping of our very concept of truth.'

In consequence of this reshaping, Boorstin saw that 'not truth but credibility is the modern [American] test. We share this standard with the advertising men themselves'. He considered that all American 'citizen–consumers are daily less interested in whether something is a fact than in whether it is convenient that it should be believed'. As a nation, Boorstin observed that Americans

> have come to think ... that our main problem is abroad. How to 'project' our images to the world? Yet the problem abroad is only a symptom of our deeper problem at home. We have come to believe in our own images, till we have projected ourselves out of this world [so that] now, in the height of our power ... we are threatened by a new and peculiarly American menace ... It is the menace of unreality ... We risk being the first people in history to have been able to make their illusions so vivid, so persuasive, so 'realistic' that they can live in them. We are the most illusioned people on earth. Yet we dare not become disillusioned, because our illusions are the very house in which we live; they are our news, our heroes ... our very experience. (ibid.:227, 212, 241, 240)

Thus by 1960, thirty years after the *American Journal of Sociology* had published Bernays's article 'Manipulating Public Opinion',

American public opinion had been manipulated, in Boorstin's phrase, 'out of this world'. In less than another decade, the pragmatic displacement of 'truth' by desirable belief and of stubborn facts by 'warranted assertibilities' had played a manifest part in producing the outcome Russell warned about in 1945: 'a certain kind of madness — the intoxication of power ... increasing the danger of vast social disaster'.

And so to Vietnam and Watergate and the difficult road back to truth and an honouring of the democratic rights of citizens — a road which cannot be totally traversed until the subject of propaganda and its control in American society — almost entirely neglected for forty years by political scientists — is afforded an urgent priority. The key political problems confronting the United States have neither changed nor ameliorated since Professor Robert Dahl defined them in 1959. 'How much', he asked, 'of the generally, favourable attitude of Americans toward business [and the consequent] absence of any well-defined alternative can be attributed to deliberate efforts to manipulate attitudes?'

If government of the people by the people for the people has any meaningful sense and if the American Dream is not to end in a business-appointed, more adroitly managed version of Orwell's 1984, then it is of cardinal importance that the problems described by Dahl are brought to light. That light would subvert those pragmatic processes for manufacturing consent and would lead to the development of a more critical cultural consciousness.

PART II

EXPORTING FREE-ENTERPRISE PERSUASION

CHAPTER 6

GRASSROOTS AND TREETOPS PROPAGANDA

Australian adoption of US fashions tends to occur with a time-lag, and large-scale opinion management is no exception. The long period of Democratic Party rule from 1932 to 1952, and American business's responses to it, find close parallels in fairly recent developments in Australia. Some points of similarity can be illustrated in relation to what have been termed 'grassroots' and 'treetops' propaganda.

Roosevelt's election in 1932 and re-election in 1936 'shocked businessmen all over the country' (Rippa 1958:53), so business turned to 'the development of structures and techniques for "educating" the public on a nationwide basis' (Cleveland 1947:323). For this purpose the president of the National Association of Manufacturers (NAM) wrote, 'all channels through which the public may be reached must be used' (Tedlow 1976:30–1).

In Australia the election of a Labor government in 1972 'shocked Australian capitalism greatly', Geoff Allen (1976) reported. (Allen was for a time executive director of the Business Council.) In April 1973 the Australian Chamber of Commerce launched a nationwide 'economic education campaign'. Following the Whitlam government's re-election in 1974 ex-Liberal minister Allen Fairhall 'called for a national "propaganda" organisation' which would 'use all the techniques … available' to communicate with the public. Supported by some 'large initial donations' from leading corporations, the new organization, to be known as Enterprise Australia, was 'ready to take off' in November 1975. However, in deference to the constitutional coup in which Whitlam was sacked by the Governor-General on 11 November, the launching was delayed until April 1976. Enterprise Australia was expected, Allen reported, to be 'by far the most important group in the propaganda warfare for capitalism'.

Enterprise Australia (EA) is primarily concerned with popular proselytizing for a reactionary or so-called 'dry' economic viewpoint. Its principal audiences comprise schoolchildren, tertiary students, teachers, industrial employees and the general public. In recent years EA has given greatly increased attention to promotion of 'human relations'-type programs in industry, including employee participation, leadership training and quality circles.

Enterprise Australia has met some resistance from teachers and teachers' unions in the public school sector, but relatively little from other unions. For several years its head, Jack Keavney, claimed repeatedly that EA had achieved greater acceptance from unions than had any comparable management-sponsored organization overseas. Fortunately Australian unions have recently recognized the need to distance themselves from EA. Altogether EA's activities are meeting enlightened resistance from a fairly sceptical Australian society. How much these propaganda activities have contributed to the present conservative economic climate is difficult to estimate. They are, however, slowly accustoming the Australian community to the idea that it is an appropriate part of business's role in democracy to judge what beliefs we must hold in order to be 'economically educated', and to spend vast amounts of tax-deductible dollars to secure such beliefs. If the proselytizers are ever able to make that idea as acceptable here as it is in the United States, the prospects for Australian democracy, and especially for the Australian unions, will be serious.

The kind of propaganda that was employed on such a large scale in the United States in the period around World War II is known as 'grassroots' propaganda. Its purpose is to reach as vast a number of people as possible in order to change public opinion so that it is sympathetic to business interests. This is Enterprise Australia's objective also. American experience from the 1930s to the 1950s provides a useful perspective on the propaganda techniques EA and some other Australian business agencies are likely to adopt. But developments in Australia have also borrowed from a new assault on public opinion by American business during the 1970s.

The 1970s propaganda campaign in the United States largely replicated the grassroots program of 1945–50. To this extent it contains little that is novel excepts for its scale and its impact on US politics. But the 1970s campaign also involved a great expansion of a more sophisticated form of propaganda which one might call, for purposes of distinction, 'treetops' propaganda, aimed at the leaders of society.

Rapid growth in this form of contemporary propaganda is the hallmark of the neo-conservative movement wherever it appears. Indeed the sole novelty of the neo-conservative movement lies in its demonstrated capacity to recruit intellectuals who will convert, in an elite version of the factory system, millions of corporate dollars into up-market propaganda for corporate interests.

Grassroots propaganda

For more than a decade after the McCarthy period, business in the United States had little trouble with critical public opinion, or of anything else American. But first Vietnam, then Watergate, changed all that and produced a disastrous collapse in public regard for all American institutions, and for business in particular. To counter this critical public sentiment the Advertising Council in 1975 once again initiated a national program of conservative 'economic education' on a scale similar to the postwar program. In 1977 *Fortune* described the continuing Ad Council campaign as 'a study in gigantism, saturating the media and reaching practically everybody' (Weaver 1977:188). By 1978, according to an expert witness before a Congressional inquiry, American business was spending $US1000 million per annum on grassroots propaganda (Baxter et al. 1978:67). This expenditure was aimed at persuading the American public that their interests were the same as business's interests.

The effectiveness of this new billion dollar propaganda program was monitored by a standardized, vastly detailed poll sponsored by the Advertising Council and repeated every twelve months. By 1980 the annual poll showed that 'the proportion of Americans who think there is too much government regulation' — a matter at the very heart of the New Right propagandists' concerns — 'had risen from 42% ... to 60%' (MacDougall 1980). Ronald Reagan's election followed. A New York firm which specializes in monitoring public opinion for business reviewed the changed mood of American politics and wrote: 'Between Jimmy Carter's election in 1976 and Ronald Reagan's victory in 1980, the outlook of the American people underwent one of those decisive shifts that historians generally label as watershed events'. The review quaintly speculates about possible explanations for the startling reversal of public opinion it reports. Naturally it entirely overlooks business's billion dollar propaganda campaigns (Yankelovich and Kaagan 1981:696–714). Again, as in 1919–21 and 1945–50, a business-sponsored assault on public opinion brought about a dramatic nationwide swing to conservatism.

And yet the social and moral significance of buying public opinion with this kind of money and what it means for democracy has not been raised in any substantial way by social scientists.

Treetops propaganda

'Treetops' propaganda is not directed at the person on the street. It is directed at influencing a select group of influential people: policy-makers in parliament and the civil service, newspaper editors and reporters, economics commentators on TV and radio. Its immediate purpose is to set the terms of debate, to determine the kinds of questions that will dominate public discussion — in a word to set the political agenda in ways that are favourable to corporate interests.

As this tactic succeeds, public discussion no longer assumes, for example, that affluent societies have a first responsibility to provide jobs for all who want them, and the debate is instead about whether 6 or 10 percent is a 'natural' (and by implication acceptable) level of unemployment. It is no longer taken for granted that we have a right to clean air; rather the debate centres on how far the cost to industry for polluting the community is economically acceptable. The debate ceases to be about how far and in what areas it is necessary for government to be involved in the economy and centres instead on arguments for reduced government involvement and timetables for achieving this. The debate is no longer about the social role of unions but about the best way to reduce union powers. And finally, with successful treetops propaganda the debate will never be about the curtailment of the manipulative power of contemporary corporations.

The tactic by which such changes in the political agenda are secured is for the corporations to search out articulate conservative economists and amenable academics, gather them together in lavishly funded tax-deductible think-tanks and pay them handsomely to inundate relevant debate with an endless stream of books and research reports. This development proceeded at an extraordinary pace in the United States during the 1970s. From there it is now in process of rapid transfer to Australia, and it has made considerable progress in Britain also.

The principal conservative think-tank in Britain is the Institute of Economic Affairs (IEA). It has published, subsidized and disseminated a very large amount of free-market-oriented literature and is widely credited with significant contribution to the emergence of the Thatcher era. In 1978 Lord Ralph Harris, the director of the

Institute, provided a succinct account of the two levels of propaganda activity that I have distinguished, and their relationship. 'A growing army of IEA economists in the broad classical liberal tradition', Harris reports (1978:10–12), 'have kept up their long range, long-term, scholarly bombardment of one enemy position after another'. Harris rejects the view of some businessmen that 'all effort should be concentrated on simple propaganda aimed at the man in the street'. This approach, he objects, is like supposing 'that ground troops could advance without support from the intellectual artillery to soften up the enemy's entrenched strong points'. 'Would an army commander send in his best infantry before aerial bombardment?' The business-supported output of Harris's 'army' of free-market economists is distributed in Australia by the business-funded Centre for Independent Studies (Sydney) among others.

In the United States the work of many private think-tanks which develop policies on a range of national issues is known as 'policy research.' Such organizations have been around for a long time, some more right-wing, like the Conference Board and the Hoover Institute, others less so, like the Brookings Institution and the Committee for Economic Development. The 1970s saw the emergence of an aggressive new breed among these organizations, which were lavishly funded by corporations and produced an endless flow of market-oriented studies. Perhaps most importantly, the new think-tanks placed a quite new emphasis on promoting and disseminating their products nationwide — that is, on proselytizing. It is this aspect of their work which justifies the label 'treetops propaganda'. The new, or revitalized, think-tanks and the scholars they recruited virtually created the neo-conservative movement of the 1970s (Rosen 1976:39–40). I shall discuss three of the more prominent among the think-tanks.

US think-tanks

The most important of the new think-tanks is the American Economic Institute for Public Policy Research (AEI). It is the home base and long-time patron of Irving Kristol, guru of the neo-conservative movement. AEI's board of trustees is comprised 'almost entirely of representatives of major corporations'. Its budget grew from less than $1 million in 1970 to over $7 million in 1978, its staff from 24 to 125, and in addition it has 100 adjunct scholars working on AEI-sponsored studies. In 1977 its 'vast outpouring of material and activities', the *New York Times* reported, 'included 54 studies, 22 forums and conferences, 15 analyses of important legislative proposals, 7 journals and newsletters, a ready-made set of editorials sent regularly to 105 newspapers, public affairs programs carried by more than 300 television stations and centers for display of AEI material in some 300 college libraries'.

In 1978 Irving Kristol was co-chairman of a new drive to raise a $60 million endowment for AEI (Crittenden 1978a:9). Although among the largest, AEI is only one among many business-sponsored centres of policy research in the United States.

The Heritage Foundation, established in 1973, and a little smaller than the AEI, is a particularly vigorous proselytizer for neo-conservatism. It is the recent home of Professor Owen Harries, sometime adviser to Malcolm Fraser. As a cheer-leader for the market economy, the Heritage Foundation organizes communication among what it calls a 'Resource Bank [of] a thousand academics and several hundred other policy research groups' (Gruber 1986:126).

In 1978 the president of the foundation, Dr Edwin Feulner, addressed an international conference of corporate opinion managers which were assembled in London. 'The American public policy arena', he reported happily, 'is awash with in-depth academic studies'. He went on to explain how the dominance of public debate by free-market think-tanks is effective 'in keeping ... debate within its proper perspective'. To assist this result the foundation provides newspaper columns,published as local editorials, to 'several thousand newspapers' throughout the United States (Feulner 1978:21–4).

The last American think-tank I shall discuss is the Business Roundtable. Founded in 1972, the Roundtable comprises the chief executive officers of 194 of America's largest corporations. Its membership represents approximately half the GNP of the United States (McQuaid 1981:115). The Roundtable's GNP is greater than the GNP any country in the world apart from the United States. It is a prototypical treetops propaganda and lobbying organization. In the same year it was founded, Justice Lewis Powell (shortly afterwards elevated to the Supreme Court by the Nixon administration) wrote a famous memorandum for the US Chamber of Commerce which was a virtual manifesto for the neo-conservative movement. In it Powell urged business 'to buy the top academic reputations in the country to add credibility to corporate studies and give business a stronger voice on the campuses'. In the following decade business founded and funded more than forty chairs of Free Enterprise, with appropriately selected incumbents (Green and Buchsbaum 1980:15; Montgomery 1981:C1, C5).

The Roundtable has added prestige and a powerful political focus to the mobilization of intellectuals on behalf of corporate interests. It maintains fifteen 'task forces' which produce 'position papers' on various issues. A study by Ralph Nader's organization says that the Roundtable buys supporting research 'through the hiring of expensive consultants and the sponsoring of academic studies'. Economist Arthur Okun of the Brookings Institution has observed in this connection: 'Of course much of the evidence will be self-serving. Some briefs I have seen ... just couldn't represent the earnest professional judgement of their authors'. The development and dissemination of information, the Nader study concludes, 'is a cornerstone activity of any lobbying group, especially the Roundtable. Money generates information in the form of studies [and] position papers ... And the Roundtable has access to all the money it needs' (Green and Buchsbaum 1980:32, 95).

The Roundtable maintains an image of statesmanlike moderation. However, 'the dominant purpose leading to [its] formation', the Nader report finds, 'was a desire to combat and reduce union power'; and 'it proclaims moderation while sabotaging moderate reform'. Officially the Roundtable does not engage in grassroots propaganda, preferring 'to pressure Congress with the best information money can buy'. But covertly it works closely with grassroots activists like the NAM and the Chamber of Commerce. Roundtable members consider their defeat of labour law reform and consumer protection bills in 1977–88 'to be their largest victories'. It is instructive to consider some of the means the Roundtable and its allies employed to achieve these victories (ibid.:115–17, 98–9, 79).

The defeat of labour law reform

The proposed labour law reform act sought to secure some limited reduction in the peculiarly American handicaps which affected the capacity of a declining union movement to recruit new members. It sought to do this by preventing managements from indefinitely delaying representation elections and by allowing unions access to the workplace and to present the case for unionization wherever managements called meetings of employees to argue against unionization. The Business Roundtable joined the NAM, the Chamber of Commerce and others in a National Action Committee to wage all-out war on the bill.

While its associates flooded Congress with stimulated mail running to millions of letters and postcards 'attacking the power and
legitimacy of organised labour', the National Action Committee
kept a relatively low profile. It hired a public relations firm to
manage its 'enormous grass roots efforts' which, in an update of the
Mohawk Valley Formula, were directed at stimulating public sentiment hostile to unions. To this end opinion surveys were used for
publicity 'as quickly as the pollsters could produce the right result.
In addition, 329 pages of editorials opposing labour law reforms
were prepared and distributed to local papers country-wide'
(ibid.:119–23 and Appendix C). In December 1977, as though to
signal an all-out war on labour, the president of the NAM
announced the formation of the 'Council on a Union Free
Environment' which would, he said, be the first 'single-purpose
national organisation devoted to the maintenance of a union-free
environment in the United States' (Mills 1979:98).

The Roundtable and its allies also organized a national distribution of cartoons, pamphlets, ads and newsletters in opposition to the
Consumer Protection Agency (CPA). The Roundtable hired a public
relations firm to distribute canned editorials and cartoons to 1000
daily newspapers and 2800 weeklies. Portions of the distributed
materials were published — without indication of source — approximately 2000 times. The Roundtable also sponsored a fraudulent
poll which claimed to show 81 percent of Americans opposed to the
CPA in opposition to independent polls which claimed to show 2 to
1 in favour. The Chamber of Commerce exploited the fraudulent poll
by promoting its results in full-page ads in the *New York Times* and
elsewhere. (Green & Buchsbaum 1980:111–14, 38–9; Percy
1977:20). The chamber also 'gathered editorials from hundreds of
newspapers, including ... Chamber-originated editorials, and distributed them to law-makers in an effort to show widespread grassroots support for the Chamber's positions' (MacDougall 1980).

Despite the Roundtable's covert involvement in grassroots
propaganda, its most important role by far remained at the treetops
level of policy research and related pressure on Congress. By 1976
the Roundtable was already, *Business Week* reported, 'the most powerful voice of business in Washington', eclipsing the NAM and the
Chamber of Commerce ('Business' Most Powerful ...' 1976:60). The
defeat of the bill for a consumer protection agency was, *Fortune*
reported in 1980, 'a signal victory' for the Roundtable and 'in retrospect a watershed in the history of consumerism' (Guzzardi
1980:49). A review of the Roundtable's history in *The Nation* sums

up the Roundtable's achievements. After a decade of defeat for the trade union movement, segments of a divided and weakened labour movement 'are now negotiating with key Roundtable figures for a separate peace. With this final twist, the New Deal comes full circle. In the late 1970s, as in the late 1920s, the business of America is business, and the populace cannot imagine it otherwise' (Ferguson and Rogers 1979:625).

As in 1919–21 and 1946–50 so in 1976–80: complete business hegemony over American society was re-established. On each occasion the same propaganda and public relations methods (if only with increased sophistication) have accomplished the same result: the closing of the American mind.

Education and the free market

Intervention by corporate interests in the American educational system for the purpose of checking the growth of tolerant values opposed to free-market conservatism had influential support in the late 1960s. Lewis F. Powell was (until his elevation to the Supreme Court in 1972) an early and influential advocate of the view that business should restrict its financial support to educational and research centres of an adequately conservative temper. George Will, perhaps the most widely read and influential of American columnists, has, for almost a decade, advocated a similar economic purge of colleges and universities whose temper is insufficiently right-wing. So also has William Simon, secretary to the Treasury from 1973 to 1977. Simon's contributions will serve to illustrate, if a little flamboyantly, the values and scale of the more intellectual component of the campaign to reshape the political agenda that has led to the dominance of the neo-conservative movement.

In 1978 Simon published a best-seller entitled *A Time for Truth* — presumably with a little help from his neo-conservative friends and certainly to applause from Nobel Prize winners Friedman and Hayek, who both contributed forewords. It sold 180 000 copies in hard cover alone. Written for a popular audience, the book concentrates on evoking fear and a sense of crisis: fear that everything Americans hold dear is under immediate threat from subversive intellectuals who seek to perpetuate the allegedly dangerous purposes of Roosevelt's New Deal. Its 240 pages endlessly reiterate a central fraudulent claim: 'The connection between economic and political freedom ... is real and unbreakable ... to lose one is to lose the other ... A nation that decreases its economic freedom must be less politically free'. In consequence, so the argument went, unless government regulatory intrusions on corporations are halted and rolled back American democracy will shortly collapse under a social-ist dictatorship (Simon 1978a:14, 32). Simon applauds a 'brilliant' film on this theme, *The Incredible Bread Machine* (to which both he and Milton Friedman contributed commentaries). He observes with satisfaction that fifteen million people in the United States have seen the film and that 1200 prints of it are still circulating the country (ibid.:224). A paperback edition of Simon's book was published in Australia by McGraw-Hill in 1979. It was reviewed with pre-dictable hyperbole by Peter Samuel, who claimed it was having a great impact on federal parliamentarians.

Simon (1978a:191, 222; 1978b:6) offers an analysis of economic-political problems in 1978 and solutions to them. The Carter admin-istration is, he asserts, 'careening with frightening speed towards collectivism'. The regulatory agencies of 'an economic police state' are spreading 'terror' among the corporations. Simon, explicitly following Irving Kristol, attributes this crisis of American democra-cy to the pervasive influence of un-American intellectuals (Simon 1978a:193–5; Kristol 1975). He asks 'What then can we do?' and responds that 'funds generated by business must rush by the multi-millions' to the rescue. Some major foundations (he instances the Ford Foundation) have been 'taken over'. By whom? By the 'philo-sophical enemies' of capitalism, people of egalitarian outlook. The only possible solution is to create new foundations which will 'serve explicitly as intellectual refuges for the non-egalitarian scholars and writers in our society ... They must be given grants, grants and more grants in exchange for books, books and more books' (Simon 1978a:228–31).

Simon also proposed that business support must be withdrawn from (among others) 'America's major universities [which] are today churning out young collectivists by legions'. But business support 'must flow generously' to teaching and research centres that promote correct doctrine. Similarly, media sympathetic to conservative busi-ness views must be supported, but 'if a newspaper or magazine or broadcasting station wishes to serve as an ... agency for those who assault the capitalist system it should be entirely free to do so. Without capitalist money' — by which Simon means without adver-tising ('Simon: Preaching ...' 1978:1).

In the same year (1978) Simon became president of the Olin Foundation, established by the former chairman of the $1 billion Olin Corporation. The foundation concentrates on support for 'scholarship in the philosophy of a free society and a free market'. As reported by the *New York Times*,

> that means ... grants to such institutions as the American Enterprise Institute, the Hoover Institution, support for the Friedman and Wattenberg television programs and funding of centres for the study of free enterprise. In all the foundation and Mr Olin ... give some $3 million a year to such projects. (ibid.:1)

In 1978 Olin and Simon were in the process of establishing yet another foundation which would be 'based on a suggestion by Irving Kristol'. Its distinctive role would be to 'encourage corporations not yet involved in promotion of the free-market system to open their coffers'. The new organization, the Institute of Economic Affairs, would be administered jointly 'by scholars and business and foundation people' and would act as a consulting body for 'corporations wishing to finance conservative research projects' (ibid.:9).

IEA's board of trustees is comprised almost entirely of representatives of major corporations. It is headed by the vice-chairman of Mobil Corporation, which in 1975 was already spending $5 million per annum on advocacy advertising (Sethi 1977:17). IEA's budget grew from less than $1 million in 1970 to over $7 million in 1978, its staff from 24 to 125 plus 100 'adjunct scholars' working on IEA-sponsored studies.

The following year (1979) Irving Kristol was co-chairman of a new IEA drive to raise a $60 million endowment. Since 1983 the list of IEA-sponsored scholars has included the Australian Prime Minister Malcolm Fraser. IEA is only one, although among the largest, of many privately financed policy research centres in the United States.

I spent 1977 in the United States and could scarcely avoid observing that most university libraries I had occasion to use contained about a foot of index cards to publications by the IEA. Returning to Australia, I believed I had got some measure of IEA's activities substantially ahead of its influence reaching Australia. I was in consequence disconcerted to find on entering the library of my home university (the University of New South Wales) that an entire foyer was occupied with a display of selected books from 250 titles which had been donated to the library by the IEA. These donations established the University of New South Wales Library as an IEA Public Policy Research Centre. Four years later the donated titles had reached 400.

Before returning to the Australian context brief mention must be made of another significant — and certainly symbolic — American academic development. From early in the 1960s American corporations began to fund chairs of free enterprise with the explicit purpose of promoting and defending the free-enterprise system. Examples of these 'chairs for propaganda' are the Goodyear Chairs of Free Enterprise at Kent State University and the University of Akron, the W. H. Davies Chair of the American Free Enterprise System at Ohio State University and the Irwin Maier Chair of American Enterprise at the University of Wisconsin. The first such chair was established at Georgia State University in 1963; the next was not established till 1974. By 1978 there were twenty; by 1981 there were more than forty (Thompson 1977:19; Alsop 1978:1, 37). In Australia the first proposal for a chair of free enterprise came in 1981 from the country-based National Party in Queensland, with 'substantial financial support' promised by sympathetic businessmen (Broadbent 1981). To date [1976] negotiations on the matter with the University of Queensland and the Queensland Institute of Technology have been unsuccessful.

Australian treetops propaganda

Early in 1980 Anne Stewart, research officer with the Vehicle Builders Employees Federation, described — with an admirable breadth of vision — the anti-union offensive of the 1970s which so badly weakened labour in the United States, and warned that a similar offensive was in prospect here. Stewart's analysis (1980:484–9) provides a perspective that extends from the American Business Roundtable to its Australian counterpart and is as instructive for what it got wrong as for what it got right.

Stewart identifies the anti-union drive in the United States with the Roundtable and especially with its success in using the law and Congress against unions. She reviews the extensive anti-union legislation passed by Australian parliaments between 1975 and 1980 and sees this legislation as the build-up to a comparable business offensive here. While Stewart sees this development as the 'spread' to Australia of 'the business offensive in the United States', she regards it as primarily indigenous, a reaction by business to 'economic pressures'. These pressures (and native inclination) are sufficient, she believes, to generate and unify an anti-union drive by Australian business. Stewart suggests that the absence from the Australian scene of 'an indigenous Business Roundtable' to lead and urge business's attack does not indicate any lack of anti-union militancy; on the contrary, it may only signify that there is no need for one. Later that same year (December 1980), and before Stewart's paper reached publication, an Australian Business Roundtable was established.

Stewart's account of the expression in parallel legislation of business's anti-union drives in the United States and in Australia was accurate and timely. But the analysis went astray at two points. She identified the strength and effectiveness of the anti-union drive with the amount of legislation and other anti-union moves, *rather than identifying the anti-union drive with the amount of popular support it was able to create.* For this reason her analysis overlooked the importance of the propaganda activities of the American Business Roundtable and associated business agencies. Consequently she also overlooked the likelihood that similar bodies will be/are established in Australia (e.g. Enterprise Australia and the Business Roundtable) for precisely the reason of managing public opinion on the subject of unions. Malcolm Fraser obtained all the anti-union legislation he needed. But he never could use it because his specially conducted opinion polls continued to tell him that such action would not have enough public support to be politically viable. (This information comes from a source inside the political establishment of the period who has insisted on anonymity.) Had the Australian Business Roundtable been established five years earlier, public opinion against Australian unions would have been greater and so Fraser's legislation could have been put into practice.

The Australian Business Roundtable was modelled precisely and explicitly 'on the American organisation of the same name'. Initially it comprised the CEOs of Australia's twenty-nine largest corporations. The Roundtable immediately established 'task forces' (one on industrial relations and two others) which would be responsible for developing unified policies ('Twenty-nine Largest Corporations ...' 1981:1, 4).

The Roundtable's interest in sponsoring free-market-oriented policy research after the American manner surfaced briefly almost at its inception. A proposal reached the Industrial Relations Research Centre at the University of New South Wales in December 1980 that the Roundtable would be prepared to provide $500000 to fund an extended inquiry into the views and attitudes of heads of large corporations in Australia. The purposes of the inquiry would be to identify the principal problems and related policy issues seen by CEOs to face Australian business in the near future, and to develop as large a consensus as possible about what policies business should push for and about priorities among policy issues. The published record of the American Business Roundtable led to questions about the propriety of a university research centre undertaking work for its

Australian counterpart. Before these questions could be resolved the Business Roundtable withdrew its offer and was replaced as a prospective sponsor of the proposed research by the Committee for Economic Development in Australia (CEDA).

Two years later the Business Roundtable merged with the Australian Industries Development Association (AIDA) to become the Business Council (following but reversing the name change by which, in the United States, the Business Roundtable had substantially emerged from the membership of the older Business Council).

The Australian Business Council, headed by Geoff Allen, displays most of the hallmarks of American policy research organizations. Like the American Business Roundtable it is comprised of the CEOs of the largest corporations of the country (about seventy at recent count). It was established with the double purpose of research and promotion, that is, 'to conduct research on public policy questions that affect business' and to encourage the council's prestigious members (with support from its research and other services) 'to speak out to governments, unions and the community'. After the standard fashion of all treetops propaganda organizations the council publishes a *Bulletin* which is distributed to 'a wide audience of decision-makers in politics, the bureaucracy, the media, academia and business' (Burgess 1984:15).

Until the appearance of the Business Council, CEDA had long been the most important business-funded policy research organization in Australia. It was modelled on its American namesake, the Committee for Economic Development, with which its leaders maintain 'close and regular liaison' (ibid.:77) In 1980 CEDA published a book-length review by Dr Ian Marsh of business-supported policy research institutes in the United States, United Kingdom and Canada. The review, based on research supported by CEDA, was undertaken for the explicit purpose of discovering what 'lessons' might be learned from US experience about the development of private think-tanks in Australia. Dr Marsh, it should be acknowledged, brings an Australian frankness to his task that is not commonly found in American work. He describes the output of policy research think-tanks, which are concerned with shaping the political agenda, as 'invariably tendentious', but does not on that account question his own commitment to their development in Australia (Marsh 1980:1).

In 1984 CEDA established a 'Strategic Issues Forum' with responsibility for setting up 'task forces' and organizing research in a number of policy areas (Utz 1984:4). CEDA's Annual Report for

1984 suggests it should take the American Enterprise Institute as a model for 'the direction in which we should try to move'. CEDA (1984b) allows, however, that 'Australia is probably not yet ready' for a rapid shift in that direction. Nonetheless CEDA's role in tree-tops propaganda was rapidly expanding. In 1984–85 its income and expenditure rose by about 30 percent to $1.6 million. It established a comprehensive 'communications' program which includes book-length research reports on policy issues, articles, pamphlets and cassettes for wide distribution and, importantly, regular private briefings with key financial journalists, and regular luncheons with editors of newspapers and executives of TV and radio stations. As well CEDA organized seminars, conferences and overseas speakers, to give status and publicity to its views. Like all the new breed of think-tank proselytizers CEDA places great importance on timing — on completing and publishing its studies and reports so as to obtain a maximum impact on commissions and committees of inquiry and thus, in CEDA's phrasing, to 'play a positive role in shaping the political agenda'.

Timing, for instance, was a factor in 1984–85 when CEDA produced three major research reports to coincide with government-sponsored reviews of immigration policy, taxation reform and the industrial relations system. It will come as no surprise that these reports, commissioned from selected academic experts, concluded respectively that even when half a million Australians are out of work, increased immigration does not cause more unemployment; that indirect taxes should be increased and personal and company taxes reduced; and that union power should be reduced by cutting back the role of the arbitration system in favour of decentralized collective bargaining. 'The timing' of these three reports, CEDA (1985) concludes, 'was impeccable'. The last of them, under the authorship of Professors Niland and Turner of the University of New South Wales, 'was used in draft form as a contribution to the deliberations of the Hancock Committee [on Industrial Relations]'.

There are numerous other business-supported or -funded think-tanks which are contributing to the new prominence of neo-conservative ideas in economic debate in Australia. Most have been founded or revitalized during the last decade. All have 'communication' programs more or less after CEDA's fashion. A recent article by Anthony McAdam (1985) in the Sydney *Bulletin* provides an overview of this development. McAdam notes the rapid growth in influence of neo-conservative ideas until it is now 'undeniable that the New Right is mainly setting the agenda of the economics debate'. This 'is not surprising', he finds, 'since it is supported by a network of well-funded institutions staffed mostly by market-oriented economists'.

In the non-government arena McAdam sees the leading think-tanks responsible for this development to be the Centre for Independent Studies in Sydney and the Centre for Policy Studies at Monash University. Other think-tanks include the National Institute of Labour Studies (located at Flinders University, but wholly funded from outside), a revitalized Institute of Public Affairs in Melbourne and the Australian Institute for Public Policy, recently established in Perth by Liberal Party 'dry' John Hyde. This contingent of treetops propagandists is, of course, supplemented at the more popular level by nationwide proselytizers such as the chambers of commerce — which McAdam omits — and Enterprise Australia, which, as he acknowledges, 'propagates the same [free market] message'.

The total budgets of these bodies which promote New Right ideas and attitudes (and the list is far from complete) is of the order of $6–8 million per annum for treetops propaganda and $2–3 million for grassroots propaganda (Carey 1987a). But these figures give little idea of the actual resources expended. For at least some of the organizations involved, the donations in kind they receive from their corporate supporters (loan of executive personnel, clerical and printing assistance, accommodations, etc.) far exceed their official budgets. Enterprise Australia, for example, received donations of radio time in 1979 worth $1 million and in 1984 worth $5 million. In 1982 a business-funded 'foundation' spent $500 000 to produce a New Right textbook for schools which it then passed to Enterprise Australia for distribution (ibid.).

A corporate vision of guided democracy

Dr Ian Marsh, CEDA's expert on think-tanks, recently observed [1986] that 'the most recent phase of think-tank development has been associated with the advance of the neo-conservative movement. Think-tanks have been the principal sponsors of the neo-conservative program'. It is evident that a similar business-funded campaign to secure the dominance of a neo-conservative movement is under way here. This development must concern all Australians who value our traditional form of democracy sufficiently to heed Professor Dahl's warning, quoted in Chapter 2, that if 'political preferences are simply plugged into the system by leaders (business or other) in order to extract what they want from the system, *then the model of plebiscitary democracy is substantially equivalent to the model of totalitarian rule'* (Dahl 1959:37–8, emphasis added).

Nonetheless it is not the proliferation of conservative think-tanks in general to which we must respond. Rather it is the entire corporate approach of socially engineered democracy which is the problem. Over a long period in the United States business has honed its social engineering methods into an art-form so as to ensure that the dominant values and direction of American society conform to its preferences. Yet there are diverse aspects to this social engineering of opinions and attitudes. A notable instance was seen in the 'Project Australia' campaign launched with the purpose of inculcating in all of us the kind of mindless, unquestioning patriotism that is so readily exploited by conservative politicians and propagandists generally. Malcolm Fraser's governments spent $15 million on this project 'to make us proud of Australia'.

The Labor government in 1983, to its credit, terminated support for Project Australia. Nonetheless Hawke has continued, and if anything increased, Fraser's practice of buying full-page ads at public expense in newspapers all over Australia, ostensibly to explain his policies, but more commonly to sell them. This not only an indefensible practice for a democratic government but it is a particularly stupid one for a Labor government. For it gives encouragement, and indeed a moral right, to those who oppose Labor policies and have the necessary resources (notably big business) to take competing ad space. If ever Australian business chooses to compete in this way it will swamp the field and Labor, having led the way, will be able to make no objection.

Exactly this development has occurred in the United States, where so-called 'issue advertising' or 'advocacy advertising' has become a $100 million industry and a major aspect of business's grassroots propaganda. For example, during the conservative assault on public opinion that occurred between Carter's election and Reagan's election, Mobil Oil spent $5 million per annum on advocacy advertising, which included full-page ads in the *New York Times* once a fortnight. Even without Prime Minister Hawke's encouragement, advocacy advertising by business had been spreading to Australia. Almost all of it pushes policies that Australian trade unions would not support. Some of it has been explicitly hostile to unions, a recent instance being John Leard's full-page ads headed 'The Unions Are Taking Over Australia!' (*Australian* 28 January 1986) There is no novelty about this, of course. Prime Minister

Fraser took out ads to attack a strike in the Department of Social Service, and throughout October 1985 Australia Post took many full-page ads to attack striking mail-sorters. But the incidence is increasing as the general growth in advocacy advertising, long expected by the advertising industry, takes place. Advocacy advertising of course does nothing to help the public image of the trade union movement.

From shortsightedness or ignorance the present Labor government, instead of learning from American experience and setting its collective mind to protect Australian democracy against an assault by business-sponsored advocacy advertising, is paving the way to just that result. In the United States the Carter administration attempted, too late, to restrain business's advocacy advertising by taxation and other methods (Ehrbar 1978:68). In 1978, when American business was spending $1 billion per annum on grassroots propaganda (a significant part of it in the form of advocacy advertising) the Supreme Court in a 4 to 3 judgment overturned a law restricting such expenditure. In a dissenting opinion that the Australian Labor Party should take closely to heart, Justice Byron White wrote:

> the issue is whether a State may prevent corporate management from using the corporate treasury to propagate views having no connection with the corporate business. Shareholders in such entities ... certainly have not invested their money for the purpose of advancing political or social causes ... Corporations are artificial entities created by law for the purpose of furthering certain economic goals. It has long been recognised, however, that the special status of corporations has placed them in a position to control vast amounts of economic power which may, if not regulated, dominate not only the economy but also the very heart of our democracy, the electoral process. The State need not permit its own creation to consume it. (Baxter et al. 1978:68)

The grassroots and treetops proselytizing programs that are under way in Australia are only at their beginning, only a few years old. If American experience is any guide we must expect that corporations will come to regard the political stakes as so high that the programs will undergo whatever expansion is necessary to obtain their objectives. Moreover, because the cost of the programs is tax-deductible, Australian citizens will bear half the expense of their own indoctrination by the corporations.

As a direct consequence of business's experience during the Whitlam years (but also as part of a worldwide expansion of American techniques for managing democracy: Ivens 1978) Australian society confronts, in the 1980s, precisely the problem anticipated by Wallas and Lowell seventy years ago:

> Popular election ... may work fairly well as long as those questions are not raised which cause the holders of wealth and industrial power to make full use of their opportunities ... [to manipulate public opinion] ... If they did so there is so much skill to be bought, and the art of using skill for the production of emotion and opinion has so advanced, that the whole condition of political contests would be changed for the future. (Lowell 1926:43)

There should be no doubt that the objective of corporate grassroots and treetops propaganda is an expansion of neo-conservative doctrine which, in Justice White's words, is directed towards dominating 'the very heart of our democracy, the electoral process'. Business sponsors and supporters of the proselytizing programs have been remarkably frank on this point, as the following examples demonstrate.

In 1977 Sir Robert Crichton-Brown, president of the Institute of Directors in Australia, addressed fellow directors on the future role of the institute. The institute should, he proposed, 'publicise and sell the benefits of the system it espouses. This can be done by cooperation with and support of such bodies as Enterprise Australia'. 'We cannot relax', Sir Robert concluded,

> until ... we have convinced society at large that our influence is indeed for its good. That ... will take up some of your time and some the corporate system's money. The expenditure of both will be well worthwhile if it succeeds in obtaining for the corporate system society's seal of approval thus relieving our successors of the need to spend their resources of time and money on further promotion of the system. (Crichton-Brown 1977:13, 15)

Sir Robert's explicit purpose is to bring about the permanent subordination of a nominally democratic society to the whims of 'the corporate system', by however much propaganda and proselytizing it takes.

In 1979 Bart Cummins, head of the US Advertising Council's (1975–80) national program for 'economic education', visited Australia under Enterprise Australia's auspices to explain to corporate leaders and others how to organize a comparable program in Australia. 'As Enterprise Australia has been telling you', he affirmed to business audiences in every state, 'you've got to persuade the electorate that they've got a great system ... the greatest system the world has ever known' (Cummins 1979:3).

Crichton-Brown and Cummins were referring only to the grass-roots propaganda campaigns. The purpose of the more recent rise of think-tanks and treetops propaganda is acknowledged with a similar frankness. Hugh Morgan, head of Western Mining Corporation, is the noisiest (if not the most literate) of apostles for the vision of a democracy where minds are safely guided by the dominance of cor-poration-sponsored think-tanks (a sort of Jehovah's Witness for a new Social Darwinism). According to an interview which Morgan gave to the *Sydney Morning Herald* early in 1982, the goal of the new think-tanks and their corporate supporters is 'to reshape the politi-cal agenda in this country'. Politicians, Morgan observes, 'can only accept what is accepted in the public opinion polls. So you have to change public opinion'! Morgan is convinced the growing output of corporate-funded intellectuals (in think-tanks and elsewhere), and efficient dissemination of the output, is well on the way to achieving this result. His dangerous political ingenuousness is strikingly revealed by the fact that, while he endlessly inveighs against the allegedly excessive power of unions, it does not occur to him that the power he claims for corporations, of using their wealth to remake public opinion to their own design, might be considered excessive (Sheehan 1982:37).

Finally, we return to Dr Feulner, head of the American Heritage Foundation, who in 1978 rejoiced to a London conference of cor-porate democracy-managers from around the world that the American public policy area was 'awash with in-depth academic studies' of a New Right bent. Dr Feulner visited Australia in late 1985 under the auspices of the magazine *Quadrant* and the ill-named Association for Cultural Freedom, to explain how to use think-tanks to control the political agenda. According to McAdam (1985:45) much of the success of the neo-conservative revival in Australia 'depends on a small but tenacious group of academics and writers associated with *Quadrant*'. So it not surprising that Feulner was sponsored by *Quadrant*.

Feulner's basic thesis (1985) was that while academics and intel-lectuals are necessary for the initial production of ideas (strangely, he instances Milton Friedman among intellectuals), 'it takes an institu-tion to help popularise and propagandise an idea — to market an idea'. This is the role, Feulner says with frankness, of 'organisations like the Institute of Economic Affairs or the Adam Smith Institute in London, my own Heritage Foundation in the United States and the Centre for Policy Studies and the Centre for Independent Studies in Australia'. Marketing an idea has to be done with simple examples, so Feulner demonstrated by making the point as simple as possible for his conservative audience: 'Proctor and Gamble does not sell Crest toothpaste by taking out one newspaper ad or running one television commercial. They sell it and resell it every day by keeping the product fresh in the consumer's mind. The institutes I have mentioned sell ideas in much the same manner'.

Feulner goes on to describe in detail how the Heritage Foundation and others applied this approach in the successful 'selling of the idea of Supply Side economics'. However, he warns, success does not come overnight. Indeed, 'it takes time' for the think-tanks, following Heritage's lead, 'to become credible and for their ideas to filter into and re-direct policy'. But apparently not an excessive amount of time. For Feulner sees 'the strength of President Reagan's 1980 and 1984 victories' as reflecting the impact on public opinion by Heritage and other marketeers of ideas as if they were toothpaste.

Finally, Feulner distinguishes between 'electoral politics' (that is, the campaigns to influence public opinion that are conducted at election time) and 'policy politics', by which he means the continuous treetops and grassroots campaigns to influence public opinion and set the political agenda which American corporations fund continuously between elections. 'The latter', he says, 'is my specialty and is, in my opinion, the more important of the two' (ibid.:24). It should be noted that this development renders virtually meaningless the concept of a 'free society' of ideas.

If Feulner's plan of campaign succeeds the result will be a society where, like the United States under President Reagan, the dominance of corporate interests is subject to little or no restraint from government or union power. The Australian union movement will be reduced to the impotence of its American counterpart. The business of Australia will be business, our relatively egalitarian traditions will be seriously eroded, and 'devil take the hindmost' values will prevail. In this sense the neo-conservatives are correct in claiming that they are a radical movement.

I should like to conclude on a somewhat more optimistic note. Australian society differs from American society in many ways which offer considerable resistance both to the inculcation of neo-conservative values and to the successful transplantation of the massive American system of control by corporate propaganda. Marsh (1980) has written at length about the obstacles the Australian political system presents to corporate-sponsored political think-tanks coming to play the dominant role they play in the United States. In addition,

Australian society and culture has always been more egalitarian, more collectivist and more seriously ironic than American society and culture. Moreover, there is considerable evidence that even among Australian corporate leaders there are many people who do not favour the kind of manipulation of Australian democracy by means of corporate opinion management that Morgan and Feulner advocate. These circumstances and others will be of great assistance in resisting these new corporate threats to Australian democracy and unions.

CHAPTER 7

EXPORTING PERSUASION

This chapter is about the introduction to Australia of techniques for taking the political risk out of democracy that have long been developed, refined and applied in the United States and — more recently and to a much lesser extent — in the United Kingdom.

Virtually nothing of these developments is indigenous to Australia. A considerable amount of them has been imported direct from the United States, commonly retaining the name of the model US institution. For example, this has happened in the cases of the Committee for Economic Development, the Business Roundtable, the Business Council and the Foundation for Economic Education. To a lesser extent American techniques have reached Australia via Britain, as in the case of Enterprise Australia's promotion of the free-enterprise system via special annual reports for employees and courses in 'economic education' designed for corporate employees and schoolchildren.

Walter D. Scott (later Sir Walter) (1950:429–51) was, in 1950, the first Australian to make a study of the combination of public opinion monitoring and corrective 'economic education' employed by US business and to propose that Australian business follow American practice. Scott refers in this connection to the American Economic Foundation (AEF), whose economic education activities would be taken as a model twenty-five years later when Scott's proposals at last gained serious support from Australian corporations. A short account of AEF's history is necessary here.

The American Economic Foundation was established in 1939 to promote 'research of simplified vocabulary in the field of economics at the mass level, including primary and secondary classrooms' (Fisk 1974:805). From 1939 to 1975 it specialized in creating materials for use in business's propaganda campaigns, for example slogans, pictures, posters, cartoons, free-enterprise 'commercials' for radio (and later TV), canned editorials, leaflets and booklets for use in schools. It also distributed some material produced by others, for example an 'evangelistic program of economic education' produced by Inland Steel and comprising four one-hour sessions. Under AEF's aegis this program was, during 1950– 53, distributed nationwide to businesses and corporations, where it was given, in work time, to some four million employees (Cooke 1954:105, 110). In 1975 AEF decided to extend its activities to include the communication (as well as production) of its 'free enterprise messages to millions of people'. Within twelve months AEF achieved some positive results in this area. It conducted a pilot test of its new program on a local community and established that the program produced substantial doctrinal improvement. Buoyed by this success it launched its main program, which used print media, radio, TV and face-to-face discussion to reach audiences of several million persons in five states, with five to follow (AEF 1976:110, 16). Community indoctrination was again working to keep right-wing political values safe.

Scott believes that although many organizations in Australia enjoyed unprecedented prosperity, the system of free enterprise was at risk because of popular dissatisfaction with it. Private enterprise, he warns, 'cannot survive without public support' but 'the public can survive without private enterprise'. He conceded that with the coming of the Cold War and McCarthyism there had been a change for the better. But 'the reason for such change is much more likely to be found in an opposition to communism than because of a new-found friendship for business'. The change had occurred only because the communist issue had become prominent and the public 'cares [even] less for communism than it does for business'. Scott concluded that 'propaganda is the order of the day'. He came to believe that if management desired to re-establish itself in the faith of the general public 'it has to use the methods that will reach the public ... Propaganda must be directed primarily to change the opinion of those who, it is felt, have been misled or do not understand and, secondly, to reinforce the opinions of that section of the public which has already been persuaded' (Scott 1950:11, 12, 437–9).

Scott was at pains to underline the difficulty and the magnitude of the task which, in his view, Australian business must undertake. To emphasize this point, and to indicate how far Australia lagged behind the United States, he drew attention to a claim by the AEF that it had spent 'five years and two million dollars' just to 'develop a functional description of ... capitalism' — to develop, that is, a way of talking about capitalism that had enough appeal to serve propaganda purposes (ibid.:432).

The Institute of Public Affairs

Scott's book was apparently written before the Australian Labor Party lost government in November 1949. Once the conservative Prime Minister Robert Menzies was at the helm, and exploiting anti-communism to great effect, Australian business no doubt felt satisfactorily secure again, and Scott's pleas fell on deaf ears. Little was heard during the next twenty years of conservative rule about the public's misunderstanding of business or about the need for reformative economic education campaigns.

Indeed silence on this front was broken only by the Institute of Public Affairs (IPA). The IPA is the oldest Australian organization created solely to conduct popular proselytizing on behalf of free enterprise (and indeed the only such permanent organization prior to Enterprise Australia). It was established by a group of prominent businessmen in direct response to the 'overwhelming victory of the Labor Party in the Federal election in 1943'. The central purpose of this new body, the IPA later confirmed, 'was to resist the trend to socialism' which the 1943 elections were taken to confirm. As in the United States before McCarthyism, it was especially in intellectual circles that the drift towards socialism was believed by businessmen to have occurred ('About the IPA' 1968:35).

In 1955 the secretary of the IPA was sent to the United States to study business's economic education programs. His report attempted to convey some idea of the 'vast sums' spent on the American operation and its enormous scale. He was able to inform us that General Motors produced more booklets as part of its 'economic education' program for employees than it produced automobiles; that the US Chamber of Commerce produced a 'colour cartoon film' which had been seen by more than sixty million people and conducted a 'Business-Education Day' annually on which 300 000 teachers had been given in-plant acquaintance with the free-enterprise viewpoint; that Sears Roebuck spent $1 million on a film about 'the economic facts of life' which was shown, in work time, to its 200 000 employees; that US Steel produced an economic education program for its 250 000 employees which was also used widely in schools and elsewhere; and that the NAM produced a weekly series of films for TV which was shown nationwide ('Understanding Free Enterprise' 1956:9–14)[1]

The IPA concluded that the main lesson to be learned from the various methods of disseminating 'economic education' that have been 'tried and tested overseas' was that individual companies in Australia must do 'far more to promote ... free enterprise' by providing economic education for their own employees. The IPA offers the standard argument as to why companies must do this: if they do not the country will succumb to 'unscrupulous propagandists' who have 'the sole aim of undermining the existing economic order' (ibid.:16). Like other business-oriented propaganda organizations IPA provided no detail (beyond a few slogans) of the unscrupulous campaign directed at undermining the free-enterprise system. It never seems to occur to these propaganda organizations that the 'free-enterprise system' is itself an artificial construction which is only kept in place by artificial means, that is, by their own enormous propaganda machine.

The Australian Chamber of Commerce

In 1955 the IPA was not optimistic about business's likely response to its appeals for 'economic education', but it was prophetic. 'There is', it observed before dispatching its secretary to the United States, 'still a widespread apathy about the whole matter', but this condition no doubt would be rapidly dispelled 'should political and economic conditions, which are at present favourable, become adverse' ('Economics for the People' 1955:16–17). As anticipated by the IPA, an active interest in economic education for the masses did not develop until the election in 1972 of the Whitlam Labor government.

And so in April 1972 the Australian Chamber of Commerce (ACC) began detailed planning for a 'program to promote free enterprise' (more formally described as a 'three years Economic Education Campaign'). As first steps the chamber conducted a national survey of school leavers' attitudes to various aspects of the free-enterprise system (e.g. profits, prices, competition) and an essay competition for schoolchildren on the same general topic. These projects were used as a basis for deciding what corrective material to prepare for circulation through the schools (ACC 1973:13).

Other activities in the first three years included TV training for ninety-five business spokesmen, kits to help with speeches, video-tapes for use in schools and with employees, and school visits by businessmen. Two further economic education campaigns followed, each of three years' duration. The total cost in financial contributions by corporations (as distinct from contributions in kind) was about

$500 000. In all, some fifteen videos and films were completed (some in conjunction with IPA) on topics ranging from 'Profits' to 'The Market Economy' and 'Advertising'. With the agreement of departments of education, all this material was included in teaching resources centres and made available to schools throughout Australia.

During this period the Chamber sent the director of its economic education program to the United States 'to study economic education programs being carried out there'. A 170-page US-produced guide to 'Employee Economic Information Programs' was distributed to 470 companies as part of a project in 'Opinion Forming Among Employees'. In addition, chambers in all capital cities conducted their own economic education programs. These included special conferences for teachers and businessmen, the establishment of links with curriculum development centres, and chamber presentations of videotape shown to tens of thousands of schoolchildren. For example, in Western Australia during 1977–78 video presentations were made to an estimated 10 000 students 'in almost every high school and all teachers colleges' (ACC 1975, 1978, 1979).

In 1981 the ACC decided the program should continue but with new projects, a new format and a new name. Now known as the 'Understanding Business' campaign, the overall program was maintained and its fundamental aim, 'to secure a wider public appreciation of the Australian market economy', was unchanged (ACC 1973:22).

The other propaganda organizations

In 1976 the director of the Chamber's Economic Education campaign produced a review of business-sponsored economic education in Australia which was published by the Committee for Economic Development in Australia (CEDA). The report identifies eight bodies who were most active in the field of social engineering. Four of these represented specific industry groups:

◆ the Australian Bankers Association,
◆ the Australian Financial Conference,
◆ the Life Officers Association of Australia, and
◆ the Australian Mining Industrial Council.

All of these had a program to 'carry a free enterprise message … to secondary schools and colleges across Australia'. They 'make their presence felt', the report says, 'through a wide range of printed and audio visual materials'.

The other four bodies found to be most active in economic education are:

◆ the Australian Industries Development Association (AIDA), which has since merged with the Roundtable to form the Business Council,

◆ the American Chamber of Commerce in Australia (AmCham),

◆ the Committee for Economic Development in Australia (CEDA), and

◆ the Institute of Public Affairs (IPA).

All of these were similarly active in both schools and the community. Only the IPA, however, provided any quantitative measure of its activities, and then for schools only. IPA claimed in 1976 that 50000 copies of its monthly pamphlet *Facts* and 15000 copies of its quarterly *IPA Review* were used in more than 1200 high schools throughout Australia (Dawson 1976). Elsewhere IPA was reported to be 'channelling hundreds of thousands of copies of publications to employees through firms' (Allen 1976). AmCham (1977) claimed to have 'carried the business story to more than 20,000 students in hundreds of high schools across the country'.

Of all these propaganda organizations probably the most important development in business's enlarging effort to control public opinion occurred in 1975 with the establishment of the Australian Free Enterprise Association Ltd. Funded by donations of $35000 from CIG, Esso, Kodak and United Permanent and (a little later) from Ford Motors and IBM (Finnegan 1984:1), the formation of the association was a direct response (as its prospectus reveals) to the 'threats to free enterprise' constituted by 'recent events', that is, by the election of the Whitlam government.

The Australian Free Enterprise Association launched its proselytizing arm (Enterprise Australia) in April 1976. Geoff Allen, subsequently director of AIDA and then of the Business Council, described Enterprise Australia as resulting from initiatives by IPA and the ex-conservative minister Sir Allen Fairhall.

The first action taken by EA's new chief executive, Jack Keavney, was to travel overseas to study the activities of similar organizations (Allen 1976). Of the organizations he visited, Keavney appears to have been most impressed by the American Economic Foundation, which gave him a great welcome and every assistance. 'We owe much of what we have done to Americans', he acknowledged five years later on a return visit to the AEF in New York, 'and especially to this organisation' (Keavney 1981b:264). Shortly after EA's launching in 1976, Fairhall (1976:2) referred to AEF's 'transposing into simple economic terms the story of business' for general proselytizing use, and he proposed that EA should follow AEF's lead.

In August 1976 Enterprise Australia brought out to Australia a director of AEF, John Q. Jennings. Jennings was an expert in 'employee communication' and especially in the production of 'annual reports for employees' which make clear how little surplus is left after wages and other costs are paid. His most famous achievement is to have used employee communications to produce a dramatic conservative shift in opinion among employees of the large English engineering firm Guest, Keen & Nettlefold (GKN); that is, a shift *against* nationalization and toward the company's view (Keavney 1977:3).

Jennings brought with him 3000 copies of GKN's annual report for employees for 1975 as a teaching model (Keavney 1978b:67). Under EA's auspices Jennings met Prime Minister Fraser and the Minister for Industrial Relations. Both thereafter publicly endorsed the use of the Jennings formula. EA subsequently reported that between 200 and 300 Australian companies were producing employee reports 'similar' to the Jennings model ('Company Employee Reporting' 1977:1–2).

Jennings was the first of a long series of conservative economists, trade union leaders and expert 'communicators' that EA imported who obtained media coverage for tours around the national circuit of business forums and conferences. The following list covers only the communication technicians (after Jennings's fashion):

◆ Dr William Peterson, a colleague of Jennings (and subsequently professor of free enterprise at the University of Tennessee). Peterson (1980:664) believes that redistribution of wealth by any means 'is basically immoral'. He was brought out in 1977 to give further assistance with annual reports for employees.

◆ Pitt and Elliott, two academic consultants to GKN, were brought out in 1978 to demonstrate an 'economic education' course for employees that was developed for GKN. Entitled 'Work and Wealth', the program comprised 640 coloured slides and synchronized tapes. EA assures us that Pitt and Elliott conducted the course 'with great skill and came across as unbiased'. This had 'enabled the program to be continued [in the UK] without any hint of resistance from the unions' ('Work and Wealth' 1978:1–2). EA proposed the course should be

'Australianized' and used with employees and schoolchildren ('Reaching Every Segment of Society' 1978:2).

◆ In 1979 Bart Cummins of the Advertising Council was brought out, as already mentioned, to help transfer the council's national economic education program to Australia.

On the mass media front there was also a great deal of so-called 'unbiased' education taking place. By 1979 EA had been instrumental in the production of a series of twelve half-hour TV films ('Making It Together') on the general theme that what helps business helps everyone. This series was broadcast in all states and a further series was in production ('Television Documentary Series' 1978:4). EA had also secured about $1 million of free radio time each year. Every day more than a hundred radio stations broadcast free-enterprise 'commercials' — which, as EA explained, 'relate that free enterprise benefits the entire community' (Meagher 1979:13; 'Radio Spots' 1978:2; 'Action 1980' 1980).

By 1980 Enterprise Australia's plan to become the leading national disseminator of popular grassroots ideology appeared to be going well. EA was, Keavney (1979:10) pronounced, 'encouraged by the success of ... its approach to promoting free enterprise'. In a buoyant mood it had set the goal of obtaining from corporate donations (tax-deductible) an annual budget of $2.5 million (Carr 1978:41). Moreover there was little sign of community resistance to EA's advance. The NSW Department of Education, where resistance might have been expected, had agreed to co-operate with EA on production of the 'Australianized' version of GKN's economic education program ('Audio-visual economics ... ' 1979:2; 'Action, 1981' 1981).

Overall there was, it appeared, significant progress towards the realization of a brave new world foreshadowed by Sir Robert Crichton-Brown (1977:13, 15), president of the Institute of Directors. As an inducement to his fellow directors to give generously in support of Enterprise Australia, Sir Robert had described a utopian vision for the permanent pacification of the ideological restlessness that characterizes democracy: '[the Institute] needs to publicise and sell the benefits of the system it espouses. This can be done by cooperation with and support of such bodies as Enterprise Australia ... ' Apparently we cannot relax until threats to the free-enterprise system have been removed. This appears to happen when 'we have convinced society at large that our influence is indeed for its good. That ... will take up some of your time and some of the corporate system's money. The expenditure of both will be well worth while if it succeeds in obtaining for the corporate system society's seal of approval'.

From 1980 the machinery of ideological management at the grassroots level had a range of programs in place to indoctrinate the community at large as well as for specific areas.

Schools

The year 1980 saw publication by the National Mutual Life Insurance Company (NML) of the first annual report for children. The report, entitled *Curly and the Bald Hairies*, was in virtual comic-strip form, and modelled directly on American practice. (Another idea I picked up in America, Keavney told the AEF in January 1981, was the idea of young people's reports: NML 1980; Keavney 1981b:264.)

In 1981 EA appointed a full-time director of its Schools and Colleges Programme (Ted Hook) and in 1982 took over distribution of a school textbook entitled *The World of Business* (Hook and Harding 1982). Based on a Canadian text of the same name, the book had been compiled by Hook under a contract funded by various business corporations and the Queensland Confederation of Industry.[2]

In 1982 EA took over Young Achievement Australia (YAA), which had been introduced to Australian schools in 1978 by the American Chamber of Commerce in Australia (AmCham) as an adaptation of an American program called Junior Achievement. In America, Junior Achievement had reached a membership of 250000 schoolchildren each year, and a target of 12000 was set for Australia ('The Facts on the EA ... ' 1982; 'Young Achievement Companies ... ' 1977; 'AmCham's Young Achievers ... ' 1978:11; Batten 1979:85).

Under American auspices YAA had not flourished (AmCham 1977). After being taken under EA's umbrella in 1982 YAA involved only 1400 high school students in four states ('The Facts ... ' 1982). In 1983 the 'Australianized' economic education program 'Work and Wealth' was made available to secondary schools throughout Australia through the education departments. Also in 1983 a board game called 'Poleconomy' was successfully marketed and 100000 sets were sold. 'Poleconomy' was produced under EA's auspices on the grounds that it improves understanding of the free-enterprise system. And in 1984 seminars were initiated in high schools at which businessmen explain to teachers and children the merits of the free-enterprise system.

Universities

In 1981 EA appointed a full-time director of its Universities Programme (John Warr) and Jack Keavney addressed formal meetings of university staff on the merits of the free-enterprise system. In 1983 Monash University employed a full-time officer, with special educational duties which included encouraging schools to use EA materials ('The Capitalist Crisis ... ' 1983). A business 'executive-in-residence' program was begun (at Monash) under which senior business executives spend up to a week explaining the merits of the free-enterprise system to formal meetings of staff and students. In 1984 twelve universities accepted arrangements of this kind.

Employees

In 1981, Prime Minister to be, Bob Hawke presented the awards to NSW companies in the competition, sponsored by EA, for the best annual reports to employees. (Hawke's conservative opposite number, Andrew Peacock, performed a like service in Victoria.) In 1982 EA appointed a full-time director to its Employee Communications Programme, and the economic education program 'Work and Wealth' was made available to corporations for use with their employees.

The general public

The $1 million per annum of free-enterprise slogans broadcast by radio was continued. In 1981 a second series of twelve half-hour television programs on industry ('Making It Together') was broadcast by forty TV stations. In 1983 production of 30-second TV spots was begun. In 1984 the value of free radio spots donated by 136 radio stations was increased to $5 million; that is, to approximately 136 000 30-second spots per annum. The topic of the spots was changed to stress the individual employee's responsibility for making the economic system work (by increasing output, quality, and hence — it is argued — jobs).

Under the rubric 'Australia for Quality Campaign', the new radio onslaught was launched on 2 April 1984, with a 3-minute speech by Prime Minister Hawke which was broadcast by all 136 commercial radio stations. In 1984 EA also improved its provision of free-enterprise speakers and of 'canned' speeches and notes for business spokesmen in general. It also made training available for these spokesmen. John Warr became chief executive officer of EA and Jack Keavney was released to operate full-time as a travelling orator for free enterprise.

Also in 1984, EA published a 59-page booklet, *Private Enterprise: The Winning Way*, written by Jack Keavney and intended for wide distribution. After six months about 4000 copies had been sold, largely to big companies (Finnegan 1984:12). The basic political theme of the book is the same as William Simon's *Time For Truth*, and may be summarized as follows: extensive interference by governments in the affairs of business (no matter how democratically sanctioned such actions may be) will bring an end to freedom and democracy. It is argued that our economic system is closely bound up with our system of parliamentary democracy and therefore there is an 'essential link between our personal, political and economic freedoms'. Therefore we cannot impose restraints on the behaviour of corporations without at the same time reducing our own personal and political freedoms.

The stunning logic of this contention means that the threat to freedom comes not only, or even primarily, from 'extremists'. Rather, 'a major threat ... is created by well intentioned people ... of altruistic aims' who wish to 'intervene excessively in the play of market forces'. In other words, the threat comes from small 'l' liberals. Elsewhere (and less generously) all critics of the present economic system are lumped together as 'an implacable minority of detractors'. In any case all such critics represent an imminent threat to 'the freedoms we enjoy' as a legacy from the sacrifices of our forebears. Hence if we are to avoid the 'opprobrium' of 'coming generations' we must, in 'our turn', join EA in its struggle to defend our traditional freedoms ('Private Enterprise ... ' 1984:10, 15–16, 58).

In April 1984 Allan Moyes (chairman of EA and head of IBM) wrote to EA's corporate supporters as follows:

> The 1984 program ... which is more extensive than for any previous year, is designed as part of a long term strategy to assist in improving the understanding in the community of the role and benefits of private enterprise. It is not possible for companies and individuals to undertake this work effectively on a national scale.
>
> The program has been developed so that it does not duplicate the aims or efforts of organisations such as the Institute of Public Affairs but uses the experience and facilities of such organisations to a maximum possible extent.

In this century the vast US propaganda campaigns which have been conducted by corporate interests have always been publicly justified as a defensive response to even more extensive propaganda activities allegedly conducted by left-wing opponents of free enterprise. Moyes (1984) adopts this same straw-man tactic on behalf of EA. Without providing details he nevertheless warns us that each year 'millions of dollars are spent by active organisations and individuals to disseminate information aimed at undermining private enterprise and its infrastructure. Our work is therefore vital to the whole community'.

Overseas connections

During his seven years' tenure of the position of chief executive of EA (1976–83), Jack Keavney made at least three circuits (1976, 1978 and 1981) of what EA calls its 'counterpart organizations' overseas. On these trips Keavney reported on progress in Australia, sought advice and expressed thanks for ideas adopted. In December 1977 and January 1978 Keavney undertook a study tour during which, EA reported, 'he established contact with many counterpart organisations ... in the UK, on the Continent and in the USA' ('Overseas' 1978). On this trip (about which there is most on the public record) the counterpart organizations in the United States to which Keavney reported included the NAM, the US Chamber of Commerce, the Roundtable and the AEF (Carr 1978:41; Keavney 1978a:7–9).

It deserves special notice that according to Keavney's report the many overseas organizations he visited 'were greatly impressed with the line that Enterprise Australia has taken, particularly in the achievement of a good working relationship with moderate unions'. According to Keavney, 'few organisations throughout the world [of EA's kind] have achieved such credibility' with unions. EA was, in consequence, 'encouraged by international endorsement of the line it had taken' ('Overseas' 1978).

On a later trip to the United States Keavney (1981b:264–6) rejoiced in the fact that Ralph Nader had described EA as 'the most dangerous organisation he had met in Australia' and that President Reagan had publicly endorsed EA's 'philosophy' and 'methods'.

In June 1978 Keavney returned to London to address an international conference comprising delegates from EA-type organizations — and policy research organizations — in fourteen countries. In justifying the London conference, the editor of the conference papers subsequently wrote that 'the free societies' (read free-enterprise societies) 'may not need their Cominform but they do need to work together' (Ivens 1978:v). Perhaps it is not surprising that delegates from American organizations who contributed papers to the conference exceeded all other overseas delegates combined.

Some comment on four American contributions can provide some flavour of the conference. A contribution from the United States Industrial Council (USIC), which claims a membership of 4500 companies) described its massive communication effort through 350 newspapers and 250 radio stations and rejoiced that the AFL–CIO had come to fear the USIC as 'one of the major corporate associations most dedicated to union-busting and most vigorous in carrying it out' (Lever 1978:71–2).

A campaign adviser to US President Gerald Ford reported that there had been 'a steady decline in voter participation in Western societies' and urged that those committed to a free-market society should recognize this as a 'golden opportunity to take the offensive around the world today [because] we are dealing with smaller numbers and thus our efforts can have greater impact on influencing the outcome of elections' (White 1978:1–2).

Cold War/free-market ideologues had a field day. An American ex-editor of *Atlantic Monthly* (who is almost matched by Brian Crozier for Britain) warned about a 'globe-encompassing fifth column' which constitutes a 'cephalopodic monster whose subterranean tentacles and coils are activated by the brain centre of the KGB in Moscow'. He lamented that virtually all Western leaders, including Giscard d'Estaing, Carter and Kissinger were more or less accomplices of this Soviet apparatus (Cate 1978:42–4; Crozier 1978:59–60).

Jack Keavney, for Australia (sounding a little colourless in this company), described EA as 'a strong national movement to preserve and promote the free enterprise philosophy', and again stressed the importance of establishing 'credibility with moderate unionists'. He acknowledged indebtedness to Aims for Freedom and Industry (publisher of the collected conference papers and the oldest of Britain's free-market proselytizers) for the idea of a Free Enterprise Week — which had been implemented in October 1977 with Prime Minister Malcolm Fraser officiating. Keavney (1978b:66–9) also reviewed EA's already considerable catalogue of contributions to the free enterprise cause.

Perhaps the most significant British contribution came from Ralph Harris, general director of the Institute of Economic Affairs, whose remarks on the 'scholarly bombardment of one enemy position after another' have already been quoted (p. 103).

Policy research in Australia

Historically and in terms of total output, CEDA appears to have led in the growth of corporate-funded economic policy research in Australia. On a visit to CEDA in Australia, David Rockefeller (1979:50), of Standard Oil and the US CED, observed that 'organisations like CEDA [are] precisely the right approach' to promoting private enterprise with less government regulation and control while at the same time protecting the public interest.

In the twenty years to 1984 CEDA has published an enormous amount of material across a broad range of issues. This material includes twenty-three 'major research projects' on aspects of economic policy and over 300 lesser research projects and papers relevant to economic policy (CEDA 1984a:8; 1984b). From 1976 to 1984, CEDA published (though it did not initiate) the only general review of corporate-sponsored 'economic education' in Australia (Dawson 1976), the only comprehensive review of bodies engaged in corporate-sponsored economic policy research in Australia (Burgess 1984), and the only Australian study of the political role of privately sponsored policy research in the United States. This last study asked the explicit question of the 'lessons' that might be learnt in pursuit of a comparable development in Australia (Marsh 1980).

The US CED was established in 1942 with a membership representing a substantial part of the US economy. Its principal purposes were to develop and promote (publicly and to government) policies for the postwar period that would both avoid a return to prewar levels of unemployment and reverse the growth of government involvement in the economy that had occurred under the New Deal and continued under wartime conditions (Schriftgeisser 1960). CED was arguably the first corporation-funded economic policy research organization in the modern manner, that is, self-consciously bringing together the resources of American business and universities for the purposes of planning and persuading the public to its business agenda (ibid.:9–20, 28; Marsh, 1980).

The 1984 CEDA review of 'Economic Policy Research in Australia' lists twenty 'privately-funded organisations' having some engagement in policy research. But the list in fact comprises predominantly sectional interest groups within the business community, or business advisory services which are provided on a commercial basis. Only four organizations, apart from CEDA, are more than incidentally concerned with broad promotion of conservative policies and ideologies. These are:

◆ the Business Council of Australia,

◆ the Centre for Independent Studies,

◆ the Australian Institute for Policy Studies, and

◆ Malcolm Fraser's 'Think Tank'. (Burgess 1984:7–29)

The first of these, the Business Council, has been described in Chapter 6. The Centre for Independent Studies (CIS) is a Sydney-based body which sponsors, publishes and promotes studies supporting a libertarian-cum-laissez-faire philosophy (Sawer 1982:7–9), for example Professor Wolfgang Kasper's recent book (1984) arguing for deregulation of foreign investment. CIS also distributes literature from British and American libertarian and laissez-faire sources. CIS is reported to have an annual budget of $250000 (Burgess 1984:17).

The Australian Institute for Policy Research (AIPR) was founded in 1983 and is headed by John Hyde. (Hyde is the leader of the Liberal/conservative Party 'dries'. The term 'dries' is slang for economic rationalists.)

Prime Minister Fraser's Think Tank was founded in 1984. It is described (somewhat generously) as 'a scaled down version of Mr Fraser's earlier hopes of establishing a research foundation along the lines of ... the American Enterprise Institute' (Burgess 1984:26) (to which organization Mr Fraser has since became officially attached). The Think Tank's membership includes Hugh Morgan of Western Mining Corporation and the conservative academic Dame Leonie Kramer.

As this chapter neared completion Hugh Morgan acknowledged, indeed proclaimed with unconcealed satisfaction, that Australian corporations are in the process of adopting American methods for controlling public opinion (Sheehan 1982:37–8). Morgan makes specific reference in this connection to the provision of generous corporate funding to such bodies as the CIS, the Institute for Policy Research and the IPA. He affirms that the expansion of the work of these bodies relates to a decision by their corporate supporters 'to change public opinion' and thereby 'reshape the political agenda' to a form that would delight the hearts of Ronald Reagan and Margaret Thatcher. Morgan seems wholly confident that a radically conservative transformation of Australian politics can be achieved, given sufficient corporate backing for policy research and popular proselytizing.

This summary of corporate-sponsored activities which are directed at managing the political agenda at a treetops level contains a number of omissions. Nothing has been said, with the single exception of the Niland and Turner study, about cognate research conducted both in universities and by university personnel but under direct external sponsorship (most notably the Centre for Policy Studies at Monash University). Nor have I yet commented on the studies on Australian society by American institutes, such as the Hudson Institute and the AEI. Nothing has been said about the explicit use of the media by corporations to promote particular policies or ideologies — the 'issue advertising' and 'advocacy advertising' which have for at least a decade been pervasive in the United States (Sethi 1977) and are beginning here. For example, we are beginning to see regular ads by the Uranium Mining Council. Again nothing has been said about agencies of sectional business interests, for instance the Bank Education Service, which provide materials to schools and work to influence school curricula (Barlowe 1985). All these developments deserve close attention. But the objective here is limited to establishing a broad perspective on the introduction to Australia of new methods of political ontrol — or at least old methods on a quite new scale — and to identifying the leading agencies through which this development is taking place.

Some areas of resistance

Yet what are the likely sources of resistance in Australian society and how can this resistance be made more effective? This question relates to a general community vulnerability as well as vulnerability associated more particularly with business, government, the media, schools, unions and universities.

The effectiveness of propaganda depends on the availability of emotionally charged symbols or ideas that can be manipulated by propagandists. In the Western world the most powerful of such symbols have to do with nationalism. These almost sacred symbols (if also secular) affirm loyalty to a cherished (and idealized) 'way of life'. In contrast, satanic symbols are those which signify subversion and 'threats to national security'. Manipulation of such symbols (by words and images) is, of course, the indispensable basis of conservative political rhetoric and conservative propaganda generally (see Chapter 1).

The extraordinary power of such propaganda in the United States is wholly dependent on the maintenance of popular 'patriotic' sentiments that are both intense and shallow. These are sentiments that are easily exploited by manipulating sacred and satanic symbols in relation to nationalism. Such exploitation is well illustrated by the booklet The American Economic System and Your Place In It which heralded the 1975–80 economic education campaign in the United States. The 20-page booklet, of which the Advertising Council distributed thirteen million copies by 1979 (Meagher 1979:13), is suffused with stars and stripes, patriotic rhetoric and Peanuts cartoons.

In Australia the relatively low level of 'patriotic' excitability together with a widespread scepticism towards inflated patriotic rhetoric represents an important barrier to an early duplication of American techniques of public opinion management. I believe it is for this reason that EA's plans, which were announced in 1979, to 'Australianize' the American booklet for similar distribution here never got off the ground. But it is also for this reason, in my view, that so much effort has recently been given to creating just the intense and shallow patriotism so essential to the work of the mind-managers. Through 'Project Australia' the Fraser governments (which also gave full support to EA's 'economic education' activities) spent $15 million to stimulate patriotism of the 'I love Australia' T-shirt variety. Although the Hawke government rapidly terminated such public funding we are left with the debilitating legacy of a national chain of shops (The Proud Australian) promoting their mindlessly 'patriotic' wares.

EA's publications have, from the beginning, been replete with dark references to a dangerous minority of disloyal 'extremists' who are hell-bent on destroying our economic-political system and all our cherished liberties. This equation of 'criticism of our economic system' with 'subversion of our political system' is a general characteristic of EA's 'economic education' and was, of course, the central theme in the history of business propaganda.

Australian society has been relatively free from campaigns which try to convert the whole community to prohibition, anti-communism or religious fundamentalism. As a consequence business's attempts to manage public opinion here in the same manner as in the United States are likely to result in a much more distinctive and visible performance. If this is the case then such visibility is more likely to evoke an unfavourable response from the public. Unfortunately this historical advantage is now being eroded by the increasing practice of state and federal governments paying for (at public expense) many pages of newspaper space to sell their policies to the public — always of course in the name of 'information' and 'understanding' ('Public Money, Private Goals' 1985).

There is, however, one aspect of Australian culture which we share with all other Western democracies. This is a particular kind of vulnerability to the new, sophisticated management of public opinion by conservative (but respectable) free-enterprise corporations. Populations in Western societies have for long been fed the belief that any disposition to undertake Orwellian mind-management on a national scale will be the exclusive prerogative of governments — especially of communist governments (see Chapter 8). The very last place we expect such a threat to come from then is the leaders of capitalist industry within their own societies. Such commonly held beliefs make a population vulnerable to corporate propaganda.

Business as a source of resistance?

There is a prospect of significant resistance — at least for the immediate future — from within business's own ranks. CEDA's leaders cannot rely on support, even from its own member companies, for a move toward an AEI role. Malcolm Fraser's proposal to establish an Australian AEI similarly failed to obtain substantial business support. EA has also met significant opposition from business quarters: Geoff Allen hardly assisted EA's credibility by publicly describing it as a 'propaganda' organization. In addition, the Bank Education Service has been critical of EA and goes to some lengths to overcome 'suspicions' of any 'possible link with EA' (Kerr 1983:32). And the Australian Chamber of Commerce takes sharp offence at any suggestion of similarity between its economic education programs and the activities and methods of Enterprise Australia. (Meanwhile EA has shifted further to the Right. Jack Keavney, whose combination of goodwill and naivety enabled him to believe that EA could and should be politically non-partisan, has lost his executive role in EA to hardliners — and the prospects of union co-operation have in consequence much diminished.)

In two conferences about business and society which were organized respectively by the Australian Council of Social Services and the American Chamber of Commerce in Australia, leading representatives of Australian business expressly rejected the propagandist and opinion-managing tactics of American business (Paech 1980; AmCham 1981). Against all this there must be set, of course, the whole-hearted endorsement of such tactics by Hugh Morgan and his supporters.

Overall, resistance from within Australian business may be expected to delay, but cannot be relied upon to prevent, the long-term control over public opinion and the management of the political agenda.

The role of governments

Malcolm Fraser's governments contributed notably to a general progress towards an opinion-managed state. A long leap forward in this direction was made by four strategies: the use of public funds for the promotion of government policies; the funding of Project Australia; actively supporting EA; and urging corporate leaders to proselytize their employees. It must be expected that whenever this conservative Coalition is returned to power it will assist, in every way open to it, the expansion of business-funded popular propaganda and policy research.

There are two ways in which the Labor government could, if it had the will, move to place some constraints in the way of such a development. First, it could firmly forswear its own practice of proselytizing its own policies by advertisements paid for out of public funds, and appeal to the Opposition to make a similar commitment. Second, it could review present taxation laws to prevent corporations from obtaining tax deductions for contributions to proselytizing organizations like Enterprise Australia. It is ridiculous that members of a democratic society should be obliged to subsidize their own indoctrination by a partisan interest group just because that group chooses to label its program 'economic education'.

Similarly, corporate expenditure on policy research should not be tax-free. It is essential that the federal government give attention to the need for some legal restraint on the expenditure of funds by corporations for the purpose of influencing public opinion before that expenditure (as has happened in the United States) becomes so vast and effective that political control of it is virtually impossible. It is crucial that we study and take warning from American experience in this regard.

Media and advertising

Both media corporations and advertising agencies can expect to benefit greatly from an expansion of political propaganda. Hence resistance from that quarter is unlikely. The economic commentator Max Walsh (1981:43), when asked at the AmCham Conference (already referred to) how the media felt about 'advocacy advertising', replied 'we love it'.

In 1983, shortly after Malcolm Fraser had announced a plan to spend $800 000 to sell the wages freeze, it was revealed that Margaret Thatcher's government planned to spend $1.6 million 'to soften up the British public to the prospect of cruise missiles outside their cities'. The Thatcher government was embarrassed by the head of a London advertising agency who went on TV to denounce the proposed use of public money. When Australian advertising executives were questioned on the matter few acknowledged any reluctance at all to use taxpayers' money to promote party-political decisions (Milliken 1983:5).

The attitude of advertising agencies is of strategic importance. In the United States since World War II the initiative for vast corporate-funded proselytizing campaigns has come from advertising and public relations agencies more than from business itself — to which, indeed, the campaigns have in large measure been sold by the advertising agencies. This US background is especially relevant for reasons made clear some years ago by John Cumming, the owner of an Australian advertising agency. Warning that the Australian Association of Advertising Agencies had been under American control since 1976, Cumming described the industry as a 'wooden-horse' for the cultural invasion of any country. Cumming anticipated that Australia would be 'turned into the 52nd state … as a result of the comparatively small advertising industry' (Blanket 1978).

By 1980 two-thirds of Australian advertising was handled by agencies which were wholly or partly US-owned ('US Fondness … ' 1980). Cumming's fears may be exaggerated, but we must certainly expect the advertising industry to employ its persuasive skills to lead Australian business towards opinion-monitoring and management — as for instance, John Clemenger Ltd have already been doing for a decade (Clemenger 1975, 1980). Finally, if Australian business follows the US path, we can sooner or later expect to hear a factitious clamour from corporate sources about how unfairly and incompetently business is reported in the media.[3] We can expect that this clamour will be followed by expenses-paid, corporate-sponsored seminars and conferences in holiday surroundings where assorted journalists are assisted to 'understand' the business viewpoint (Dreier 1983).

Reaction in schools

Departments of education throughout Australia have shown a remarkable readiness to assist Enterprise Australia's varied efforts to 'penetrate' schools. This is so despite a report by the Bank-Education Service that EA has 'a questionable reputation with curriculum areas of most education departments' (Kerr 1983:32). Much the most vigorous and vocal of all opposition to EA has came from teachers in state schools and their unions (Bell 1982; 'In the Name of All ... ' 1982; Keavney 1982a; Moran 1981, 1982; Shanahan 1982) As a consequence EA is slow to make progress in public schools but may be faring a lot better in private schools. In neither case is reliable information available.

Some sort of publicly visible safeguard is necessary against undue invasion of the public schools by ideologically inspired public relations material produced by business and industry agencies and their followers. Something of the kind could be provided if departments of education were required to collect information from all state schools that would enable them to publish annually an estimate of the overall amount of 'outside' material used in schools and the percentage deriving from each significant source.

If US experience is repeated here we can expect that business in general and EA in particular will eventually launch a campaign to have economics made a mandatory subject in high schools. Just such a campaign flourished in the United States following the discovery by the Opinion Research Corporation in 1960 that the more courses in economics a student had taken the greater was the commitment to conservative free-enterprise beliefs ('Why Too Many College Students ... ' 1960; Neal 1962). By 1976 more than half the American states had made high school courses in economics mandatory for all students.

Universities and colleges

The response from researchers in universities and colleges of advanced education will be an important determinant to the degree to which Australia is a guided democracy. There is no defence so effective against propaganda agencies which masquerade under the name of 'education' and 'research' as repeated exposure of their real purposes through detailed critical examination of their activities and output. Once effectively tagged with the propaganda label, the 'credibility' of such agencies and their influence is almost irremediably destroyed. (Even the little I have myself published about EA has had, in the judgement of Jack Keavney (1982b:1), their former chief executive, a very serious impact on its reputation and credibility.)[4]

The disastrous consequences for critical thought and American democracy resulting from corporate propaganda could not have happened but for an almost unbelievable neglect by liberal scholars and researchers to give critical attention and exposure to the extent, character and consequences of this development (Carey 1983:13–17). On the other hand American scholars and researchers by the thousand have wittingly and unwittingly assisted in every imaginable way to make the monitoring and management of public opinion more effective (Albig 1957). A great deal will depend on whether or not Australian academics in the social sciences are able to produce a very different track record from their US colleagues. It is already clear, I think, that corporations, with the advantage of relatively abundant funds, will have no difficulty in finding academics who will give the seal of professional credibility to the invariably tendentious policy research conducted from business's viewpoint.

A case in point was the survey sponsored by the American-owned insurance company Sentry Holding Ltd on attitudes of workers, union officials and managers (Sentry Holdings 1978). Its sampling, interpretation and subsequent promotion were all clearly biased so as to yield results adverse to union interests (Gill 1979; Carey 1979b:33–5). The survey of management's and unions' views about industrial relations that was sponsored by CEDA provides another example (Niland and Turner 1985). By a systematic disregard of contradictory data this study was interpreted to reveal a high level of dissatisfaction with the present industrial relations system among corporate executives. In fact any such conclusion accords much more closely with the known views of the study's sponsors than it does with the evidence produced by the study (Carey 1984).

Given Australia's lack of history in the propaganda business there is a certain natural resistance still operating in the community which appears to be blocking the establishment of an AEI-type policy research institute. It therefore must be expected that universities and university scholars in the social sciences will be subject to increasing pressure — and temptation — to become more deeply involved in politically motivated research on behalf of corporations. This is a prospect which should profoundly concern academic staff associations and professorial boards.

Union resistance

Much will depend on how quickly unions come to appreciate that the essential weapon will not be strikes, or the crude economic power of employers or the sympathy of the government in office or the form of the system for settling disputes. As was the case with American corporations thirty-five years ago (Whyte 1950), the essential new weapon in the armoury of Australian corporations will be what managements call 'communications'. The purpose of the new weapon will always be represented as a benevolent concern with improvement in mutual understanding. But its real purpose, as revealed in the US context, is the mass communication of management's viewpoint and values to 'target' audiences inside and outside industry in order to both weaken support for unions among the general public and to weaken the tie between unions and employees in each particular firm.

The decisive upward and downward turning-points in the history of American unions were the Wagner Act of 1935 and the Taft–Hartley Act of 1947. These reflected one condition above all others: favourable public opinion in 1935 and unfavourable public opinion in 1947. Malcolm Fraser built up an armoury of legal weapons for use against unions. One thing only prevented him from using them: his polls showed that he would not have the support of public opinion if he did so.

In the United States, industrial relations are still formally conducted by direct negotiation between the parties. In reality management's freedom of action and the terms that unions will have to accept are, to a major degree, predetermined by the level of effectiveness achieved by management's two-pronged 'communication' activities. More than thirty years ago Whyte described American management's unprecedented preoccupation with domestic 'communications' as union-busting. And Peter Drucker acknowledged that the main purpose of a major aspect of this communication program — the 'human relations' crusade of the previous ten years — had been to 'bust the unions' (Whyte 1950; Drucker 1950:7).

In brief, the major part of American business's industrial relations policies has long been conducted via public relations and 'human relations' conceived as psychological weapons in a struggle to undermine the power and appeal of unions. This policy has proceeded via various forms of management-initiated and management-controlled 'communications'. The success of this strategy over the last thirty years has brought disastrous consequences for the union movement. Fortunately the use of a similar strategy in Australia is seriously hindered by the arbitration system as it exists at present. In any case I doubt whether Australian corporate managers would carry exploitation to the lengths US managements have carried it. Nonetheless unions must expect that many Australian corporations will try to follow the American course.

These prospective developments require new responses from unions, both with respect to their own members and with respect to the public at large. Unions should warn their members to have nothing to do with any management-initiated communications project (for example, annual reports for employees, economic education programs, surveys of the opinions of union officials and members) unless people with the inclination and qualifications to look after union and worker interests are involved. In particular, workers should on no account participate in polls or surveys initiated by employer agencies or university researchers unless qualified representatives of union interests are involved in both the design of the survey and the interpretation of results. Unions could well provide themselves with valuable feedback (and possibly with political and public relations ammunition) by periodically polling their own members. They could well provide union-designed polls of first-line and middle management and then publicize management's unwillingness to co-operate.

Generally, unions need to develop more capacity to counter management's 'communications' and public relations activities with competing union initiatives, including policy research. On the public relations front unions will continue to be at a great disadvantage until they can educate their members to appreciate the need to pay for at least some public opinion monitoring. Unions badly need reliable feedback from polls on their public profile and the use of strikes. In recent years a high proportion of strikes have occurred in publicly owned service industries, where they inconvenience a maximum number of people and discredit public ownership. In private industries strikes would show neither of these results. This appears to indicate a grossly inadequate appreciation of the importance of public relations. It must never be forgotten that, no matter how many strikes the union movement wins, it will in the long run come to disaster if it loses the support of public opinion. If American union history has not conveyed persuasive warning on this point nothing ever will.

CHAPTER 8

THE
ORWELL DIVERSION

In the nineteenth century Matthew Arnold described the aim of literature as to perceive life 'steadily' and as a 'whole'. In the twentieth century the social sciences have challenged this traditional role of poets and writers as the most influential source of enquiry and reflection upon human life and values. It is my contention that the producers of our social science have largely abandoned Arnold's goal. In consequence all of us now see the world more unsteadily than we need and, in a double sense, in a manner more partial and fragmented.

I would argue that the abandonment of an interconnected view of the community is deeper and more dangerous than ever before. Its cause is not due to a natural inevitability but is held in place, almost artificially, by the bitter divisions of our world. This predilection for division, a division which maintains a binary morality of 'them' and 'us', finds its traditional expression in the terms 'communist' and 'anti-communist'. I would suggest that this division has become a kind of global disease that scars and corrupts the best and most humane aspects of our liberal Western traditions.

The communist craze has been created and sustained for so long that we are in danger of believing in it — believing for instance, that we should take George Orwell's warning about 1984 seriously. Orwell warned that a crude and brutal totalitarianism would come from the Left of politics and subvert the liberal democratic freedoms we are all supposed to enjoy. Such a prospect is no more than part of the communist craze of the twentieth century, for while the freedoms of liberal democracy are certainly threatened, the danger has always come from the Respectable Right. It has come in the form of a widespread social and political indoctrination, an indoctrination which promotes business interests as everyone's interests and in the process fragments the community and closes off individual and critical thought.

This chapter will discuss briefly four developments in the last hundred years which have combined to produce this 'democratic propaganda': the growth of democracy; the growth of free-enterprise corporations; the emergence of a major communist state; and the growth of propaganda as a democratic instrument of power.

The growth of democracy

Between 1880 and 1920 the proportion of the population in major Western societies who enjoyed the right to vote approximately trebled. Thereafter the beliefs and opinions of the less privileged majority in these societies took on a quite new importance and value (Lippman 1955:39–40).

As early as 1909 the leading students of democracy in Britain and the United States, namely Professor Graham Wallas at the London School of Economics and A. L. Lowell, president of Harvard University, saw in this new situation some significant consequences for the traditional holders of power. Wallas observed:

> Popular election may work fairly well as long as those questions are not raised which cause the holders of wealth and industrial power to make full use of their opportunities. But if the rich people in any modern state thought it worth their while ... to subscribe a third of their income to a political fund, no Corrupt Practices Act yet invented would prevent them spending it. If they did so there is so much skill to be bought, and the art of using skill for the production of emotion and opinion has so far advanced, that the whole condition of political contests would be changed for the future. (Lowell 1926:43)

In the United States Lowell expressed summary agreement: 'Graham Wallas', he wrote, 'is probably right in thinking that property [if challenged on a matter of great importance to it] would resort, not to resistance by force, but to corrupting the electorate' (ibid.).

The main point I wish to establish here is that a rapid expansion of democratic franchise over the last hundred years created an unprecedented concern on the part of people who controlled resources. Corrupting the electorate rather than opposing the extension of franchise became the strategy of businesses for protecting themselves against the public. And the method for this corruption was the use of techniques for manipulating public opinion — that is, propaganda.

In the last hundred years, as previous chapters have described, there has been a remarkable growth of huge corporations, with a corresponding increase in propaganda techniques. A few statistics will provide a perspective. In the United States in 1870 there were only three private corporations with more than 1000 employees. By 1914 there were 557. In 1973 a UN report observed that many multinational corporations, such as AT & T, Standard Oil, and United Fruit, 'are bigger than a large number of entire national economies', for example Chile, Madagascar, Haiti or Fiji (Carroll 1981:2; TNEC 1941:9; UN 1973:13).

The emergence of a communist state

The arrival in 1917 of a major communist state on the world stage as a functioning alternative to the system of free enterprise had immediate and enduring consequences worldwide. It united every existing species of capitalism (to which the Nazi and fascist varieties would shortly be added) in implacable hostility to the new state. It is now widely unknown or forgotten that in 1918 thirteen Western nations and Japan concerted an invasion of the Soviet Union by armies which totalled 100 000 troops. Between May and September 1918 troops of the Western Allies drove into the new republic from east, north and west and fomented civil war with the intention of destroying the Bolshevik regime (Kennan 1958).

Rather than destroying the Bolsheviks, the invasion clearly established the circumstances of the Soviet Union's continued existence. As E. H. Carr (1963:913) tells us, 'from 1925 the need to industrialise as a defence against the menace of international capitalism ... was constantly stressed' by Russian leaders. This threat provided justification for Stalin's ruthless suppression of all opposition. In a famous speech of February 1931, Stalin warned 'the pace must not be slackened ... To slacken the pace would be to lag behind ... the advanced countries. We must make good this lag in ten years. Either we do it or they crush us'. Hitler invaded Russia just ten years after that speech. In summarizing the Russian experience of the West in the crucial decade up to World War II, Professor D. F. Fleming (1966:127) states:

> The motives of the appeasers in London and Paris in the decade before 1939 were mixed. But a desire to stop Hitler and Mussolini and Tojo by an alliance with the Soviet Union was not one of them. All through this period Litvinov, the Soviet Foreign Minister, argued and pleaded with the West to enforce the law of the League of Nations against aggression. In the

long series of surrenders to the aggressors Soviet collaboration was offered and invariably rejected. There was a fundamental conviction in the minds of the appeasers that Fascism, with all its gangster qualities, could be lived with better than Communism.

Indeed, almost until the time when Russia signed a non-aggression pact with Germany in 1939, the Western allies continued to rebuff appeals by Litvinov for an agreement on joint military action in the event of further aggression by Hitler. Failure to reach a collective security arrangement with the West brought first Litvinov's dismissal and then the infamous Stalin–Ribbentrop pact (Shirer 1960). Western attitudes during this decade were epitomized in comments by the then Australian Attorney-General on his return from a visit to Germany on 8 August 1938. As reported in the *Sydney Morning Herald*, Robert Menzies said: 'I do not believe war is possible in Western Europe ... Germany can only expand towards the East', that is, into Russia. Menzies stopped short of making this prospect an explicit ground for commendation of Nazi Germany. But he plainly did not regard it as a kind of behaviour that should be discouraged, for he continued: 'I hope the understanding between Great Britain and Germany will grow. No German wants war. There is a great deal of spirituality in the willingness of the young Germans who are devoted to service to the state' ('European War Unlikely ...' 1938). The next day the *Herald* carried a caption, over one column only, which read 'Jews Beaten to Death. Persecution by Nazis. The Buchenwald Camp'. The article described, with the detachment of a weather report, horrifying details of the torture and death of hundreds of Jews, Social Democrats and Bible students. Even detailed knowledge of Hitler's atrocities was not sufficient to permit a defensive alliance across the schism of capitalism and communism.

Alexander Werth (1971:37) provides a simple but essential perspective on the division that has degraded our century: 'When one examines carefully the origins of the Cold War one almost inevitably comes to the conclusion that it began, not at some relatively recent date, but simply in 1917, the year the Soviet regime was established'. Fifty years of blinkered Cold War Manicheism led, logically enough, to Vietnam. And Vietnam brought us what should have been, if Arnold's goal still stood, unforgettable symbols of the corruption of our culture and sensibilities by the long global schism: B-52s blessed by priests as they took off from Thailand to bomb unseen peasants in their own countryside from twice the height of Mount Everest; Lieutenant Calley's chilling and unanswerable defence at his trial in the wake of the My Lai massacres: 'nobody ever told us they were human' (Bigart 1971:1).

If we continue in this long-habituated path, as President Reagan would have us do, there remains no reason at all why we should not find our way to the ultimate corruption of a global Vietnam and the darkness of nuclear winter. If that result comes, we can no doubt expect there will be anti-communist madmen who, wrapped in the Stars and Stripes, will explain the destruction of our world as they explained the destruction of a village in Vietnam: 'We had to destroy it in order to save it'.

In the meantime, how many of the leaders of our literary and social science fraternities have made any serious attempt to see steadily or see whole what has been happening to our world over all these years, let alone inform popular consciousness about it?

The growth of propaganda

With the growth of corporations and democracy there came a vast growth in corporate propaganda as a means of defending corporate interests against democracy. 'As industrial power grew', V. O. Key (1956:104) writes, 'the conscious policy of manipulating public attitudes to retain that power came to be adopted'. Apart from the Great Depression, there have been three occasions when this policy went into action on a vast scale. A comment on the context of these occasions is necessary.

Major wars always create major problems for defenders of the established order. For modern wars require the support of everyone; and so wartime propaganda idealizes the humane, egalitarian, democratic character of the home society in a way that no elite or business interest has any intention of allowing actually to come about. In consequence, at the end of major wars there is a public temper that expects reforms in the direction of the democratic and egalitarian ideals for which people have been told they sacrificed and suffered.

This was the situation in the United States at the end of World War I in 1918, World War II in 1945 and (in a complex way) the Vietnam War in 1975. In every case a massive campaign of business propaganda went into action directed at arousing fear of a communist threat and in the process discrediting liberal and democratic critics of business and corporate interests. In every case there was a successful indoctrination of the community — successful in the sense of closing off widespread critical consciousness and by the marginalization of liberal and democratic thought. Thus in each of these periods there followed within two or three years a dramatic shift in public opinion towards conservatism, chauvinism and/or an intensification of Cold War anti-communism. There were, in consequence, McCarthyist periods from 1919 to 1921 and from 1948 onwards, and a sudden swing to conservatism after 1976 which culminated in Ronald Reagan's presidency and Cold War policies (Carey 1987a, 1987b).

I have documented (in Chapter 5) the growth of propaganda sponsored by industry as a means for managing democracy until it became by 1950 a significant American industry in its own right. This Orwellian industry combined an intensive surveillance of public opinion to detect early signs of ideological drift and the employment of a large corpus of experts from all the social science professions on the refinement and dissemination of corrective persuasion through all media and all parts of the society. The program was relatively simple: if the public begins to identify their own interests as different from business interests then flood the media with corrective propaganda until the public changes its collective mind. For example, the Great Depression, with its millions of hungry and jobless, brought widespread hostility and considerable weakening of business's ideological control. The NAM campaign launched in 1934 to recapture American minds for business was largely suspended during the 1939–45 war, but was resumed on an even vaster scale immediately the war ended. 'The apparatus itself is prodigious ... the output staggering', wrote sociologist Daniel Bell (1954:254), who was clearly awed by the scale of the mind-bending program that continued from 1945 to 1953. It produced, Professor Key (1958:75) observes, 'an almost overwhelming propaganda of doctrine'.

The contribution of social science may be illustrated by the work of Dr Henry C. Link, psychologist. Link was the head of an organization appropriately named 'The Psychological Corporation', which from 1932 monitored public opinion for the corporations and tested the effectiveness in influencing public opinion of alternative tactics which their propaganda system might adopt.

Link (1947a) reported that in 1945 a series of large-scale 'experiments in the "Techniques of Communicating Ideas"' was sponsored by ten of the nation's leading companies. The experiments showed that the way to sell the conservative vision of free-market 'free enterprise' to the American people was not on its own values and characteristics as such, but by having these identified with 'Americanism' and then by linking New Deal policies to 'un-Americanism'. The following year (1946), the US Chamber of Commerce distributed, nationwide, a million copies of a 50-page pamphlet, *Communist*

Infiltration in the United States. In 1947 a similar pamphlet, *Communists Within the Government* (that is, the Truman government), was similarly distributed.

With 1984 three years past it is evident, I believe, that George Orwell's warnings about future threats to liberal democracies were largely, even dangerously, misconceived. Influenced by Orwell's erroneous views, popular consciousness has been drilled in the expectation that the subversive Left, supported by influences from 'outside' the country, is about to control public and individual thinking. (This is the corporate-sponsored narrative which provides the justification needed for managing democracy in the interests of business.) Meantime the real attack is in stark contrast to Orwell's expectations. It has come, for most of this century, from the Respectable Right. But this actual threat is more or less ignored by the community, for it is vastly sophisticated, appears uncoercive yet is dedicated to corporate interests.

Whatever Orwell's intentions, his work has been exploited so as to misdirect and confuse the public into looking in the wrong places for the 'brainwashing' instinctively felt by many. Ever since World War I this circumstance has so blinded or intimidated the public that few writers and social scientists have attempted to see our world clearly or see it whole in its political-economic dimensions. Almost forty years after Orwell wrote *1984* no writer has attempted to update it so as to make clear the seriousness of Orwell's misguidance for democratic societies. Worse still, in the name of free enterprise and anti-communism, a great number of social scientists, sponsored by corporations, are willingly engaged in advancing Orwell's thesis by way of a corporate-managed democracy.

PART III

PROPAGANDA IN THE SOCIAL SCIENCES

CHAPTER 9

THE HUMAN RELATIONS APPROACH

In the United States theory and research about worker motivation and behaviour has, from the 1940s to the 1970s, been dominated by one broad school of thought and practice. This movement was known until about 1955 as the 'human relations' school. In its earlier phases it was particularly associated with the Hawthorne studies, Elton Mayo, George Homans, and Roethlisberger and Dickson; in its later phases it was associated with Kurt Lewin and his students. From about 1955 this movement broadened, changed certain emphases, and was renamed first the 'neo-human relations' and subsequently the 'human resources' school. Douglas McGregor, Frederick Herzberg and M. Scott Myers have been among the leaders of this latter-day revision of the 'human relations' school.

As I have shown elsewhere (Carey 1976a), this entire tradition, extending from Mayo to Myers, has exhibited three characteristics of particular interest.

1   It has endlessly produced theories and 'evidence' which are alleged to show that the motivation and behaviour of industrial workers are more importantly influenced by something other than monetary and material reward (by, for example, social satisfactions, ego satisfactions, 'creative' or 'self-actualizing' satisfactions and so on).

2   The studies or experiments which are claimed to have substantiated these conclusions about the relative unimportance of economic reward for workers have commonly become 'classics' and gained fame and influence in industry and in academia.

3   The actual evidence produced in the classic studies of this tradition is consistently found, on examination, to have failed to support, and even to have contradicted, the now-famous conclusions drawn from the studies.

The consistency of this discrepancy between evidence and conclusions in this 50-year tradition of work, together with the widespread acclaim accorded it, raises questions about what purposes, other than scientific, this work (wittingly or unwittingly) might serve (see Carey 1967, 1977). This chapter introduces the work and the political role played by the human relations school in America, especially since 1945.

Background

We could capture the essence of this relationship between industry and social scientists in the assertion that the objective of most applied social science connected with industry is to help take the risk out of political democracy.

In democratic countries political power, and indeed economic power, is vulnerable to public opinion. This may be put more concretely. From time to time in Western societies the belief that capitalist industry is exploitative gains wide popular acceptance. Specifically, business and industry are seen to be governed by considerations of power and profit, to the neglect of important social and human concerns. When this belief prevails the popular base exists for higher corporation taxes and many other legislative interventions undesired by business leaders. Such a state of public opinion is understandably regarded as highly threatening by the leaders of our 'free-enterprise system' (Robinson 1939; Sethi 1977:58). At such a point, in the United States at least, the stakes are regarded as being so high that virtually unlimited funds become available to meet the perceived threat from the general public. That is where many kinds of social scientists come in: poll-takers, experts in group dynamics, in attitude-change, in advertising, in 'selling' ideas — experts, that is, in democratic propaganda.

As is evident from the figure below, there have been two occasions during the last three or four decades when American business (and, to a lesser degree, British and Australian business) has felt especially threatened by adverse public opinion: the first immediately after World War II, the second from 1968 onwards. The figure shows the percentage of affirmative responses to the question 'Does business achieve a good balance between profits and service to the public?'

In the United States the response of business and its associations to the opinion trough of 1946 was to call for help from social scientists who specialize in public relations and industrial psychology (though they scarcely needed to be called). At such times the 'problem' confronting business is defined as one of 'misunderstanding', of failure of 'communication', between business, managers and corporations on the one hand and workers and the public on the other; or — and this is regarded as an equivalent formulation — as a problem of improving the 'image' of business, corporations, etc.

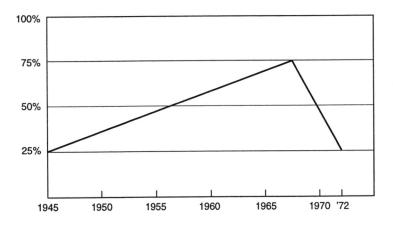

This chart reveals that as far as the United States is concerned, there was a steady growth over a 20-year period, and then ... ! As Yankelovich (1972) predicted, the tide of public opinion turned against the business world What took twenty years to build has been destroyed in less than five years. Source: Yankelovich 1972.

In the conditions of the late 1940s an intensely symbiotic relationship developed between American business and social scientists (Mills 1948; Moore 1947). In 1946, according to the *New York Times*, business and industrial leaders concluded that only by investing great financial resources in research in the social sciences could the 'free-enterprise system be saved' from the threat of the welfare state, socialism, collectivism and associated disasters (Porter 1946b:3). In consequence, from 1946, American business provided vast funding for research by social scientists into the measurement, development and change of attitudes and opinions and related study of industrial relations. Wherever studies or alleged findings by social scientists were judged to have use in improving industry's 'image' and acceptability to public opinion, these studies and findings were officially adopted by industry leaders, publicized and dramatized.

Social scientists themselves were no less enthusiastic or explicit about their intensified alliance with business. The American Psychological Association (1962) eventually offered industry a bill of sale which included the following:

> The task of keeping the image of the company clear and valid ... is a continuing one ... [However,] the industrial psychologist is increasingly helpful in bringing psychological devices and insights to the aid of management in the effort to create and maintain a positive reputation. Essentially what the industrial psychologist attempts to do is to help the employee come to ... a recognition of how his interests and management's coincide ...

This adjustment of everyone's opinion to accord with a management prescription is to be sought by 're-education and restructuring of perceptions', a field of activity regarded as lying well within the province of social science expertise.

The kind of format for such a 're-education' program is provided by S. Prakesh Sethi (1977:58), who lists the following strategies for business to undertake when dealing with adverse public opinion in a democracy.

Business Strategies

1. Do not change performance, but change public perception of business performance through education and information.

2. If changes in public perception are not possible, change the symbols used to describe business performance, thereby making it congruent with public perception. Note that no change in actual performance is called for.

3. In case both (1) and (2) are ineffective, bring about changes in business performance, thereby closely matching it with society's expectations.

Some key terms

A brief glance back to the 1920s and 1930s will afford some perspective on the path by which business leaders and social scientists converged to a point of common interest in propaganda.

The calculated subservience of social scientists to business and corporate interests dates at least from 1921. In that year twenty 'leading psychologists' established 'the Psychological Corporation' to promote and sell the services of psychology to industry (Cattell

1923, 1937). From 1937 the Psychological Corporation began a systematic and continuous monitoring of public opinion on all questions of political importance to business and corporations (Link 1948). Over the next fourteen years the results of many of these surveys were published in the *Journal of Applied Psychology* (e.g. TPC 1937; Link 1947b; Link and Freiberg 1949).

The possibility of this new service to industry came from the development in the mid-1930s of reasonably reliable small-sample polling techniques. The demand for the service arose as a direct consequence of the shock to business occasioned by F. D. Roosevelt's landslide second-term victory in the 1936 presidential elections (Bernays 1937; Walker and Sklar 1938; Lasswell 1939). After 1936, for the first time, all American business combined to use all media in a sustained campaign to discredit the Roosevelt Administration and proclaim the merits of laissez-faire capitalism in the face of the New Deal's 'creeping socialism' (Walker and Sklar 1938). Thereafter the continuous feedback from public opinion polls about changes of public opinion in response to propaganda campaigns brought a new sophistication to the production and distribution of business-sponsored propaganda. In 1939 Lasswell (1939:357) announced that 'for better or for worse, the future of business is bound up with propaganda'.

The more strident and divisive business-sponsored propaganda was suspended during the war. With the war's end business returned to its battle with the public and found it had problems. Unions, protected by the Wagner Act of 1935, had grown apace in membership and strength. Many people felt, in the aftermath of a war fought to preserve democratic values, that the authoritarian structure of industry should be modified 'to provide greater economic democracy ... to match our political democracy' (Porter 1946b:3). Moreover a review in November 1945 of a dozen surveys carried out in the previous five years concluded that

> [people] have two serious reservations about industry; that great industrial corporations lack warmth and friendliness in their human relationships; and that the owners of industry, the stockholders, realise too great a return on their contribution to industry.
>
> [Thus] two counts on which industry is most vulnerable are (1) its human relationships and (2) the widespread public misunderstanding about corporate profits. (Ellison 1945:25)

In May 1946 a national conference of social scientists endorsed an ambitious plan to expand 'human relations' training and research.

At the annual meeting of the American Management Association in 1946 its president, Alvin Dodd, mounted a virtual crusade to proclaim industry's undying commitment to 'human relations', and this human relations clamour was carried across the country. Dodd announced (on no particular evidence) that

> American business is taking concrete steps to ensure that its management in all echelons ... is thoroughly conversant with intelligent and enlightened human relations policies ... Top executives ... are stating flatly that a knowledge of human relations is one of the most important, if not the prime requisite, to management at all levels.

As the *New York Times* observed in some bewilderment, this intelligence was a 'requisite, never [before] seriously considered by practical businessmen as of paramount importance' (Zipser 1946:1).

The several volumes published on the Hawthorne studies during the 1930s (all replete with human relations doctrine) appear to have made no great immediate impact. Indeed they were accorded, as late as 1947, a distinctly mixed reception, especially by academic reviewers (Kornhauser 1934; Dodd 1946; Moore 1947; Landsberger 1958). But that was to change very rapidly, first among business leaders, and then among academics. By 1948 Lyndall Urwick, director of the International Management Institute, Geneva, observed (on behalf of management) that there is no thought about personnel management 'that has not an echo or a reflection in the vast treasure house of the work at Hawthorne' (see 'The Fruitful Errors ... ' 1946; Urwick and Brech 1949).

In addition to the loaded phrase 'human relations', two other words were much promoted in and about postwar industry: 'democracy' and 'participation', and especially 'democratic participation'. Just as the 'human relations' doctrine was given a (false) aura of science by its linkage with the Hawthorne studies, so each of these newer words was indissolubly linked with a 'classic' social science study. Thus the 'classic' study which proclaimed a beneficial connection between industrial productivity and 'democracy' was Lewin's 1939 study. Similarly Coch and French's 1948 study found a beneficial connection with industrial productivity and 'participation' (Carey 1976a).

Five further observations or commentaries by experts in the fields of industrial management and propaganda should be noted. In 1952 Asch (1952:516–17) observed of the studies by Kurt Lewin and his associates that were most influential in the postwar period (and of Coch and French's 'classic' participation study published in 1948 in particular):

The studies examined refer to the methods used as 'democratic' participation ... [because they] stress informing and arousing interest ... This should not obscure the fact that the procedures were one-sided and that the decisions to which the workers were said to have assented in democratic discussion had been reached by management in advance ... There is danger of confusing democratic procedure with the manipulation of groups by persuasion that retains only the external forms of freedom.

The second commentary concerns the generally propagandist character of the human relations-cum-democratic participation movement in American industry. Jaques Ellul (1973:23–4, 287) has percipiently observed in this connection:

> Public Relations and Human Relations ... these are precisely the form propaganda takes in the United States.
>
> Even in the actual conduct of human relations, at meetings [etc.] ... the propagandist ... is nothing else and nothing more than the representative of the organisation — or, rather, a delegated fraction of it. He remains a manipulator in the shadow of the machine. He knows why he speaks certain words and what effect they should have. His words are no longer human words but technically calculated words; they no longer express a feeling or a spontaneous idea, but reflect an organisation even when they seem entirely spontaneous.
>
> We know how important human relations can be to the individual ... personal contact ... the warmth of a personal presence. This is exactly what puts the human-relations technique of propaganda into play. But this human contact is false, and merely simulated; the presence is not that of the individual who has come forward but that of the organisation behind him. In the very act of pretending to speak as human to human, the propagandist is reaching the summit of mendacity and falsification, even when he is not conscious of it.

It should be remembered, however, that in addition to its general propagandist function, the human relations–democratic participation campaign begun in 1946 was also directed at the unions. In 1941 Roethlisberger (1941:128), in a book which sought to spell out for management the full implications of the ideas developed in connection with the Hawthorne studies, raised certain substantially rhetorical questions about workers at the 'lower levels' of industry:

> If deprived of certain [human relations-type satisfactions] might they tend to seek associations which would provide them? Might they get this kind of human satisfaction through their union activities? Might this opportunity for social participation be as important to some of its members as the formal purposes for which a union is organised?

Studies in the late 1940s explored these questions and claimed, indeed, to establish the anticipated relationships between 'participation' and 'union–management polarity'. Morris Viteles, doyen of academic industrial psychologists, reports in this connection thus:

> The advantages to management of a 'climate' in which employees can become active and participate are illustrated in [the] findings of [a study conducted in an automobile company] ... Preliminary analysis [of these findings] ... has revealed a number of significant trends, viz., *'Uniformly, in departments where the foreman is active in involving the men and the steward is not, the workers are more likely to be high on the managemen*t [loyalty] *index and low on the union* [loyalty] *index*; [and vice versa].'

Viteles concludes:

> Such findings, and those from other studies, clearly suggest that *any management which wants its employees to be management-minded must take steps to provide the opportunity for and to encourage active participation by workers* in arriving at decisions pertaining to the work process and the work situation ... Employee participation refers to participation by the employee as an individual or as a member of a small work group or team. (1954:453–4; emphases in original)

Finally, in 1950, Peter Drucker (1950:7), long-time consultant and confidant to US business, observed:

> The human relations policies which American management has been buying wholesale in the past ten years have been a conspicuous waste and failure, in my opinion ... Most of us in management ... have instituted them as a means of busting the unions. That has been the main theme of these programs. They are based on the belief that if you have good employee relations the union will wither on the vine.

We may now sum up developments in industry–social science relationships in the postwar period.

(1) Widespread use in and about industry of certain key terms like 'human relations', 'democracy' and 'participation' was justified and dramatized on the basis of studies by social scientists. The studies were supposed to have shown (but did not) that certain kinds of management supervisory behaviour described by these key terms (in large part speciously) led to dramatic improvements in productivity and in worker–management relations.

(2) A whole new, controversial theory of worker 'human nature', developed by social scientists, was adopted to provide a 'scientific' basis for management's unending preoccupation with 'busting the

unions', but nicely, with key terms in speeches, literature and press reports about industry. Accordingly it was 'human relations', 'democracy', 'participation' that workers primarily sought from industry — rather than more money or more material benefits. Indeed this new theory was so vigorously promoted that even some leading management strategists apparently came to believe it. Thus W. H. Whyte (1950:78), then an editor of *Fortune* magazine, wrote: 'What does the worker really want? ... More than anything else, Elton Mayo and those who have followed him, have pointed out, he wants ... the psychological security that comes from good work, the recognition of it and the esprit de corps of the group about him ... ' But for Whyte the business executive is different: 'Is the top executive the same man? ... He has different motivations ... more than the worker he thinks in terms ... of economic incentive ... He is, in short, a different man'. Ironically this piece of managerial metaphysics occurs in the course of a widely influential article which is primarily occupied with exploring the reasons for the alleged failure of business's massive postwar propaganda campaigns! Given Whyte's views, one might conclude that if these campaigns were half as successful in converting their popular audience as in converting business's own experts they were very effective.

(3) All of the key words associated with the human relations movement were intimately linked with business's public relations problems. The words used and the human relations movement more generally were concerned primarily with cosmetic rather than real change in the authoritarian power relations within industry; with new images rather than new relationships; with protecting industry against effective (e.g. legislative) demands for real democratic change rather than with providing it. Thus the deployment of these words powerfully illustrates Sethi's second business strategy for dealing with adverse public opinion: 'Change the symbols used to describe business performance', thus bringing it into line with how the public should think, and 'note that no change in actual performance is called for'.

C. W. Mills (1948:199–204) was one of very few who recognized the 'human relations' developments of the late 1940s for the propagandist exercise they are. In 1948 he described the recent, much-publicized industrial interest in 'democracy' and 'human relations' as illustrative of a new 'sophisticated conservatism' whose distinguishing feature was its 'stealing of liberal symbols for conservative purposes' — a characterization which may be taken as a summary statement of Sethi's second 'strategy'.

(4) The use of terms like 'democracy' and 'participation' outside the firm or factory had a primarily public relations, image-making purpose; but inside the factory the situation was a little more complicated. It was widely believed that some form of active 'participation' in low-level decisions could be introduced that would be insignificant in affecting management's power and authority but would nevertheless weaken the loyalty of workers to unions.

Thus overall the human relations movement and the use of key words hoped to provide three purposes simultaneously:

◆   to change, and improve, the public's perception ('image') of industry without requiring actual change in management's performance; and in particular

◆   to forestall popular or legislative demand for change based on a public sense of incongruence between the authoritarian structure of industry and the values of a political democracy; and finally

◆   to weaken unions and to make workers 'management-minded'.

If the human relations movement could serve all these crucial political objectives then complaints about the veracity of supporting 'experiments' were of no particular interest to business. Moreover the claims by business-oriented social scientists that human relations techniques do improve productivity had a political usefulness which outweighed the validity of such statements. Human relations practices could not, of course, be openly stated to be used for the purpose of weakening unions and manipulating public opinion. Such overt assertions would weaken the propaganda value of the human relations movement. Hence industry needed these 'experiments' as an ostensibly solid, scientific base from which to build an erroneous picture of the interests of employees and the role of unions.

CHAPTER 10

THE INDUSTRIAL PREACHERS

Max Weber tells us that employers continually invoked God and his divine intentions throughout the Industrial Revolution to provide their employees with an ideal attitude to work. This divinely sanctioned view of industrial life became known as the Protestant ethic. Its chief effect was to turn older Christian traditions and values on their heads (Tawney 1938:241–66; Burns 1969:15–23).

In the Genesis story of the Garden of Eden, Adam and Eve knew perfect happiness in a place where idleness (if not dalliance) abounded. This perfection had God's approval. Thus work came as a bane, not a boon — a punishment and a burden that restricted enjoyment and fun. But this view of human nature provided no ideological basis on which to launch and sustain an industrial revolution. From the seventeenth century a profound moral revision developed, and by 1800 the new work ethic was well established (Tawney 1938; Thompson 1968).

With the Protestant ethic work ceased to be represented as a punishment imposed on man by God. Rather, to work now became man's peculiarly human distinction. It was discovered to be God's will that man should find grace in work, that he should make his work a vocation and a ruling concern of his life, that he should give his body and mind willingly for the intrinsic vocational satisfactions it provided, and should abjure sloth and idleness if he hoped to escape eternal damnation.

The puritan preachers of the Protestant ethic are the spiritual ancestors of today's industrial psychologists. The main effect, if not the conscious intention, of their sermons was to reconcile men to the values of modern industry. Industrial psychologists in general perform a similar function. Many American industrial psychologists, perpetuating an especially missionary tradition, have gone further still. American industrial psychologists since the time of F. W. Taylor affirm that people should carry out industrial work in accordance with the basic contract by which they sell their time, labour and skills. In addition, employees should like what they do — even love it — and identify wholly with the institution that hires them (Whyte 1960:35–59).

All technologically underdeveloped countries (including Britain during the Industrial Revolution) have experienced great difficulty in persuading workers to accept the values and discipline of modern industry, of subordinating impulse and spontaneity to a rigid time schedule, or exchanging imaginative ritual and fantasy for a concept of life where usefulness and worth are exclusively material criteria. Such an exchange could lead one to reasonable doubt about the appropriateness of modern industry to fit the natural needs and inclinations of human beings. But industrial psychologists, particularly American industrial psychologists, have shown little disposition to any such doubts.

US dominance

Australia, Britain, and the United States, though with some important variations in history and popular values, share the same puritan, Protestant ethic and free-enterprise heritage. This heritage provides a wider perspective within which the subordination of the industrial psychologists' work to managerial criteria finds a natural home. The consequences of this background for industrial psychology and industrial sociology in the United States have been documented by Leon Baritz (1965:210), who concludes that social scientists in US industry have been 'servants of power' and have 'served power instead of mind'.

In Britain, V. L. Allen (1961:51) attributes a similar though less complete subordination to management's control over both the access of social scientists to industry and over what they have studied. In Allen's account, employers 'turned to social scientists for help' when from 1939 onwards, unionism and full employment seriously threatened management's traditional right to control in industry. In consequence, 'when social scientists entered the field of industry they did so on employers' terms and concentrated largely on their problems' (see Kornhauser 1947; Mills 1948; Smith 1961:36–7).

Australian industrial psychology shares with its British and American counterparts the general conditions of development described by Allen.[1] Three related characteristics, however, distinguish it: a relatively embryonic state of development as a profession, a very limited base in indigenous research or theory, and a consequent extreme dependence on imported research, theory and textbooks.

A recent Australia-wide survey of members of the Australian Psychological Society (Bordow 1971) indicates that about a hundred members can be reckoned to have some claim to description as industrial psychologists, and that about a third of these do some basic research. About half of this hundred are employed in teaching and management consultancy (equally divided); some 10 percent (i.e. about ten) are employed full-time in business or industry. The remaining third are employed by government agencies.

Thus the principal occupations of industrial psychologists in Australia are teaching about industrial psychology and consultative services to managements. The latter services are comprised mainly of personnel work (selection, assessment, motivation, and morale problems) and management development and training.

The small number of Australian industrial psychologists and the nature of their principal occupations have prevented the development of any substantial body of indigenous research or theory. In 1969 Dr Bruce Yuill's *Organisational Principles of Management* (1966) was 'the only Australian textbook on this subject' (Byrt 1969:104) — that is, the only Australian approximation to a textbook on industrial psychology. But two years earlier Professor E. J. Willett (1968:57–80) wrote that all management education in Australia (including its psychological component) 'is far too dependent on overseas teaching materials and research concepts. Teaching is therefore derivative and Australian research is urgently required ... The future position [of management education] is not satisfactory'.

A fairly cursory inspection of library shelves or catalogues will confirm the overwhelmingly imported content of every kind of management education in Australia, and of industrial psychology in particular. For example, the subject catalogue in the library of one university specializing in the area (the University of New South Wales) contains about 150 entries under industrial psychology. Of these some 80 percent are published in the United States and draw almost wholly on American theory and research. About 15 percent are published in Britain by British authors, the majority of whom rely heavily on American research. About 3 percent are produced by resident Australian authors, but in general around 90 percent of these depend on imported research — overwhelmingly American.[2]

Perhaps there is passing comfort in the fact that something not very different from the present Australian condition was common to the Western world until at least as recently as 1961. A UNESCO report of that year (Smith 1961:36–7) concluded that while in the United States 'industrial sociology has been little affected by foreign influences', elsewhere 'the pioneering influence of the United States has been too great' to allow any strongly independent development of industrial sociology; and that in consequence 'in nearly every [country] the teacher of industrial sociology must depend quite heavily on material derived from research conducted by social scientists in the United States'.

Australian industrial psychology has existed for only twenty-five years. During all of that period such intellectual foundations as the subject has possessed were imported — overwhelmingly, and in large part uncritically, from the United States.

It would matter less that the intellectual foundations of industrial psychology were imported if they were imported from a society with an industrial history not too dissimilar from our own. In fact Australian and American industrial histories vary greatly. Australia's industrial history has been marked by nothing comparable to the sustained vigour — frequently extending to violence — with which, until quite recently, American management sought to combat the growth of unions and guard against the development of public attitudes or ideologies that would present a serious challenge to management's traditional rights and prerogatives, or to the free-enterprise system in general.

It is only by a full appreciation of the social and political context within which American industrial psychology has developed that we can begin to estimate the consequences for related disciplines in Australia. From 1904 onwards, the Australian arbitration system gave some protection even to weak unions and cushioned the confrontation between management's and labour's interests. In contrast, US corporations employed violence and intimidation on a large scale to combat the growth of unions, and this condition continued until the 1950s. For example, in the sixteen years to 1949 there were 143 deaths in the United States which were officially attributed to labour–management disputes (Streuben 1950:300ff.).

In the United States industrial psychologists do not appear to have a conflict of interest between management and labour, for their role has been to assist management to advance economic and political goals. Thus a leading American industrial psychologist, writing in a widely used and highly regarded textbook on industrial psychology, is clear both about the inequity of the existing American

economic system and about his own willingness to assist in the per-
petuation of this inequity:

> Both management and labour have certain social responsibilities which
> they must meet if the system of private enterprise is to operate unhampered
> by governmental restrictions, or even to survive at all. Since it is more to
> the interests of the owning classes than to that of the masses of labour to
> preserve this system, the former, especially, should have an understanding
> of their responsibilities and take a long range point of view. (Maier
> 1946:30)

In an essay entitled 'The Psychologist in Industry' the American
Psychological Association (1962:1–16) warns managers that there
are limits to what can be achieved on their behalf through even the
most skilled promotion campaigns (for sometimes popular attitudes
can be so averse to the product being marketed that 'even the truth
will be rejected'). But the association leaves no doubt about the willing subservience of psychologists to management's political purposes: 'Industrial psychologists are', the APA assures American business, 'probing such questions as how to build a favourable "company image"'. And while

> the task of keeping the image of the company clear and valid among the
> various strategic sub-publics and among the population at large is a con-
> tinuing one ... The industrial psychologist is increasingly helpful in
> bringing psychological devices and insights to the aid of management in
> the effort to create and maintain a positive reputation. [Moreover] while
> the psychologist's basic interest is human behaviour, he can help with
> management's most basic aim, increasing profitability ... General accep-
> tance [i.e. by rank-and-file employees] of management's aims requires that
> each group be educated to see things in proper perspective and to under-
> stand its role in the broad setting. (ibid.:11)

This alignment of everyone with management's aims is to be sought
not by objective changes which reduce the real conflict of interests
between operatives and management but by 're-education and
restructuring of perceptions' (ibid.:14).

In a passage which, despite a heavy infusion of benevolence, has
overtones of political re-education centres in Orwell's *1984*, we learn
that industrial psychologists also help employees: 'Essentially what
the industrial psychologist attempts to do is to help the employee
come to ... a recognition of how his interests and management's
coincide ... [to] help the employee adjust to the requirements of a
successful enterprise' (ibid.:12).

The ideological and political interests of US industry have meant that industrial psychologists have avoided exploring basic questions about the structure of power and authority in American industry. Such exploration would invite the discovery that basic changes in these areas would better serve the needs of employees, workers and society at large. In contrast, industrial psychologists have developed theories and skills designed to hold the hearts and minds of workers and the general public in favour of the free-enterprise businessman and in opposition to government regulations and unionism.

In the context of the fervent pro-democratic and anti-authoritarian rhetoric that accompanied the 1939–45 war against Germany, the obviously authoritarian structure of US industry made it a potentially vulnerable target for strongly aroused democratic, egalitarian sentiments. It was therefore politically important to management to appropriate the term 'democratic leadership' so that it could be used as a plausible veneer for their own authoritarian power structures. To make this appropriation shift plausible psychological expertise was required. If it could be scientifically established that workers primarily want social satisfactions rather than money from their jobs then it follows that there is no need to raise basic questions about the present power and authority structure of industry. Nor is there any need to view salary increases as being in the best interests of employees.

Economic education

By the postwar years there was a systematic attempt (with the assistance of ex-service psychologists) to apply what had been learned from wartime propaganda to the objective of indoctrinating employees throughout the United States in an unqualified commitment to the free-enterprise system (Viteles 1953:14–36).[3] In general these exercises went under the name of Courses in Economic Education for Employees. They were given in management time (hence were virtually compulsory) with crude pre- and post- tests from which improvement in 'information' and 'education' was assessed.[4]

By 1952 'systematic company training in economics [stood] out as one of the fastest growing and most significant management developments in recent years' (Opinion Research Corporation 1952:5). Nationwide surveys of employees showed large apparent improvement, where economic training had been given, in 'views ... which are consistent with the ideology of an economic system of free enterprise' (Viteles 1953:426). However, Viteles concludes, there are 'many methodological problems', and 'much remains to be done in establishing the relationships between economic indoctrination ... and ... changes in ideology, morale [and] productivity ... ' if 'maximum results in the way of changed attitudes' are to be obtained 'from employee information and similar programs' (ibid.:428–9). For example, there is evidence from a major wartime study that, for the best results, one side only of an issue or argument should be presented to poorly educated people. Two-sided presentations, however, are more effective in influencing better educated people and those initially opposed to the desired view.[5] These results, Viteles concludes, 'suggest that different programs — perhaps "one-sided" for rank and file employees and "two-sided" for technical and supervisory personnel — may be required' (ibid.:433–5).

It therefore appears to Viteles that 'propaganda or indoctrination programs must be based upon an extensive and detailed knowledge of existing employee attitudes and opinions obtained through the application of appropriate survey techniques'. Both the wartime experiment cited, and others which compare 'the effectiveness of lectures, group discussions, and other procedures, point to the need for *research designed to establish for industry the types of programs which will produce most effective results in the way of attitude change*' (emphasis in original). As part of such research employees should be asked what they like or dislike about specific programs, for such enquiries will not only yield information useful to designing new programs but will 'produce ... a feeling of participation on the part of employees' — in planning programs covertly aimed at their own indoctrination — 'which can in itself contribute to [success] in moulding and modifying [their] attitudes' (ibid.:435–6; emphasis added).

In 1954 the American Management Association (AMA) published a report and appraisal of programs for education of employees in a sample of fifty firms and corporations (Williams and Peterfreund 1954).[6] The report found that 'so much in the way of economic education is ... going on [that] "employee education" and "economic education" have become virtually synonymous to many people'. Moreover 'a good number of respondents actually stated that "propaganda" and "economic education" are synonymous in their companies. We want people to think right' (ibid.:12, 31).

The principal technique used for changing beliefs and attitudes of employees consisted of small-group discussion sessions (15–20 people) supported by films (or other teaching aids) and, usually, by trained discussion leaders.

The study of ostensibly free discussion, in small groups led by democratic supervisors (i.e. 'group dynamics'), as a means of changing attitudes has a remarkable academic history, to which we shall return later. In the immediate postwar years this work led to packaged discussion programs on economic education produced by Du Pont (HOBSO — How Our Business System Operates) and others.

In 1954 the AMA report found some employee education to be almost universal in American industry (ibid.:49), while in some companies 'the total costs of presenting a discussion-type program such as HOBSO ... came to as much as a million or even two million dollars' (ibid.:40). There were a few objections by management personnel that such employee education was 'a propaganda effort to manipulate opinions and perceptions in the interests of management' and that 'people should ... not be subjected to "propaganda devices" on a "capture basis"' (ibid.:13, 32).[7] More surprising, to an Australian viewpoint, managements were, by and large, able to secure the active co-operation of workers and local union officials[8] in indoctrination sessions that had the aim of weakening unions. Moreover, in general, workers or their colleagues voluntarily made up the production lost through work time spent in economic education sessions.[9]

The purpose of the education programs was frankly political.[10] 'Many companies ... want to integrate the employee with his work group, to develop his "sense of belonging" to get him to identify his own welfare with the company's. Some employers view this kind of program as a sort of "battle of loyalties" with the unions' (ibid.:29). Still other employers 'believe strongly that morale (and productivity) improves' as a result of such programs. But for the vast majority increased productivity was plainly secondary to political objectives.

The AMA found no cause for unease in all this, except for the practical consideration that 'millions on millions of dollars are being spent on education for employees ... without any systematic or deepseated appraisal' that could provide reassurance that the education was producing political and other changes in employee attitudes commensurate with its great cost (ibid.:49).

The report identifies a major problem in this area. Most surveys that attempt to assess the effects of employee education concentrated on whether the employee has learned the (more favourable) facts provided in the programs. But almost nothing is known about the relationship between changes in the facts people accepted and changes in their attitudes (feelings, emotions) and behaviour. The report notes uneasily that 'it is possible that as people learn more facts about our economic system' — even facts selected by management — 'they could just as easily become more critical of it ... as not' (ibid.:47).

The report recommends that intensive research in two areas should be urgently promoted:

1 Intensive study, through interviews in depth with a variety of workers, of the facts, attitudes and behaviour to establish how changes in information affect attitudes, behaviour in the plant (productivity, grievances, unions) and away from the plant (voting).

2 Large-scale research and surveys are required to produce national and local pictures of present employee information, attitudes and behaviour. A base line representing the present situation can then be drawn against which future changes in each area — information, attitudes and behaviour — can be continuously charted. Within this frame the interrelationships between information and attitudes etc could be closely monitored and explored and the effectiveness of different education programs for different purposes could be determined (ibid.:49–53).[11]

The report proposed that study was particularly necessary of the way in which the emotional content of employee attitudes limits changes that can be obtained through information-oriented education,[12] and of how such resistance by employees to changes in their attitudes desired by management might be overcome. The report suggests that employee reactions to projective tests made from pictures of 'executive offices, a new factory, a company's annual report, a manual worker ... , a new stock issue, etc.' might be used to explore emotional barriers to the production of attitude change in the direction of increased loyalty to, and indentification with, the free enterprise system (ibid.: 51–3).

It may or may not be a matter of coincidence that the questions the AMA report identifies as problems for politically oriented employees have constituted the main preoccupations of research and theory in social and industrial psychology from the end of the war to 1976, that is, techniques of communication and leadership as these affect attitudes and attitude change — especially in a small-group context — and associated problems of measurement.[13]

The main purpose of this excursion into the relationships between the political interests of American managements and social and industrial psychology is to point up the political context of the work of American industrial psychologists. A consequence of

this is the likelihood that the political interests of American managements will largely influence both the information about industry
and the theories about industrial behaviour that find their way into
textbooks.

The human relations school

To explore this question further it will be necessary to distinguish
the school (or tradition) of social science research which has long
held a dominant place in management textbooks in America and
abroad. Thereafter we will examine the most celebrated studies in
this tradition to bring out the consequences for Australian teaching
in the management area of using American textbooks and theories
with a naive disregard of the political context that has produced
them. From UNESCO (Smith 1961) to the United States (Korman
1971), Britain (Lupton 1971) and Australia (Bucklow 1966) there is
general agreement that one, primarily American, school of social and
industrial psychology has dominated the field for some forty years.
Known as the 'human relations' school, it has, in Britain as in
Australia, provided 'the only ideas from the social sciences that many
managers may have encountered' (Lupton 1971:17).

The human relations tradition of work and theory had its origin
in a series of research projects carried out at the Western Electric
Company's Hawthorne works, near Chicago. Under the general
direction of Elton Mayo, professor of business administration at
Harvard, the 'Hawthorne studies' continued intermittently from
1927 to 1935. These studies have long been celebrated as the scientific coming of age of industrial psychology (Blum 1949:47). A textbook in wide use in Australia for almost twenty years describes them
as providing 'a foundation on which all future research must be
based' (Brown 1954:85), a view shared by Colonel Lyndall Urwick.
Indeed Urwick, whose influence in Australia has been considerable,
waxes almost rhapsodic in praise of the Hawthorne studies and their
abiding importance for all managements for all time (Urwick and
Brech 1948).[14]

The UNESCO report referred to above finds these studies 'probably the best point from which to date the development of industrial
sociology', and concludes that 'it is unlikely that any subsequent
investigations could have so great an impact as the Hawthorne studies' (Smith 1961:23, 56). The distinctive conclusion reached by the
Hawthorne researchers was that economic incentives are of relatively
little importance for workers' motivation and productivity compared

with attention to their social needs. Worker discontent, the researchers concluded, is often emotionally — indeed irrationally — based. Managements should therefore 'guard and develop' the 'social sentiments' of workers (Whitehead 1938a:205). If management gives greater attention to the social and emotional needs of the worker the reward, in terms of increased output and increased loyalty to the firm, will be great. Management can achieve this result by training supervisors to exercise authority in a paternalistic, human relations style and to foster satisfying social relations within work groups. The implied neurosis and maladjustment which underlie worker disaffection toward management (e.g. the disposition to support militant unions) can be dissipated by providing a quasi-clinical counselling service which enables workers to let off steam by telling their problems as often as they like to sympathetic listeners (Wilensky and Wilensky 1951).

An editor of *Fortune* magazine later described the key import for management of the Hawthorne studies and their conclusions in the following manner: 'the workers were a social system; [this] system ... determined the worker's attitude towards his job. The social system could work against management, but if the managers troubled themselves to understand [it] ... the system could work for management' (Whyte 1956:37). Put more crudely but more honestly, members of tight-knit work groups are subject to powerful conformist pressures. With the help of social scientists management can create such work groups and use these pressures to further management's interests (Thompson 1961:122–8).

Until at least 1955 the human relations movement consisted mainly of a search for techniques of persuasion through which such group pressures could be fostered and made to work in the service for management (Goldthorpe et al. 1968:43–5).[15]

After Mayo and the Hawthorne studies the next most influential figure in the human relations tradition is Kurt Lewin (Caplow 1964:238–9; Homans 1968:259). 'Although perhaps generally less well known than Mayo, Lewin had, if anything, an even greater impact within social science' (Pugh 1971:213). Lewin's influence derives both from the research studies he directed and from a number of his students who, long after his death in 1947, continued to dominate much of social and industrial psychology (Homans 1968:259; Korman 1971:9). Lewin largely continued the Hawthorne tradition (Benoit-Guilbot 1968:233; Smith 1961:32). He emphasized the importance of social needs and extended the exploration of ways in which group situations could be used to control individual behaviour (group dynamics). But Lewin was also innovative in his approach.

Mayo and the Hawthorne researchers had been frankly paternalistic toward workers. They believed that management (with the help of social scientists) knew better than the workers what the workers wanted (Whyte 1956:40–3). It was therefore in everybody's interest that management (whose behaviour is governed by logic) should employ social scientists to help it control workers (whose behaviour is governed by irrational sentiments) (Roethlisberger and Dickson 1964:255–69, 563–8, 574–5). Lewin, by contrast, while similarly exploring ways of managing small work groups that would increase managerial control over their behaviour, made much use of the word 'democracy' and called his recommended tactics for democratic leadership 'democratic participation' (Kariel 1956; Pateman1970:71–3).

Bucklow (1966:60) notes that 'Lewin's influence on industrial practice came largely from three field studies directed by him with children's play groups, housewives and young girl pyjama machinists'. The first and last of these studies (Lewin et al. 1939; Coch and French 1948) have long enjoyed the status of 'classics'. We shall return to them later.

The study with housewives occurred during the war (National Research Council 1943). In it Lewin compared the effectiveness of different techniques for changing the attitude of housewives towards consumption of greater amounts of liver and kidneys (meats not required for the troops abroad). His experiments were claimed to show that democratic discussions with housewives, in small groups, produced greater changes toward the desired behaviour than did more conventional lecture or instruction sessions. These experiments, though apparently trivial, were an important influence on a decade of postwar research in social and industrial psychology. For they were taken to hold promise that intensive psychological study of groups (group dynamics) would uncover new techniques for controlling behaviour. 'These researchers', wrote J. G. Miller (1948:287), 'contain the first glimmerings of evidence that we have means to control scientifically the mass behaviour of human beings in a matter concerning which they feel they have freedom of action'.

We can therefore say that two propositions underpinned the work of the human relations school up to 1955:

1   that a certain *style* or *manner* of supervision and of reaching decisions with subordinates (variously called friendly, democratic, participatory, consultative, considerate, team-oriented, etc.) will

greatly increase the morale and satisfaction of workers; and

2 that the happier, or more satisfied, a worker is (e.g. with social relations with his work group) the harder he will work (Strauss 1971:110).

The second proposal was essential, of course, if the human relations approach were to retain any appeal to management's interest in output and efficiency. From 1955 onwards accumulating industrial research, observation and practical experience slowly forced the abandonment of this belief, with consequent rapid decline in the popularity of the human relations movement (Strauss 1970:145).[16] It became evident that there was little relationship between satisfaction and productivity (Brayfield and Crockett 1955; Vroom 1964). It was discovered that workers may be miserable and productive and conversely happy and idle (Whyte 1956:58).

Industrial psychology was in danger of losing its appeal to management. How was this 'fall from grace' resolved? The solution was to discover (or decide) that there are different kinds of worker satisfaction — some related to productivity, others not. There was, for instance, the now discredited satisfaction that comes from social and other conditions associated with the work context, and then there is another more individual (or egotistic) kind of satisfaction that comes from characteristics intrinsic to the job itself, such as interest, challenge, opportunity for responsibility, and self-direction etc. Increase in satisfaction from the former source, which the old human relations doctrine had emphasized, does not, it was discovered, cause increased effort and productivity. Increase in satisfactions of the latter kind, which the 'neo-human relations' (or 'human resources') doctrine would henceforth emphasize, does cause increased productivity.

Thus between 1955 and 1960 job enlargement and job enrichment gradually replaced social needs as the alleged key to unlocking (without expensive salary rises) the energy of employees. Most industrial psychologists had long given some attention to such things as 'challenge', 'self-direction' etc. and so regarded the shift as a change in emphasis only. Herzberg (1959) dramatized the shift in a theory which expressed it in a very extravagant form. He produced a vast confection of putative evidence in support of his theory and a suitable range of homespun metaphors in which to express it (Herzberg 1968; Ludwig 1973). Herzberg thereby established, in popular reputation, an appearance of having invented, and taken out patent rights on, the concept of job enrichment.[17]

Field studies

In textbooks of industrial and social psychology published during the last twenty years certain sets of studies or experiments are commonly referred to as 'classics': the Hawthorne studies, studies directed by Lewin, Coch and French's Harwood experiments, and a study by Herzberg published in 1959. This last work was the foundation for the pre-eminent reputation Herzberg enjoyed; although it is not commonly described as a classic, its influence has been vast. Each of these studies was marked by a number of salient features. Chief among these were:

1   an insistent minimizing of the importance of money or material reward as an influence on work behaviour in general and on productivity in particular, and

2   a disposition to view low output, lack of co-operativeness, absence, grievances, strikes or other uncongenial worker behaviour as neurotic or maladjusted behaviour. Herzberg in particular accounted for these two features in an unprecedentedly extravagant manner.[18]

The Hawthorne studies

The Hawthorne studies concluded that 'none of the results gave the slightest substantiation to the theory that the worker is primarily motivated by economic interest', and that 'a wage incentive system was so dependent on its relation to other factors' — especially supervision and related social factors — 'that it was impossible to consider it as ... having an independent effect on the individual' (Roethlisberger and Dickson 1964:160, 575–6).

These are the most celebrated conclusions in the history of industrial psychology. Through American (and English) textbooks countless Australian students and managers have for thirty years been taught these nonsensical conclusions, along with a nonsense account of the Hawthorne studies.

For Australians there is a kind of inverted justice in all this. The man chiefly responsible for the Hawthorne studies, Elton Mayo, professor of industrial research at the Harvard School of Business, was an Australian who graduated in psychology from Adelaide University. The building which housed the first School of Applied Psychology in Australia, the Mayo Building at the University of New South Wales, was named in his honour. (The Hawthorne Studies are considered in detail in Chapter 11.)

Lewin, Lippitt and White

The second set of 'classical' studies was carried out at Iowa University and published in 1939 by Lewin, Lippitt and White. It comprised four groups, each of five boys aged around ten years. From these groups four after-school clubs were constituted which engaged in a variety of hobby activities, such as mask-making and soap-carving.

A balanced experimental design was planned in which each of the four clubs would continue in operation for eighteen weeks divided into three experimental periods of six weeks' duration — making twelve experimental periods in all. There would be six experimental periods under 'democratic' leadership and six under 'autocratic' leadership. Each of four adult leaders would play both democratic and autocratic roles, and each club would, in different periods, have democratic and autocratic leadership by turn. Observers would keep detailed records of the social behaviour of the boys (e.g. frequency of 'aggressive acts') and of productive output.

The first six weeks of democratic leadership, however, turned out badly. The boys (Charlie Chan Club) behaved in an 'individual anarchic way'. So a new category of laissez-faire leadership was specially created, and the results from the first period of democratic leadership were relegated to that category (White and Lippitt 1960:20–2). In the end five experimental sessions were designated democratic, five autocratic, and two laissez-faire.

The Charlie Chan Club in its first democratic-cum-laissez-faire period produced 34 'acts of aggression' per 50-minute meeting. With considerable consistency it produced scores of 27 and 30 under further democratic and autocratic leadership. To adjust this 'bad' result the experimenters allowed that this consistent aggressiveness might be due to the personalities of the boys (Lewin et al. 1939:281).

The other three clubs underwent a total of four (six-week) periods of democratic leadership, and four of autocratic leadership. Every autocratic period produced less aggression than any democratic period. The former averaged 2 'acts of aggression' per 50-minute meeting, the latter 20 (Lewin et al. 1939:281). Under autocratic leadership the boys spent 74 percent of their total time absorbed in work, under democratic leadership 50 percent (White and Lippitt 1962:510). Output was higher under autocratic leadership (though we are not told how much higher); instead, 'a large quantity of work [was] done' (White and Lippit 1960:65, 87). These are the only results of the study which have any (and then dubious) claim to objectivity.

It is a considerable tribute to the experimenters' attachment to the word 'democracy' (both in its political connotations and in the sense in which a human relations supervisory style in industry is called 'democratic'[19]) that they are able to interpret this evidence in a way favourable to democracy, and then conclude that democracy was more efficient and produced less frustration and less aggression than autocratic leadership. But it is even more remarkable that for thirty years subsequently, unending versions of this trivial and worthless study have been spread over literally thousands of pages of journals, books, textbooks and citations, ranging from education and industrial psychology to international relations. It should be no surprise then that after a while it was widely reported, in textbooks and articles, that output was highest in the democratically led groups (see Jacques 1948:128–9; French et al. 1960:3; Benoit-Guilbot 1968:23; Raven 1968:289).

In 1971 I read a paper on this study to the Annual Conference of the Australian Psychological Society. Subsequently one of Australia's best known industrial psychologists, who is head of a human relations unit in a large corporation, sought a copy of my paper. He offered no objection to its analysis but suggested 'toning down the ironic or sarcastic comments [for publication], because the prestige of Lewin, Lippitt, and White is so high that editors might possibly turn down your paper as being too aggressive'.

Coch and French

The third 'classic' series of studies was conducted among women sewing operatives at Harwood Manufacturing Corporation, Marion, Virginia. The president of the company was a psychologist, Dr A. J. Marrow. Marrow had worked closely with, and greatly admired, Kurt Lewin and his theories. The best known report of the studies was published in 1948 by Coch and French, pupils and disciples of Lewin.

Labour turnover and hostility toward management was very high at Harwood. In the operatives' view, management used transfers between jobs to cut price rates and to get rid of slower workers. Job changes and transfers were frequent. The company paid a 'transfer bonus' and this bonus made up the wages of half of any group of transferred workers while they learned the new job. The 'half' of the group was determined on the basis of the half which relearned fastest. The rest lost money on every transfer. Operatives who were transferred most frequently quit most frequently (in the operatives' view, for economic reasons). This behaviour the experimenters quaintly called 'resistance to change', and supposed it to be irrationally and emotionally based. The experiment was designed to show that group discussion with workers about to be transferred (i.e. 'participation') could be used to overcome such resistance to change.

Coch and French set up four work groups. One was simply told their job would be changed and what the new rate for it would be. This group's output and earnings on their new job were poor; they filed grievances about the piece-rate, and three (out of eighteen) quit. Both the output attributed to them and their earnings were, of course, a function of the piece-rate set. The other three groups were allowed to participate in 'designing the new jobs and setting the new piece rates' (Coch and French 1948:28). They were also trained in methods of work appropriate to the new job 'so they [could] reach a high rate of production within a short time' (ibid.:521). In these three groups output and earnings were high and no one quit.

Explanation of the results on straightforward economic grounds would not seem difficult. But Coch and French claimed that the results demonstrate that allowing workers to participate in discussion about proposed job changes overcomes psychological barriers and enables management 'to modify greatly or remove completely group resistance to change in methods of work and the ensuing piece rates' (ibid.:531). Coch and French's experiment has been widely celebrated on these grounds and is still widely reprinted (Faunce 1967; Cartwright and Zander 1968).

Later, French and others (1960) attempted to replicate this experiment in a Norwegian factory. They were particularly interested in exploring the influence on worker behaviour of participation (i.e. discussion meetings) which produced a 'feeling' of influencing decisions about their work situation ('perceived participation') as distinct from actual influence ('objective participation'). This time all groups received similar retraining and the setting of all piece-rates was determined by negotiations between management and unions. Under these circumstances the groups which participated in discussions prior to job changes performed no differently from the rest, indicating that piece-rates were the determining factor of production. Unsurprisingly this Norwegian experiment hasn't become celebrated.

Herzberg

The last of these classic studies concerns Herzberg, who sought to test his hypothesis that some aspects of work situations cause satisfaction and high motivation if they are good (but cannot cause dissatisfaction no matter how bad they are). Conversely, other aspects of work situations cause dissatisfaction etc if they are bad (but cannot cause satisfaction no matter how good they are). Examples of the first category are (non-monetary) recognition and sense of achievement. These are called 'satisfiers' or 'motivators'. Somewhat predictably, perhaps, money is an example of the second category and is called a 'dissatisfier' or a 'hygiene factor'.

Herzberg and his associates (1959) interviewed 200 white-collar employees about their work attitudes and motivation. Management was interested to obtain information about their employees' attitudes and motives and let their employees know they were expected to co-operate with the interviewers. Each person interviewed was first asked to recall occasions or events (in the near or distant past) which had been associated with (a) very 'good' feelings about his job and (b) very 'bad' feelings about his job. Next he was asked, in each case, to describe the good (or bad) feelings experienced and how they related to the event or occasion which produced them. Finally, he was asked what effect these 'high' and 'low' experiences had on his job behaviour.

Herzberg undertook no observation whatever of the actual work situations or work behaviour of his subjects. The empirical foundations of his theory consisted entirely in 476 selected anecdotes (or parts of anecdotes) obtained from the 200 subjects, together with their self-appraisals about why they felt especially 'good' or 'bad' on the occasions to which the anecdotes referred.

The result is a miasma of statistics in which, as in a Rorschach test, almost anything may be found, according to the motivation of the observer. However, two things are omitted from this 'evidence': first, that people are motivated by events or conditions unrelated to their job; second, that the job may be subordinate to a wider life of non-work concerns — such as meeting family needs for housing or education, building a boat, ending the Vietnam War, attending symphony concerts, or even winning a frog-jumping contest. These factors will not be found because Herzberg (1959:48) excludes from the anecdotes selected for analysis any anecdote (or part anecdote) 'in which a factor in the personal life of the individual, having nothing to do with his job, was responsible for a period of good or bad feelings, even if these feelings affected his job'.[20]

This exclusion goes a long way to ensuring that Herzberg's results will reveal a vocational attitude to industrial work, that is, will reveal that men who work in industry are motivated primarily by (non-monetary) satisfactions intrinsic to their job. Of course this exclusion works in opposition to an attitude to work which views it as a means, through the income it provides, to social and personal ends.

Herzberg's exclusive statistics also erase the motivation and satisfaction derived from monetary rewards.[21]

Voluntarily produced anecdotes about memorable occasions of high satisfaction frequently centred on 'some act such as a promotion or wage increase which was not itself accompanied by verbal recognition'. In 'many' such cases, however, the respondent, when probed further, said that he felt the promotion or wage increase had been a due recognition of his competence, or whatever. Herzberg classified all such anecdotes as instances of high satisfaction resulting not from the promotion or wage increase but from non-monetary recognition (ibid.:45).

By a variety of interpretive shifts of this kind Herzberg concluded that workers seek primarily non-monetary, vocational rewards from industrial work (e.g. recognition, sense of achievement, responsibility, opportunity for growth); and that only these sorts of rewards can provide positive motivation and satisfaction.[22] (Hence these vocational aspects of work are 'satisfiers' or 'motivators'.) On the other hand, salary, good working conditions, job security are, Herzberg concludes, of secondary importance. These cannot, in his view, be sources of positive satisfaction or motivation. (They are called 'dissatisfiers' or 'hygiene factors'.) The most that can be achieved through them is to reduce resentment or dissatisfaction to zero. Except, that is, for a supposedly unfortunate minority of maladjusted or neurotic (even pathological) employees who are unnaturally oriented to satisfaction from these sources, and admit that they obtain positive satisfaction from high wages, job security or good working conditions (Herzberg 1968:77, 90, 178–92). With cosmic presumption Herzberg offers a 'culture-free' definition of work as 'the nature of man as it is in reality' (ibid.:43, 77). It turns out that, according to his scientifically discovered definition of men (more strictly, employees), those who seek or obtain positive satisfactions from material rewards are not only sick, unhealthy and maladjusted, but mentally ill, neurotic and pathological as well (ibid.: 77, 79, 80, 84, 85, 191–2).

The appeal of this definition of 'man-as-worker' to managing directors and shareholders is understandable — not least because if employees are told often enough that science and psychologists have shown their concern about money to be a symptom of neurosis they may come to believe it, and feel guilty about asking for pay rises.

A personal anecdote about Herzberg may be excusable at this point. In 1970 Herzberg was jetting about Europe explaining to managers how unwise and unprofitable it was to suppose monetary incentives could contribute positively to the satisfaction or motivation of workers. He stopped off in London for one day to address a conference. The *Economist* (6 June 1970:66) reported the occasion in an article entitled 'Does your job bore you or does Professor Herzberg?' Four hundred and forty-four business executives paid £GB25 each to listen to Professor Herzberg. Herzberg grossed about $A25 000 for one day spent explaining the relative unimportance of money as an incentive for employees. Three years later, in an interview with the editor of *International Management*, Herzberg gave a characteristically extravagant account of his revolutionary theory about the unimportance of pay as a motivator (Ludwig 1973:22). At the end he hypocritically admitted that he himself was very expensive, concluding, 'But, hell, I believe in hygiene factors' (i.e. in high material rewards).

The propaganda function that many industrial psychologists have performed, in the name of social science, is to be deplored. We should be grateful that many of them have been so inept. I am sure that their spiritual ancestors, the puritan preachers of the Protestant ethic, served their industrial masters much more honestly, and more effectively.

CHAPTER 11

THE HAWTHORNE STUDIES: A CRITICISM

There can be few scientific disciplines or fields of research in which a single set of studies and a single researcher has exercised so great an influence as was exercised for a quarter of a century by Mayo and the Hawthorne studies. This influence has declined in the last ten years as a result of the widespread failure of later studies to reveal any reliable relation between the social satisfactions of industrial workers and their work performance. Nevertheless reputable textbooks still refer almost reverentially to the Hawthorne studies as a classic in the history of social science in industry.

One might have expected therefore that the Hawthorne studies would have been subjected to the most searching and sceptical scrutiny. Before the remarkable claims of these studies (especially the relative unimportance of financial rewards compared with purely social rewards) became so widely influential, one would have thought that the quality of the evidence produced and the validity of the inferences from it would have been meticulously examined and assessed. There have been some broad criticisms of Mayo's approach and assumptions, many of them cogent. They include charges of pro-management bias, clinical bias, and scientific naivety.[1] But no one has systematically and in detail applied a critical eye to the claim that there is scientific worth in the original reports of the Hawthorne investigators.

Background

The Hawthorne studies comprised a long series of investigations into the importance of work behaviour and attitudes. The principal investigations were carried out between 1927 and 1932, after which economic depression caused their suspension. The component studies may be distinguished in five stages:

Stage I: The Relay Assembly Test Room Study. (New incentive system and new supervision.)

Stage II: The Second Relay Assembly Group Study. (New incentive system only.)

Stage III: The Mica Splitting Test Room Study. (New supervision only.)

Stage IV: The Interviewing Program.

Stage V: The Bank-Wiring Observation Room Study.

Stages I to III constitute a series of partially controlled studies which were initially intended to explore the effects on work behaviour by varying the physical conditions of work, especially variations in rest pauses and in hours of work, but also in temperature and humidity and in the payment system.

After the studies had been in progress for at least twelve months the investigators came to the entirely unexpected conclusion that social satisfaction, arising out of human association in work, was more important for work behaviour in general and output in particular than were any of the physical and economic aspects of the work situation (Pennock 1930; Putnam 1930). This conclusion came as 'the great éclaircissement ... an illumination quite different from what they had expected from the illumination studies' (Roethlisberger 1941:15). This is the central and distinctive finding from which the fame and influence of the Hawthorne studies derive.

This 'éclaircissement' about the predominant importance of social satisfactions at work occurred during Stage I of the studies. In consequence, all the later studies are in important ways subordinate to Stage I: 'It was the origin from which all the subsequent phases sprang. It was also their main focal point. It gave to these other phases their significance in relation to the whole enquiry' (Urwick and Brech 1948:27; see also Roethlisberger and Dickson 1939:29).

Stages II and III were 'designed to check on' (and were taken to supplement and confirm) the Stage I conclusion 'that the observed production increase was a result of a change in the social situation ... [and] not primarily because of wage incentives, reduced fatigue or similar factors' (Viteles 1954:185). Stage IV was an interviewing program undertaken to explore worker attitudes. Stage V was a study of informal group organization in the work situation.

The two later studies (IV and V) resulted directly from conclusions based on Stages I–III about the superior influence of social needs. Observations made in both were interpreted in the light of such prior conclusions. Hence it is clear that, as maintained by Urwick, Stage I was the key study, with Stages II and III adding more or less substantial support to it. The present chapter will therefore be limited to a consideration of the evidence produced in Stages I–III.

The preferred incentive system and output

Stage I: Relay Assembly Test Room (new incentive and new supervision)

In Stage I five girls who were employed assembling telephone relays were transferred from the factory floor to a special test room. Here their output of relays was recorded for over two years during which a large number of alterations were made in their working conditions. These alterations included a much less variable assembly task (Roethlisberger and Dickson 1939:21, 26), shorter hours, rest pauses, freer and more friendly supervision, and a preferred incentive system (ibid.:22, 30, 73). These changes were introduced cumulatively and no control group was established. Nonetheless, it was originally expected that the study would yield information about the influence of one or another physical condition of work (ibid.:129; Pennock 1930:299).

At the end of two years the girls' output had increased by about 30 percent (Roethlisberger and Dickson 1939:160). By this time the investigators were confident that the physical changes in work conditions had been of little importance, and that the observed increase was due primarily to a change in 'mental attitude' of the employees resulting from changed methods of supervision (ibid.:189–90; Pennock 1930:297–309). This change in mental attitude was chiefly characterized by a more relaxed 'relationship of confidence and friendliness ... such ... that practically no supervision is required' (Pennock 1930:309).

However, the standard report of the study recognizes that any of several changes introduced concurrently could, hypothetically, have caused both the observed change in mental outlook and the associated increase in output. The authors of the report list the following as providing possible 'hypotheses to explain major changes' in work behaviour (Roethlisberger and Dickson 1939:86–9): (1) changes in the character and physical context of the work task; (2) reduction of fatigue and monotony consequent upon introduction of rest pauses and reduced hours of work;[2] (3) change in the payment system; and (4) changes in supervision, with consequent social changes in group relations.

The rest of this chapter will critically examine the evidence and arguments from which the investigators reached conclusions favourable to the last of these alternative hypotheses.

First hypothesis: changes in work task and physical context.

The investigators allow that 'the fact that most of the girls in the test room had to assemble fewer types of relays could not be entirely ignored. Operator 5's performance offered a convincing example. Of all the girls in the room she had had more different types of relays to assemble and of all the girls her output rate had shown the least improvement' (ibid.:87). Whitehead (1938a:65) reports that 'later [1930–31] her [Operator 5's] working conditions were in line with the rest of the group and her comparative standing in the group definitely improved'.

It was subsequently found, however, that statistical analysis of the relevant data (i.e. the varying output of five girls who were subjected to numerous cumulatively introduced experimental changes) did not show 'any conclusive evidence in favour of the first hypothesis'. On this ground the investigators 'concluded that the change from one type of relay to another familiar type did not sufficiently slow up output to explain the increased output of the relay test room assemblers as compared with the assemblers in the regular department' (Roethlisberger and Dickson 1939:89). This conclusion leads the investigators to dismiss from further consideration the possibility that changes in task and conditions played any part at all in the observed increase in output.[3]

Second hypothesis: reduced fatigue due to rest pauses and shorter hours.

The investigators recognize that 'the rest pauses and shorter hours [may have] provided a relief from cumulative fatigue', resulting in higher output. They acknowledge that the fact that the rate of output of all but the slowest worker declined once the girls were returned to standard hours was 'rather convincing evidence in favour of this argument' (ibid.:87). Yet the investigators eventually dismiss these factors on the grounds that under the new conditions of work neither work curves nor medical examinations provided evidence that fatigue effects were present. Viteles (1932:476) has commented bluntly in this connection: 'It is interesting to note that [these grounds] are exactly the same used by other investigators in illustrating the effectiveness of rest pauses by reason of reduced fatigue'.

Using these arguments, the investigators eliminated the first two of the four hypotheses originally proposed as alternative explanations of the 30 percent increase in output observed in Stage I. This left two contending 'explanations': (1) the new incentive system and (2) the new kind of supervision and related social factors. The problem of choosing between these explanations led directly to the next two major experiments.

Stage II: Second Relay Assembly Group (new incentive system only)

> The aim of [this experiment] was to reproduce the test-room situation [i.e. Stage I] only in respect to the one factor of method of payment, using another group of operators. Since method of payment was to be the only alteration from the usual situation, it was thought that any marked changes in output could be reasonably related to this factor. (Roethlisberger and Dickson 1939:129)

Five girls who were employed on the same sort of task as the girls in Stage I under normal work conditions on the factory floor were given the preferred incentive system which had been used throughout Stage I. Under this system, the earnings of each girl were based on the average output of the five. Under the regular payment system, the earnings of each girl were based on the average output of the whole department (i.e. about 100 girls).

Almost at once the Stage II girls' output increased by 12.6 percent (ibid.:131–2; Pennock 1930:307). But the experiment caused so much discontent among the rest of the girls in the department, who wanted the same payment conditions (Roethlisberger and Dickson 1939:133), that it was discontinued after only nine weeks. The output of the five girls promptly dropped by 16 percent.[4]

As Viteles (1954:187) comments, 'the increase in output during the period when the wage incentive was in effect, followed by a production decrease with the elimination of the wage incentive, represents evidence ordinarily interpreted as indicative of the direct and favourable influence of financial incentives upon output'. But the investigators reject this interpretation and, without producing supporting evidence of any substance, firmly conclude (Roethlisberger and Dickson 1939:133–4, 158, 577) that the increase was due to inter-group rivalry resulting from the setting up of this second small group.

The change in payment system alone (in Stage II) produced as much increase in output in nine weeks (possibly five weeks: Pennock 1930:307) as was produced in about nine months by change in pay-

ment system together with a change to genial supervision (Stage I).
Yet this comparison appears not to have made any impression on the
investigators' confidence about the superior importance of social factors (Roethlisberger and Dickson 1939:160, 577).

Stage III: Mica Splitting Test Room (new supervision but no change in payment system)

In Stage I numerous changes had been introduced, resulting in a 30
percent increase in output. In Stage II only one of these changes (the
preferred incentive system) was introduced and a rapid 12 percent
increase in output resulted. In Stage III 'the test-room situation was
to be duplicated in all respects except for the change in pay incentive. If ... output showed a trend similar to that noted in [Stage I],
it would suggest that the wage incentive was not the dominant factor in the situation' (ibid.:129). Stage III, then, sought to test the
combined effect on output of (1) change to a separate room, (2)
change in hours, and (3) the introduction of rest pauses and friendly
supervision. Again a selected group of five girls was closely studied
and an increase in output was recorded — 15.6 percent in fourteen
months (ibid.:148) or, if one follows Pennock (1930:307), 20 percent in twelve months.

A comparison between Stage III and Stage I had little prospect
of scientific usefulness since in Stage III the incentive system was
different from both the disliked system used at the beginning of
Stage I and the preferred system introduced shortly afterwards, the
type of work was quite different from Stage I, and the experimental
changes were quite different (Roethlisberger and Dickson 1939:156,
159). It is this comparison, however, which has been taken by
reporters of the studies (ibid.:146–9, 159–60; Pennock 1930:307)
and by textbook authors[6] to provide the principal experimental evidence of the relative unimportance of financial and social motives for
influences on output. Assuming with Roethlisberger and Dickson
that Stage I and Stage III have some minimum comparability, it is
important to examine precisely how the investigators dealt with the
evidence from these stages for the purpose of arriving at some kind
of comparison.

Comparison between results in Stages I, II, and III

Stage III produced the claimed 15 percent increase in rate of output
over fourteen months. Thereafter the group's average rate of output
declined for twelve months before the study was terminated due to

the Depression and lay-offs. The investigators attribute this decline entirely to anxieties induced by the Depression,[7] ignoring the possibility that the preceding increase might also have been influenced by changing general economic and employment conditions. They do this despite evidence that output among a group of 5500 Hawthorne workers rose by 7 percent in the two years preceding the experiment (Whitehead 1938b:35).

In Stage III the output rate for each girl shows continuous and marked fluctuations over the whole two years of the study (Roethlisberger and Dickson 1939:147). To obtain the percentage increase to be attributed to each girl the investigators chose, for each girl, a 'peak' output period within the study period and measured her increase as the difference between this peak and her output rate at the outset of the study (ibid.:148). These peaks occur at different dates for different girls. To secure the 15 percent increase that is claimed, the study is, in effect, terminated at different conveniently selected dates for different girls. There is no one period over which the group achieved the 15 percent average increase claimed (ibid.:146–8, 159–60).

In Stage I two measures of the workers' performance are used: total output per week (ibid.:78), and hourly rate of output by weeks (ibid.:76). It is not clear from Roethlisberger and Dickson's report of Stage I whether the increase is in total output or rate of output. It is described only as 'increase in output', and 'output rose ... roughly 30%' (ibid.:160), which would ordinarily be taken to mean an increase in total output. But the investigators make it clear in passing (ibid.:55, 77) that throughout the studies they used rate of output per hour as 'the most common arrangement of output data' by which to 'portray the general trend in efficiency of each operator and of the group'. Whitehead (1938a:34), who produced a two-volume statistical study of Stage I as companion volumes to Roethlisberger and Dickson's standard report, is very clear on this point: 'All output will be expressed in the form of a rate ... as so many relays per hour'.

However, Whitehead (1938b:Chart B4) employs throughout his study the description 'weekly rate of output' when he means rate of output per hour by weeks. This practice, coupled with his habit of not labelling the ordinates of his charts dealing with changes in output, and added to by Roethlisberger and Dickson's use of phrases such as 'increase in output' to mean both increase in rate of output per hour and increase in total output, has led to widespread misinterpretation of the Hawthorne results, and textbook accounts which are seriously in error.[8]

Several points are of present importance. For Stage I, it is not clear whether the 30 percent increase in output claimed refers to rate of output or total output. It does not matter which measure is used to calculate percent increase in output in Stage I since the total hours worked per week at the end of the study period is only 4.7 percent less than at the beginning (Roethlisberger and Dickson 1939:76–7). Thus an increase of the order of 30 percent would result from either method of calculation. In Stage III, however, it makes a great deal of difference which method is used, and hourly rate of output is the only measure used. Thus the 15 percent 'increase in output' (ibid.: 159–60) claimed for Stage III is an increase in rate of output per hour worked, not in total output. Indeed, it is only by this measure that any increase at all in output can be shown.

If total output per week is used to measure performance in Stage III, the 15 percent increase claimed for Stage III reduces to less than zero because although output per hour increased by 15 percent, the weekly hours decreased by 17 percent, from 55.5 to 46.5 (ibid.:136–9).

The evidence in relation to the conclusions

By subtracting the 15 percent increase in Stage III (which is an increase in rate of output) from the 30 percent increase in output in Stage I (which is all, or nearly all, an increase in total output), the investigators conclude that 15 percent remains as 'the maximum amount [of increase in output] to be attributed to the change in wage incentive' introduced in Stage I. The investigators acknowledge the wholly speculative nature of this calculation, yet go on to assert in a summary of events to date that the conclusion 'seemed to be warranted from the test room studies so far ... that it was impossible to consider [a wage incentive system] as a thing in itself having an independent effect on the individual' (ibid.:160).[9]

It is important to appreciate just how invalid these assumptions are. In Stage I friendly supervision and a change to a preferred incentive system led to an increase in total output of about 30 percent. In Stage III friendly supervision without a change in payment system led to no increase in total output, but to a less than compensating increase in output per hour over a period during which working hours were reduced from 55.5 to 46.5. This could be interpreted to mean that when working hours exceed about 48 per week such extra working time may bring little or no increase in total output — a finding which had been well established many years before (Vernon 1921).[10] This interpretation would have left the way clear to attribute the 30 percent increase in Stage I entirely to the preferred incentive system. Instead, by the rather special method of analysis and argument that has been outlined, the investigators reached the conclusion that the effect of a wage incentive system is so greatly influenced by social considerations that it is impossible to consider it capable of independent effect.

A similar situation holds with regard to Stage II. As Stage II was planned, the 'method of payment was to be the only alteration from the usual situation', with the express intention that 'any marked changes in output' could then be 'related to this factor' (Roethlisberger and Dickson 1939:129). There was a marked change in output — an immediate 12 percent increase. There was an immediate change in behaviour — the other girls in the department demanded the same conditions. This would seem to require a conclusion in favour of the importance of a preferred incentive system, but no such conclusion was reached.

As a first step in the interpretation of the Stage II results, Roethlisberger and Dickson noticed, *post hoc*, that somewhere in the 'daily history record' of the Stage I group was a reference to a comment by one member of that group that a 'lively interest' was being taken in their output by members of the new Stage II group (ibid.:134). At this point the investigators simply note this and hint at significance to come. Twenty-four pages later we are told that

> although output had risen an average of 12% in [Stage II] it was quite apparent that factors other than the change in wage incentive contributed to that increase ... There was some evidence to indicate that the operators in [Stage II] had seized upon this test as an opportunity to prove to everyone that they could do as well as the [Stage I] operators. They were out to equal the latter's record. In view of this, even the most liberal estimate would put the increase in output due to the change in payment alone at somewhat less than 12%.

Since no additional evidence had been produced, this judgement lacks any serious foundation.

Much later (ibid.:577) the matter is returned to and, with no additional evidence, we are given to understand that the increase in output in Stage II was due to certain 'social consequences' of the 'basic social situation'. This situation is simply asserted to have been one in which 'rivalry [with the Stage I group] was brought to a focus' by setting up the Stage II group, whose 'output rose rapidly' in consequence.

Stage II was 'designed to test the effect of a [change in] wage incentive' on output (ibid.:576). The preferred incentive system was introduced and output immediately rose 12 percent. It was withdrawn and output immediately dropped 17 percent. Not encouraging results for anyone who believed that wage incentives were relatively unimportant and incapable of 'independent effects'. Yet these awkward results were not only explained away but converted to positive support for just such conclusions, all on the basis of a single hearsay comment by one girl.

The investigators carried the day for the hypothesis that 'social factors were the major circumstances limiting output'. They conclude that 'none of the results [in Stages I, II and III] gave the slightest substantiation to the theory that the worker is primarily motivated by economic interest. The evidence indicated that the efficacy of a wage incentive is so dependent on its relation to other factors that it is impossible to separate it out as a thing in itself having an independent effect' (ibid.:575–6). This conclusion is a striking contrast to the results obtained in Stages I, II and III as these bear on incentive systems: (1) when a preferred wage incentive system was introduced, total weekly output per worker rose (Stages I and II); (2) when the preferred incentive system was withdrawn, output promptly dropped (Stage II); (3) when changes in supervision, hours, etc., were introduced but with no change in incentive system, no increase in weekly output per worker resulted (Stage III).

Viteles (1954:190), an unusually perceptive critic of the Hawthorne studies, has commented caustically on Stage III: 'This increase in output, representing an average rise of 15% in the first 14 months of the experiment, would ordinarily be accepted as evidence that the introduction of rest pauses and the shortening of the work day can in themselves result in increased output, even in the absence of changes in the way of enhancing the wage incentive'. Yet Viteles misses the important point that there was no overall increase in total weekly output in Stage III — only a less than compensating increase in output per hour when shorter hours were worked. It is clear that he supposes the 15 percent increase to be an increase in total output (ibid.:5). Viteles's patience is great, and his criticism of the Hawthorne studies restrained. But they eventually draw from him a testy general protest about 'the more "subtle" — certainly more subjective — form of analysis and interpretation which has generally characterised interpretation of the Hawthorn data by the Harvard group' (ibid.:256).

It remains to consider more closely the complementary

Hawthorne claim that it was friendly supervision and social factors which were the principal influences leading to the large rise in output in Stage I.

A closer look at friendly supervision in action

The whole of the Hawthorne claim that friendly supervision, work-group social relations and satisfactions are overwhelmingly important for work behaviour rests on whatever evidence can be extracted from Stage I, since that is the only study in the whole series which exhibits even a surface association between the introduction of such factors and increased output.

Stage I began with five girls specially selected[11] for being both 'thoroughly experienced' and 'willing and cooperative' (Roethlisberger 1939:21), so there was reason to expect this group to be more than ordinarily co-operative and competent. Yet from very early in the study 'the amount of talking indulged in by all the operators' had constituted a 'problem', because it 'involved a lack of attention to work and a preference for conversing together for considerable periods of time' (ibid.:53). The first indication in the report that this might be a serious matter occurs on 2 August 1927, twelve weeks after the girls' installation in the test room, when four of the five operators were brought before the foreman[12] and reprimanded for talking too much (ibid.:38). Until November, however, 'no attempt had been made to do away with this privilege, although several attempts had been made by the foreman to diminish what seemed to him an excessive amount of talking'. But Operators 1A and 2A in particular continued to fail to display 'that "whole-hearted cooperation" desired by the investigators'. 'Any effort to reprimand them would bring the reply "We thought you wanted us to work as we feel"' (ibid.:53), since that was what the supervisors had told them at the beginning of the study (ibid.:21; Whitehead 1938a:26).

By 17 November 1927 the situation had not improved and disciplinary rules were resorted to. All of the operators were required to call out whenever they made mistakes in assembly, and they were prevented from talking. By December 'the lack of cooperation on the part of some of the operators was seriously alarming a few of the executives concerned'. Supervisors were asked to give the girls a 'hint' by telling them that they were not doing as well as expected of them and that if they didn't improve they would lose their free lunches (Whitehead 1938a:16).

From then on the girls, but especially 1A and 2A, were 'threatened with disciplinary action' and subjected to 'continual reprimands'. 'Almost daily' 2A was 'reproved' for her 'low output and behaviour' (sic) (ibid.:116–18). The investigators decided 1A and 2A did not have 'the "right" mental attitude'. 2A was called up before the test room authorities 'and told of her offences of being moody and inattentive and not cooperative'. She was called up also before the superintendent (Roethlisberger and Dickson 1939:55). [13] Throughout this period output for all five girls remained static or falling (ibid.:78).

After eleven weeks of serious but ineffective disciplinary measures and eight months after the beginning of the study, 1A and 2A were dismissed from the test room for 'gross insubordination' and declining or static output (ibid.:53–7). As Whitehead puts it (1938a:118), they 'were removed for a lack of cooperation, which would have otherwise necessitated greatly increased disciplinary measures'. [14]

1A and 2A were replaced by two girls chosen by the foreman 'who were experienced relay assemblers and desirous of participating in the test' (Roethlisberger and Dickson 1939:60). These two girls (designated Operators 1 and 2) were transferred to the test room on 25 January 1928 (ibid.:55, 56, 60). They both immediately produced an output much greater (in total and in rate per hour) than that achieved by any of the original five girls on their transfer to the test room and much above the performance at any time of the two girls they replaced (ibid.:76 Fig.6, 78 Fig.7). [15]

Operators 1 and 2 had been friends in the main shop. Operator 2 was the only Italian in the group; she was young (twenty-one) and her mother died shortly after she joined the test room (ibid.:61–2). After that 'Operator 2 earned the larger part of the family income'. 'From now on the history of the test room revolves around the personality of Operator 2' (Whitehead 1938a:120). Operator 2 rapidly (i.e. without any delay during which she might have been affected by the new supervision) adopted and maintained a strong and effective disciplinary role with respect to the rest of the group (ibid.:120–9; Roethlisberger and Dickson 1939:63, 74, 86, 156, 167), and led the way in an increased output in every period from her arrival till the end of the study. In this she was closely followed by the other new girl, Operator 1 (Roethlisberger and Dickson 1939:162).

At the time that Operators 1 and 2 were brought into the test room, daily hours of work were shortened by half an hour, but it was decided to pay the operators the day rate for the half hour of working time lost. A little later, the working day was reduced by a further half-hour, and again the girls were paid for the time (one hour per day) they didn't work (Whitehead 1938a:121–2).[16] Later still, the girls were given Saturday mornings off and again they were paid for the time not worked.[17]

Summing up the experience in the test room to the time when the two operators were dismissed,[18] the investigators claim that 'it is clear' that over this period there was

> a gradual change in social interrelations among the operators themselves, which displayed itself in the form of new group loyalties and solidarities ... [and] ... a change in the relations between the operators and their supervisors. The test room authorities had taken steps to obtain the girls' cooperation and loyalty and to relieve them of anxieties and apprehensions. From this ... arose ... a change in human relations which came to be of great significance in the next stage of the experiment, when it became necessary to seek a new hypothesis to explain certain unexpected results of the inquiry. (Roethlisberger and Dickson 1939:58–9)

In view of the evidence reviewed here this would seem to be a somewhat sanguine assessment of developments in the test room up to this point. It is, therefore, necessary to examine more systematically the way in which the behaviour of the supervisors on the one hand and of the operators on the other (including their changing output) varied during the period under consideration.

It is already clear that whatever part satisfying social relations at work — resulting from free and friendly supervision — may have played in producing the increase in output, there were other influences likely to have been important, for example a period of fairly stern discipline, the dismissal of two workers, and their replacement by people of rather special personality and motivation. In order to assess these various influences on output it is necessary to consider how work performance varied during the periods when these changes were introduced. This is difficult because none of the reports of the Hawthorne studies provides actual figures covering the way in which output changed throughout Stage I. Consequently one must work with such estimates as can be derived from the various graphs and charts of output-change that are supplied, and supplemented by occasional statements in the texts which give additional quantitative information.

Variations in supervision and output

For present purposes, Stage I may be divided into three phases: Phase I: the first three and a half months in the test room during which supervision seems to have been fairly consistently friendly, casual and at low pressure. Phase II: a further interval of about seven months during which supervision became increasingly stern and close. This phase culminates in the dismissal of two of the five operators and their replacement by workers of rather special character and motivation. Phase III: a final long period during which output rose rapidly and there was a return to free and friendly supervision.

Supervision during Phase I

'Besides the girls who composed the group under study there was a person in the experimental room who was immediately in charge of the test.' This was the test room observer whose twofold function was 'to keep accurate records ... and to create and maintain a friendly atmosphere in the test room'. He 'assume[d] responsibility for most of the day to day supervision', while in other matters such as accounting, rate revision and promotion, responsibility rested with the foreman (ibid.:22, 37).

It is quite clear from Roethlisberger and Dickson's account that during Phase I the supervisors did everything in their power to promote a free, co-operative and non-coercive relationship (ibid.:32–9). At the outset of the study the girls 'were asked to work along at a comfortable pace' and were assured 'that no attempt would be made to force up production'. They were led to expect changes in working conditions which might be 'beneficial and desirable from the employees' point of view', and were told that there was no reason why 'any [such] change resulting in greater satisfaction of employees' should not be maintained, and this 'regardless of any change in production rate' (ibid.:33). 'The test room observer was chiefly concerned with creating a friendly relation with the operators which would ensure their cooperation. He was anxious to dispel any apprehensions they might have about the test and, in order to do this, he began to converse informally with them each day' (ibid.:37). Some weeks after the study began, there was a friendly talk with the doctor about the physical examinations, and ice cream was provided and a party planned. The girls were also 'invited to the office of the superintendent who had talked to them, and in various other ways they had been made the object of considerable attention' (ibid.:34, 39). Although there had been almost from the beginning a good deal of talking among the girls, a fairly permissive attitude had been taken about this (ibid.:53).

Output during Phase I

There was 'no appreciable change in output' on transfer to the test room (Pennock 1930:301, 304), but there was a 'downward tendency' during the first five weeks thereafter (Roethlisberger and Dickson 1939:58), despite facilities which 'made the work slightly easier' (ibid.:33–4, 39).

At the end of five weeks, the new wage incentive system was introduced and output increased (ibid.:58). From the output chart (ibid.:56) this increase may be estimated at 4 or 5 percent. But this increase must be accepted with some caution, for the investigators report that the 'change in method of payment necessitated a change in piece-rates' (ibid.:34). It was apparently judged that under the new conditions of work (which did not include all of the types of relay assembled on the shop floor, and where there was one layout operator to five assemblers instead of one to six or seven as on the shop floor) new rates were necessary. We are told that 'the chief consideration in setting the new piece-rates was to determine a rate for each relay type which would pay the operators the same amount of money they had received in the regular department for an equivalent amount of work' (ibid.:35). But it is well established that the unreliability of time-study ratings can be expected to yield errors of at least 5 percent between different ratings of similar tasks (Viteles 1954:30, 38). So no great reliance can be placed on the observed 4 or 5 percent increase in output following the introduction of the new incentive system and the associated new piece-rates. Indeed, there is perhaps some recognition of this in Roethlisberger and Dickson's introductory comment (1939:29) that early in the study 'a change in wage payment was introduced, a necessary step before the experiment proper could begin'. Phase I ends after fifteen weeks of friendly supervision, with a somewhat doubtful increase of 5 percent which occurred with the introduction of a preferred incentive system.

Supervision during Phase II

'The second phase ... covering an interval of approximately seven months was concerned with the effects of various kinds of rest pauses' (ibid.:40).[19] The investigators emphasize that by the beginning of this phase not only was supervision friendly, but the relation between workers and supervisors was 'free and easy' (ibid.). Their account of actual supervisory behaviour during succeeding months supports these claims. (1) On each of the four occasions when rest pauses were varied, the girls were consulted in advance, and on all but one occasion their expressed preferences were accepted. (2) The investigators decided to pay the girls their bonuses monthly instead of weekly, but when the girls were told about this decision they objected and the plan was dropped. That the girls 'felt free to express their attitudes' and that the investigators altered their plans out of regard for these attitudes is said to be 'typical of the supervisory technique employed', which 'proved to be a factor of utmost importance in interpreting the results of the study'. (3) Later the girls were given free lunches and were consulted about what should be served (ibid.:48–9, 51).

However, the problem of excessive talking among the girls worsened. No attempt had been made to prohibit talking, although four of the girls had been 'given a talk regarding their behaviour' (ibid.:38). Now this 'lack of attention to work and preference for conversing together for considerable periods' was judged to be reaching such proportions that the 'experiment was being jeopardised and something had to be done' (ibid.:53–4). A variety of disciplinary procedures of increasing severity were applied, but with little effect. Finally, the leaders in talking (operators 1A and 2A) were dismissed from the test room 'for lack of cooperation which would have otherwise necessitated greatly increased disciplinary measures'.

Output during Phase II

There was no change in weekly output during this six-month period. 'Total weekly output does not decline when rest pauses are introduced, but remains practically the same during all the rest period experiments' (ibid.:79).

Supervision during Phase III

At the beginning of Phase III[20] the two dismissed girls were replaced by two girls chosen by the foreman. Something has already been said about the way in which these girls at once took and maintained the lead in output and about how one of them, who had a special need for more money, took over the general leadership and discipline of the rest of the group. These points will bear underlining by direct quotation:

'When Operator 2 joined the group, her home was largely dependent upon her earnings, and within a few weeks her father lost his job and became temporarily unemployed. Thus, to her natural sense of responsibility was added the factor of poverty; and Operator 2 began to urge the remainder of the group to increase their output' (Whitehead 1938a:122–3).

'Operators 1 and 2 were very definitely the fastest workers of the group in 1928, and this was freely recognised by the others' (ibid.:126).

'On the whole, from January to November 1928, the Relay Test

Group showed no very marked developments apart from a growing tendency for the discipline to pass from the hands of the supervisor to those of the group itself, largely as represented in the person of Operator 2' (ibid.:124).

'Operator 2 became recognised as the leader of the group, both by the operators themselves and by the supervisor. It is doubtful whether any operator could have secured this position unless she had been the fastest worker, but the other qualifications possessed by Operator 2 were a high sense of the importance of the work for the group and a forceful personality' (ibid.:129).

'Op. 2. "Oh! what's the matter with those other girls. I'll kill them"' (ibid.:127). (This expostulation was provoked by the output curves showing operators 3, 4 and 5 on a downward trend.)

From this period on supervision again became increasingly friendly and relaxed. This friendliness of supervision often had a very tangible character. From the arrival of the new workers in the test room, the observer 'granted them [all] more and more privileges'. The preferred incentive system, the rest pauses, the free lunches, and the 'parties' following the regular physical examinations all continued (Roethlisberger and Dickson 1939:71, 72, 77). In addition, within the next eight months the girls were first paid for half an hour per day not worked, and then for an hour a day not worked, and finally for Saturday mornings not worked. Approximately eight months after the arrival of the new girls, all these privileges except the preferred incentive system and the parties were withdrawn. The girls were warned in advance about this withdrawal of privileges and were assured that the new and heartily disliked conditions 'would terminate after approximately three months'.

Despite this promise, the girls' work deteriorated immediately: they wasted time in various ways such as reading newspapers, eating candy and going for drinks, and the observer shortly 'discovered that the girls were attempting to keep the output rate low ... so as to make sure that rest pauses would be reinstated'. The observer 'again tried to stop the excessive talking' by 'reprimand and threat'. He told the girls that 'unless excessive talking ceased it might become necessary to continue the experiment without rest pauses for a longer period' (ibid.:70–2).

At this point the girls had been in the test room eighteen months and had achieved nearly all the eventual 30 percent increase in output. Yet it would seem that Operator 2, the incentive system and the other privileges, as well as 'reprimand and threat', played a significant part in determining the work behaviour and output of the group. It is also clear from Roethlisberger and Dickson's account that a great part of the time, following the arrival of Operators 1 and 2, was relaxed and friendly and relations continued to be satisfactory. But there would seem to be good grounds for supposing that supervision became more friendly and relaxed because output increased, rather than vice versa.

Output during Phase III

Output for the whole group rose markedly during the several months after the dismissal of 1A and 2A, owing chiefly to the contributions from the new operators (ibid.:78, Fig.7). Thereafter the group's total output rose more slowly for a further year (with a temporary drop when the Saturday morning shift was discontinued for a time).

Summary of evidence about supervision and output

1   Apart from a doubtful 4–5 percent increase following the introduction of a preferred incentive system, there was no increase in weekly output during the first nine months in the test room, despite a great deal of preoccupation on the part of the supervisors with friendliness towards the workers, with consultation, and the provision of a variety of privileges not enjoyed on the factory floor.

2   From the beginning of what Roethlisberger and Dickson describe as the 'experiment proper', that is, after the period in which the new incentive system was introduced, there was no increase in weekly output during the next six months. When it became apparent that free and friendly supervision was not getting results, discipline was tightened, culminating in the dismissal of two of the five girls.

3   The dismissed girls were replaced by two girls of a special motivation and character who immediately led the rest in a sustained acceleration of output. One of these girls, who had a special need for extra money, rapidly adopted and maintained a strong disciplinary role towards the rest of the group. The two new girls led the way in increased output from their arrival till the end of the study.

4   Total output per week showed a significant and sustained increase only after the two girls who had the lowest output (ibid.:162)

were dismissed and replaced by selected output leaders who account for the greater part of the group's increase, both in output rate and in total output, over the next seventeen months of the study.

5   After the arrival of the new girls and the associated increase in output, official supervision became friendly and relaxed once more. The investigators, however, provide no evidence that output increased because supervision became more friendly rather than vice versa. In any case, friendly supervision took a very tangible turn by paying the girls for time not worked and so the piece-rate was in effect increased.

Discussion and conclusions

The examination undertaken here by no means exhausts the gross error and the incompetence in the understanding and use of the scientific method which permeate the Hawthorne studies from beginning to end. Three further studies were conducted: the Bank Wiring Observation Room Study; the Interviewing Program; and the Counselling Program. These studies cannot be discussed here, but I believe them to be nearly as worthless scientifically as the studies which have been discussed.[21] This should not be surprising, for they arose out of 'evidence' found and conclusions reached in the earlier studies and were guided by and interpreted in the light of the strongest preconceptions based on the conclusions of those earlier studies.

There are major deficiencies in Stages I, II and III which have hardly been touched on: (1) There was no attempt to establish sample groups representative of any larger population than the groups themselves. Therefore no generalization is legitimate. (2) There was no attempt to employ control data from the output records of the girls who were not put under special experimental conditions. (3) Even if both of these points had been met, the experiments would still have been of only minor scientific value since a group of five subjects is too small to yield statistically reliable results. Waiving all these points, it is clear that the objective evidence obtained from Stages I, II and III does not support any of the conclusions derived by the Hawthorne investigators.

The results of these studies, far from supporting the various components of the 'human relations approach', are surprisingly consistent with a rather old-world view about the value of monetary incentives, driving leadership, and discipline. It is only by massive

and relentless reinterpretation that the evidence is made to yie
contrary conclusions. To make these points is not to claim that t
Hawthorne studies can provide serious support for any such ol
world view. The limitations of the Hawthorne studies clearly re
der them incapable of yielding any serious support for any sort
generalization whatever.

If the assessment of the Hawthorne studies offered here is coger
it raises some questions of importance for university teachers, esp
cially for teachers concerned with courses on industrial organizati
and management. How is it that nearly all authors of textbooks wl
have drawn material from the Hawthorne studies have failed to re
ognize the vast discrepancy between evidence and conclusions
those studies? How have they frequently misdescribed the actu
observations and occurrences in a way that brings the evidence in
line with the conclusions? Exploration of these questions would pr
vide salutary insight into aspects of the sociology of social scientis

NOTES

Chapter 4 The McCarthy Crusade

1   In 1954 the American Legion attacked the Girl Scouts of America, demanding that they clean up their Handbook. They obliged with forty modifications, e.g. The 'One World' badge of the 1953 edition became the 'My World' badge; 'You are preparing yourself for world citizenship' became 'You are preparing yourself to be a friend to all'. In the chapter on international friendship, 'Start not by making friends among those you think you do not like' was terminated at 'friends'. 'Make up a quiz game on the UN' became ' ... on the World Association of Girl Guides and Girl Scouts' (*Reporter* 30 December 1954:2).

2   Rovere is one of America's most widely respected political commentators. He contributes a regular column, 'Washington Newsletter', to the *New Yorker* and is co-author with Arthur M. Schlesinger of *The General and the President*.

3   Whiting had been head of the Research Department of the State Department. He carried out this study under the auspices of the Rand Corporation. It was commissioned and paid for by the US Air Force.

Chapter 7 Exporting Persuasion

1   Much of the economic activity reported by the IPA in 1956 describes programs in operation several years earlier.

2   The Queensland Confederation of Industry established the World of Business Research Foundation in 1979 to receive corporate contributions (thereby made tax-deductible) towards the cost of commissioning the manuscript of the book. Its task accomplished, the foundation ceased to exist in 1981 ('Audio-Visual Economics Course ... ' 1979; Keavney 1981b; 'The Facts ... ', 1982).

3   A strong bid of this kind was in fact attempted at the AmCham conference by a representative of a major advertising agency. In a fashion inconceivable in the United States it was dismissed with mockery and derision in a related commentary by Max Walsh (1981:38–9), managing editor of the *Australian Financial Review*.

4   Mr Keavney (1982b:1) is, indeed, moved to hyperbole by the occasion. He observes that 'attacks on Enterprise Australia in the journals of teachers unions have spread like a bushfire in 1982', causing 'great damage'. He notes that bushfires may be started 'by nothing more than a discarded cigarette butt' and goes on to attribute a similarly culpable incendiary role to my article (i.e., Carey, 1980).

Chapter 10 The Industrial Preachers

1   The unquestioned ideological boundaries to Western sociological thought in this are often indicated with a surprising naivety. Thus Frank Heller (1971:41) discusses the 'important British structural school of industrial sociology and the work of the Tavistock Institute of Human Relations', which are distinguished for having escaped from the usual total preoccu-

pation with 'face to face or interpersonal relations' to an interest in 'the systems nature organisations and the analysis of some of their constituent parts'. One wonders how long will be before a majority of Western 'industrial sociologists' recognize that their variables a their theories ought to be able to accommodate industrial experiment and experience in W Germany and Yugoslavia (not to mention 800 million Chinese) as 'case examples' of son thing or other.

2   Bruce Yuill (1966) provides a 'selective bibliography' of almost 100 items. These divic American 76 percent, British 12 percent, Australian 6 percent. Other Australian books management and organization show a similar breakdown.

3   As examples of 'principles [from] research and practice in the field of propaganda [that] ha value as general guides in planning programs designed to influence employee attitude Morris Viteles (1953:431) mentions: 'Repetition, simplicity and emotional appeals ... whi touch ... attitudes deeply embedded . .. by past conditioning ... '

4   Employees were judged 'well-informed' (or 'educated') if they believed (or claimed to believ that (1) 'the consumer rather than the company sets the price'; (2) 'labour-saving machine makes jobs'; (3) 'stockholders and employees' interests are allied'; and (4) if they oppose price controls, limits on profits, limits on salaries, government ownership and strong unions (Viteles 1953:23–5).

5   'This finding contrasts with studies which have generally been accepted as demonstratir that, with few exceptions, promotional campaigns that present first one view and then t opposite — perhaps on the theory that the public should decide rationally between them – are not effective' (Young 1945:514).

6   Based on a survey and field work covering about fifty companies and relevant universities an conferences.

7   HOBSO was originally developed by Du Pont, then made generally available through th NAM and other sources. It is a current favourite and is enjoying wide use, although it to has its critics (Williams and Peterfreund 1954:38).

8   There was 'very vocal opposition raised by many international union officers', but this wa 'not reflected by the more cooperative position taken by most local union officers. There little evidence to show that the unions as a whole have viewed management's educationa efforts as a serious threat'. 'Only two or three companies out of fifty cited [have] active unio opposition' (ibid.:27, 28).

9   'When discussion programs involve taking employees away from their jobs on company tim for meetings, etc., the production output for the day generally is maintained. [All but one company ... reported higher output before or after the meetings to sustain total output, o said that where members of a group were out for the meetings in turn, the rest of the grouj picked up the slack' (ibid.:40).

10   Many political considerations were found to lead to 'educational activities' by management Among them the growing strength of unions, which was felt to threaten 'infringement c management perogatives'; high taxes; 'the many [public] references to high profits'; succes of the German unions in obtaining co-determination; the nationalization of industries i Britain (ibid.:21).

11   It should be noted that public attitudes (and changes in attitudes) on a wide range of ques tions of political/ideological importance to management had already been closely monitored through six-monthly national polls, for a long time. From at least the time of US entry int the war in 1941, and the consequent increased regulatory role of government in industry, the Psychological Corporation conducted six-monthly polls (based on samples of 5000) covering public attitudes, by economic class and union membership: to unions and their control by law; to government regulation of prices, profits etc.; to increase in the government payroll to the 'threat' of socialism and communism; and covering also comparative public confidence in union leaders, business leaders and associations of businessmen (NAM and Chamber of Commerce). See Link (1946) for detailed comments.

12   For example: 'A movie was made by a large organisation to acquaint its employees with the fact that the company stock was widely held. In a test being made of the effectiveness of the film (by interviewing employees on their reactions to it) one said: "I understand the point of the film. It shows all kinds of people from all walks or life can own our stock and do own our stock. I believe that all right. Anybody can be a capitalist. Even a young newspaper boy like in the movie can be one. Still I wouldn't want anybody to call me a capitalist"'. These studies

are reported in Williams and Peterfreund 1954.

13 After World War II there was 'an explosive and rapidly mushrooming interest in small groups'. The number of studies carried out with small groups between 1950 and 1960 exceeded by more than four times the total number of studies carried out prior to 1950 (Deutsch 1968:265). In 1950 'communication' as a subject was 'hardly mentioned in textbooks on management'; by 1960 it was 'among the most popular management subjects in America'; and there had been 'a great change in the amount and nature of communications research'. In 1960 small-group leadership 'was still the most popular topic for research in industrial social psychology' (Vroom and Maier 1961:461). By 1964 'the work on small groups ... continue[d] to be voluminous' and had been extended to management groups (Leavitt and Bass 1964:379). 'The chief questions' to which research on small groups 'sought answers' were: 'What determines whether a man changes his behaviour or opinion under the influence of others? In particular what determines whether or not he conforms to the norms of a group?' (Homans 1968:260).

14 '[The Hawthorne] investigations have not yet attracted (in Britain) especially among the ranks of sociologists and industrial managers the degree of interest that their quality demands. Yet ... there is no thought among the newest ideas on the social and personal character of the responsibilities of the executive that has not an echo or a reflection in the vast treasure-house of the work at Hawthorne.' 'What [the] contribution [of the group who took part in the Hawthorne studies] means many managers in industry do not yet realise. Those alive today may see the knowledge that they have unfolded accepted as a commonplace or everyday practice. Or it may be left to writers of a later century to relate how this group initiative was translated from a series of books and reports into principles and methods adopted by all responsible for executive control and supervision in industry. For whether general recognition comes sooner or later their work is securely founded on scientific method and will endure' (Urwick and Brech 1948:2, 6).

15 See also Caplow (1964:156): 'We do not have to look very hard at the polar terms authority and democracy against the background of modern theories of administration to notice a curious feature: democratic decision-making permissiveness with respect to rules, the displacement of authority by consultation and group participation in selling and enforcing norms are all conceived as devices for extending the organisation's control over the individual member. When they function successfully they decrease his ability to hold private purposes opposed to those of the organisation. The autonomy conferred on the individual in small matters reduces his opportunities to deviate from the main outline of the organisational program'. See also Golembiewski (1960:207–8).

16 Compare the comment: 'Management has at long last discovered that there is greater production and hence greater profit when workers are satisfied with their jobs. Improve the morale of a company and you improve production' (Parker and Kleemier 1951:10) and 'high morale is no longer considered as a prerequisite of high productivity. [Moreover] the nature of the relationship between morale and productivity is open to serious questioning. Is it direct? Is it inverse? Is it circular? Or is there any relationship at all between the two; are they independent variables?' (Scott 1962:93).

17 Herzberg attributes to himself the achievement of 'creating job enrichment' (Ludwig 1973:20). My own judgement accords with that of Hunt (1972:348) that 'the concept of job enrichment is not new ... Many of the early management writers saw the need for enriching jobs as did most of the writers of the Human Relations school. Where Herzberg differed slightly was in his analysis of the relationship between the individual and the organisational structure'.

18 The editor of *Management International* has stated that 'brushing aside pay as a motivator was one of the most revolutionary elements in Herzberg's theory' (Ludwig 1973:22). If that is the mark of a revolutionary social scientist then the human relations movement from Mayo to Lewin and Liken has been one continuous revolution.

19 For a devastating account of the authoritarian — even totalitarian — implications of Lewin's psychological theory see Kariel (1956); for an accurate and perceptive appraisal of the curious applications of the word 'democracy' in the industrial context in general and by Lewin in particular see Pateman (1970:69ff.).

20 Again, 'the story must not be about a sequence of events that revolved around high or low spirits caused by something unrelated to the job ... We did not include a sequence in which the ... origin of a person's attitude was his social life marriage ... ' (Herzberg et al.

1959:41). Thus stories of worry or pleasure about salary increase or about promotion whe[
that concern had its origin in non-work needs for increased money are excluded fro[
Herzberg's analysis.

21   Herzberg provides some 'typical' stories told by his subjects when 'probed' for an explar[
tion about why a salary increase or promotion had (or hadn't) been an occasion of high sati[
faction to them. An accountant had previously received only rises in pay as recognition of h[
worth. Then came a compliment from the boss. 'Biggest thing', he said, 'was the person[
satisfaction with the job done and then a pat on the back'. Again, an engineer was promoted
a new job along with an unexpected salary increase ... 'Probed' as to why this caused hi[
high satisfaction, 'he was pleased mainly because it indicated that his work was appreciate[
and his superiors had confidence in him ... After many years he still feels good because
that promotion'. 'Again', Herzberg concludes, 'as with responsibility we find in this story th[
secondary nature of increased income in increasing the engineer's job satisfaction' (Herzbei[
et al. 1959:61–2).

22   The audacity of Herzberg's (1959) interpretive shifts are breathtaking. Thus 30 percent [
his subjects' 'stories' about occasions of very high job satisfaction centred on salary or pr[
motion or both (see tables 6 and 7, pp. 72, 75). Moreover, (appreciative) references to sala[
or promotion occurred 80 times in 228 voluntarily given descriptions of occasions of hig[
satisfaction, while discontented references to either occurred only 69 times in 248 stori[
about occasions of low satisfaction (pp. 64, 72). Yet from this 'objective' data (as he calls [
Herzberg, chiefly by manipulating percentages having widely discrepant bases as thoug[
they were frequencies — and indeed describing them as frequencies — is able to tread [
completely invalid path to the conclusion that monetary rewards cannot provide satisfactio[
but can only cause or diminish dissatisfaction.

Chapter 11 The Hawthorne Studies: A Criticism

1   For a review of these charges and criticisms see Miller and Form (1951:74–83). For a defenc[
see Landsberger (1958:64). Landsberger's defence is restricted to the report of the Hawthorn[
studies by Roethlisberger and Dickson (1939). Even this report, in Landsberger's view, ha[
'done the field of human relations in industry an amount of harm which, in retrospec[
appears to be almost irreparable'.

2   The investigators list fatigue and monotony as separate hypotheses. For brevity, these hav[
been combined as one hypothesis. The same sort of critical objections are relevant to the argu[
ments and evidence advanced by the investigators with respect to both.

3   The scientifically illiterate procedure of dismissing non-preferred explanations on th[
grounds that (1) the experimenters had found no conclusive evidence in favour of them and/c
(2) there was no evidence that any one of these explanations, considered by itself, accountec
for all the effect observed, recurs throughout Roethlisberger and Dickson's report of th[
Hawthorne studies. This procedure is never applied to preferred hypotheses, which ar[
assumed to be well founded provided only that the evidence against them is less than con[
clusive. See, for example, Roethlisberger and Dickson 1939:96, 108, 127, 160.

4   According to Pennock (1930:307), the increase in output was 13.8 percent, the experimen[
was discontinued after five weeks, and output then fell by 19–24 percent.

5   That is, by the end of Experimental Period 7 in Roethlisberger and Dickson's output char[
(1939:78).

6   For example, 'we cannot avoid being impressed by the fact that a wage incentive alone (Stag[
II) increased production 12%, a change in the social situation raised output 15% (Stage III[
and a combination of the two gave an increase of 30%. This looks surprisingly like an addi[
tive effect, with the social rewards being somewhat more potent in influencing behaviou[
than the monetary reward' (Stagner 1956:131–2; see also Blum 1949:26).

7   Viteles (1954:191) comments on this period of declining output: 'Both "the investigators an[
the operators were of the opinion that the rates on the new piece parts were not high enoug[
in comparison with the old." Nevertheless scant consideration is given to the possibility tha[
... a reduced appeal to economic motives could readily account in large part for the very sever[
drop in output observed during this final phase of the Mica Splitting Room experiment'.

8   For example, Ghiselli and Brown 1948:435–7 and Brown 1954:71–2. These authors incor[

rectly report an almost continuous increase in total weekly output over the first nine months of Stage I. In fact there was no increase except in the period of eight weeks immediately following the introduction of the preferred incentive system. There was no improvement in weekly output in either the preceding period or the four experimental periods extending over six months which followed it.

9   Viteles (1954:193) bluntly rejects this inference as invalid, but textbook treatments of the Hawthorne studies generally accept it without demur.

10 Ghiselli and Brown (1948:242) have summarized Vernon's findings as follows: 'In a munitions plant, when the working week was reduced from 66 to 48.6 hours (a reduction of 26%) hourly output was increased by 68% and total output for the week by 15%. This instance could be multiplied many times'.

11 Note, however, that while the five girls were 'all chosen from among those with a considerable experience in the assembly of this kind of relay ... the actual method of selection was quite informal and somewhat obscure, it appears to have been determined by the girls themselves in conjunction with their shop foreman' (Whitehead 1938a:14).

12 Foremen were on a par with departmental chiefs and four ranks above operatives (Roethlisberger and Dickson 1939:11).

13 Superintendents controlled a branch of the works and were seven ranks above operators (Roethlisberger and Dickson 1939:11).

14 In Mayo's accounts it is first said that these two operators 'dropped out' (1946:56) and later that they 'retired' (ibid.:62). It is also interesting to compare the above account of events in the test room and those drawn from the standard reports with Mayo's picture of the test room. According to Mayo's account, success was achieved 'largely because the experimental room was in charge of an interested and sympathetic chief observer. He understood clearly from the first that any hint of the "supervisor" in his methods might be fatal to the interests of the inquiry ... He helped the group to feel that its duty was to set its own conditions of work, he helped the workers to find the "freedom" of which they so frequently speak ... At no time in the [whole period of the study] did the girls feel that they were working under pressure' (ibid.:68–9).

15 Compare output curves during the first seven Experimental Periods with output from the second week of Experimental Period 8.

16 Roethlisberger and Dickson (1939:60, 62) give no indication that the operators were paid for these hours not worked. Indeed, their account clearly implies that they were not so paid (ibid.:63–4). But Whitehead is quite explicit on this point.

17 Roethlisberger and Dickson (1939:68) do report that the girls were paid for the half-day on Saturdays which was not worked. They acknowledge that this 'added a new factor to the situation which cannot be disregarded and which has to be taken into account in comparing this period with any other' (ibid.:69). They take no further account of it, however, just as they take no further account of the unworked hours paid for on the occasions when the work day was shortened.

18 That is, up to the end of Experimental Period 7 in Roethlisberger and Dickson's terminology.

19 This phase actually extends from 8 August 1927 to 21 January 1928, a period of twenty-four weeks.

20 Actually on 25 January 1928, two days after the beginning of Phase III. Thus the resulting sharp rise in output does not show fully on Roethlisberger and Dickson's weekly output charts (1939:76, 78) until the second week of their Experimental Period 8.

21 For substantiation of this judgement with respect to the Bank Wiring Observation Room Study, see Sykes (1965:253–63).

BIBLIOGRAPHY

'About the IPA' (1968) *IPA Review*, April–June, pp. 33–40
'Action 1980' (1980) Enterprise Australia, Sydney (n.p., n.d., but 1980)
'Action 1981' (1981) Enterprise Australia, Sydney (n.p., n.d., but 1981)
'Action 1982' (1982) Enterprise Australia, Sydney (n.p., n.d., but 1982)
Albig, W. (1957) 'Two Decades of Public Opinion Study: 1936–1956', *Public Opinion Quarterly* 21 (3), pp. 15–22
Allen, G. (1976) 'The Capitalist Offensive', *The Age*, March 31
Allen, V. L. (1961) 'Management and the universities', *Listener*, July 13, pp. 51–2.
Alsop, R. (1978) 'Programs to teach Free Enterprise sprout on colleges campuses', *Wall Street Journal*, May 10, pp. 1, 37
AmCham (1977) 'Directors' Report', Annual Report, n.p.
—— (1981) *Corporate Risks in the Australian Political Environment: Responding to the Growing Pressures*, transcript of Proceedings from the 20th Annual General Meeting of the American Chamber of Commerce in Australia, March, Overmeyer Ltd, Sydney
'AmCham's Young Achievers with Success on their Hands' (1978) *Commerce*, May–June
American Economic Foundation (1976) *37th Annual Report*, AEF, New York
American Management Association (1946) 'Management appraises its job', Annual Report
American Psychological Association (1962) 'The Psychologist in Industry' in H. Karn and B. von Gilmer (eds) *Readings in Industrial and Business Psychology*, McGraw-Hill, New York pp. 1–16
Asch, S. (1952) *Social Psychology*, Prentice-Hall, New York
'Audio-visual Economics Course in Schools' (1979) *Enterprise News*, Enterprise Australia, Sydney June
Auerbach, J. S. (1966) *Labor and Liberty: the La Follette Committee and the New Deal*, Bobbs Merrill New York
Australian Chamber of Commerce (1973) 'National Chamber Intensifies Programme to Promote Free Enterprise', ACC 69th Annual Report, 1972–73
—— (1975) 'ACC Economic Education Campaign: 7th Report to Contributors' (n.p., n.d. but 1975)
—— (1978) 'The ACC Economic Education Campaign, Phase 2: Report to Contributors' (n.p., n.d., but 1978)
—— (1979) 'The ACC Economic Education Campaign: Phase 3' (n.p., n.d., but 1979)
Barbash, J. (1948) *Labor Unionism in Action*, Harper, New York
Baritz, Leon (1965) *The Servants of Power*, Wiley, New York
Barlowe, K. (1985) The Ideology of the Higher School Certificate Economics Syllabus, M.Ed. thesis, Macquarie University, Sydney
Batten, M. (1979) 'How Companies Help Young Folk Learn About Business', *Rydges*, June, pp. 85–6
Bauer, R. A. (1958) 'Our big advantage: the social sciences (development in the US and the Soviet Union compared)', *Harvard Business Review*, 36 (May), pp. 125–36
Baxter, J. D. et al. (1978) 'Is Government Having a Chilling Effect on Business's Right to Speak?', *Iron Age*, October 23, pp. 65–110
Beard, C., and M. Beard (1927) *The Rise of American Civilization*, vol. 2, Macmillan, New York
Bell, D. (1954) 'Industrial Conflict and Public Opinion', in A. Kornhauser, R. Dubin and A. Ross (eds) *Industrial Conflict*, McGraw Hill, New York, pp. 240–56
—— (1982) 'Enterprise Australia — Handle With Caution', *Education*, July 5

Benoit-Guilbot, O. (1968) 'The sociology of work', *International Encyclopedia of the Social Sciences*, vol. 7, pp. 230–40

Bernays, E. L. (1928) 'Manipulating public opinion: the why and the how', *American Journal of Sociology*, 33 (6), pp. 958–71

—— (1937) 'Recent Trends in Public Relations Activities', *Public Opinion Quarterly*, 1 (1), pp. 147–51

—— (1938) 'Public Opinion and Public Relations', *Market Research*, 18 (2)

—— (1947) 'The Engineering of Consent', *Annals of the American Academy of Political and Social Sciences*, 250 (March), p. 114

—— (1952) *Public Relations*, University of Oklahoma Press, Norman

Bigart, H. (1971) 'Calley Pleads for Understanding', *New York Times*, March 31, p. 1

Blanket, L. (1978) 'The Last Angry Adman', *Advertising News*, November 10

Blum, Morton (1949) *Industrial Psychology and Its Social Foundations*, Harper, New York

—— ed. (1973) *The Price of Vision: The Diary of Henry A. Wallace 1942–1946*, Houghton Misslin, Boston

Boorstin, D. (1961) *The Image: or What Happened to the American Dream*, Weidenfeld & Nicolson, London

Bordow, Alan (1971) 'The industrial psychologist: his education, employment history and job functions', *Australian Psychologist*, 6 (2), pp. 80–90

Boyce, R. O. (1972) *Management Education in Australia*, vol. 1, Australian Institute of Management, Melbourne

Brady, R. A. (1943) *Business as a System of Power*, Columbia University Press, New York

Brandeis, E. (1957) 'Organized Labor and Protective Labor Legislation', in M. Derber and E. Young (eds) *Labor and the New Deal*, University of Wisconsin Press, Madison

Brayfield, A., and W. Crockett (1955) 'Employee attitudes and employee performance', *Psychological Bulletin*, 52, pp. 396–424

Broadbent, D. (1981) 'Sheil wants colleges to teach more profitable subjects', *The Age,* September 4

Brown, James A. C. (1954) *The Social Psychology of Industry*, Penguin, Harmondsworth

Brown, W. B. (1960) *Explorations in Management,* Penguin, Harmondsworth

Bucklow, Maxine (1966) 'A new role for the work group', *Administrative Science Quarterly*, 11 (June), pp. 59–78

Burgess, P. (1984) *Economic Policy Research in Australia*, CEDA Information Paper No. IP13, Sydney

Burns, Tom, ed. (1969) *Industrial Man*, Penguin, Harmondsworth

Bursk, E. C. (1948) 'Selling the idea of Free Enterprise', *Harvard Business Review*, May, pp. 372–84

'Business is still in trouble', (1949) editorial, *Fortune*, 39 (5)

'Business' Most Powerful Lobby in Washington' (1976) *Business Week*, 20 December, pp. 60–3

Byrt, W. J. (1968) *The Idea of Management*, Sun Books, Melbourne

—— (1969) *Organising for Results,* Sun Books, Melbourne

—— (1971) *People and Organisations,* McGraw-Hill, Sydney

Caplow, T. (1964) *Principles of Organisation,* Harcourt Brace, New York

Carey, A. (1967) 'The Hawthorne Studies: A Radical Criticism', *American Sociological Review*, 32 (June), pp. 404–16

—— (1971) Industrial psychology: nonsense or non-science?, mimeograph, Department of Psychology, University of NSW

—— (1976a) 'Industrial Psychology and Sociology in Australia', in P. Boreham, A. Pemberton and P. Wilson (eds) *The Professions in Australia*, University of Queensland Press, Brisbane, pp. 220–55

—— (1976b) 'Reshaping the Truth: Pragmatists and Propagandists in America', *Meanjin Quarterly*, 35 (4), pp. 370–8

—— (1977) 'The Lysenko Syndrome in Western Social Science, *Australian Psychologist*, 12 (March), pp. 27–37

—— (1979a) 'The Norwegian Experiments in Democracy at Work', *Australian and New Zealand Journal of Sociology*, 15 (March), pp. 13–23

—— (1979b) Worker Motivation: Social Science, Propaganda and Democracy, unpublished paper, University of NSW

—— (1980) 'Social Science Propaganda and Democracy' in P. Boreham and G. Dow (eds) *Work and Inequality*, vol. 2, Macmillan, Melbourne, pp. 60–93

—— (1983) Business Propaganda and Democracy, unpublished paper, University of NSW

——— (1984) Report on A. Carey, 'Control Consensus or Chaos? Managers and Industr[ial] Relations Reform', manuscript submitted to Industrial Relations Research Cen[tre] University of NSW, 18 May

——— (1987a) 'Capitalist Corporations and the Management of Democracy', in E. Wheelwright and K. D. Buckley, *Communications and the Media in Australia*, Allen Unwin, Sydney

——— (1987b) 'Managing Public Opinion: The Corporate Offensive', in S. J. Frenkel (e[d]) *Union Strategy and Industrial Change*, NSW University Press, Sydney

Carr, B. (1978) 'Troubleshooter with a difference', *Bulletin*, August 15, p. 41

——— (1981) 'Big Business Launches New Lobby Group', *Bulletin*, February 10

Carr, E. H. (1963) 'The Russian Revolution and the Peasant', *Listener*, London, BBC, May 30

Carroll, A. (1981) 'Current Political Environment', in *Corporate Risks in the Australian Politi[cal] Environment*, American Chamber of Commerce in Australia, Sydney, March

Cartwright, D., and A. Zander (1968) *Group Dynamics Research and Theory*, Tavistock, London

Cate, C. (1978) 'Grovellers of the World Unite!', in Ivens (ed.) *International Papers on the Reviva[l] Freedom and Enterprise*, pp. 42–4

Cattell, J. McK. (1923) 'The Psychological Corporation', *Annals of the American Academy of Politi[cal] and Social Sciences*, 110 (November)

——— (1937) 'Retrospect Psychology as a Profession', *Journal of Consulting Psychology*, 1 (1)

Cellier, F. S. (1953) 'The Story of Sears in America: An Economic Education Programm[e]' American Management Association Personnel Series No. 152, pp. 29–40

Chamber of Commerce of the United States (1947) *Communists Within the Government*, Washingt[on]

——— (1952) *Annual Report*, Washington, April

Chapman, D. W. (1939) 'Industrial Conflict in Detroit', in Hartmann and Newcombe, *Industr[ial] Conflict*, pp. 43–102

China White Paper (1967) vol. 1, with an Introduction (unpaginated) by Lyman P. Van Sly[ke] Stanford University Press

Clemenger John (1975) *What Every Corporate Communicator Should Know About His Hostile Audien[ce]* Clemenger, Melbourne

——— (1980) *The Corporate Dilemma*, Clemenger, Melbourne

Cleveland, A. S. (1947) Some Political Aspects of Organized Industry, Harvard University Thes[is] Collection, Harvard College Library

Coch, L., and R. French (1948) 'Overcoming resistance to change', *Human Relations*, 1, pp. 512–

Commission of Inquiry, The Interchurch World Movement (1920) *Report on the Steel Strike of 191[9]* Harcourt Brace and Howe, New York

——— (1921) *Public Opinion and the Steel Strike*, Harcourt Brace, New York

Committee for Economic Development of Australia (1976) 'The First National Private Enterpri[se] Convention', CEDA Information Paper No. 5

——— (1984a) 'Economic Policy Research in Australia', CEDA Information Paper No. IP1

——— (1984b) Annual Report (n.p.)

——— (1985) Annual Report

Company Employee Reporting' (1977) *Newsletter*, Sydney: Enterprise Australia, May

Cooke, B. L. (1954) Economic Education in Industry, Ph.D. thesis, University of Minneapolis

Creel, G. (1920) *How We Advertised America*, Harper, New York

Crichton-Brown, R. (1977) 'Looking to the Future — The Institute's Role in the Corpora[te] Sphere', *Australian Director*, October–December, pp. 11–15

Crick, B. (1959) *The American Science of Politics*, Kegan Paul, London

Crittenden, A. (1978a) 'A New Corporate Activism in the US', *Australian Financial Review*, July 1[?]

——— (1978b) 'The Wind's Blowing Toward the Right for Now', *New York Times*, July 16

Crozier, B. (1978) 'A Western Response to Conflicts', in Ivens (ed.) *International Papers on t[he] Revival of Freedom and Enterprise*, pp. 59–60

Cummins, B. A. (1979) The Advertising Council's Campaign on Economic Education, text [of] address to business groups, April

Cyerl, Richard M., et al. (1970) *Report of the committee of inquiry into post-graduate education for man[?] agement*, Australian Government Printer, Canberra

Dahl, R. (1959) 'Business and Politics: A Critical Appraisal of Political Science', in R. Dahl et al. *Soci[al] Science Research on Business: Product and Potential*, Columbia University Press, New York

Davis, M. S. (1947) 'Public opinion — the court of last resort', *Labor and Nation*, January

February, pp. 24–7

Dawson, A. (1976) 'Economic Education in Australia' in *The First National Private Enterprise Convention*, Information Paper No. 5, CEDA Appendix, Sydney

Deutsch, M. (1968) 'Group Behavior', *International Encyclopedia of the Social Sciences*, vol. 6, pp. 265–75

Dewey, J. (1920) *Reconstruction in Philosophy*, Holt, New York

——— (1938) *Logic: The Theory of Inquiry*, Holt, New York

Dodd, P. A. (1946) 'Book Department', *Annals of the American Academy of Political and Social Sciences*, 208 (March)

'Does your job bore you, or does Professor Herzberg?' (1970) editorial, *Economist*, June 6, p. 66

Dreier, P. (1983) 'The Corporate Complaint Against the Media', *Quill*, November, pp. 17–29

Drucker, P. (1950) 'Have Employee Relations Policies Had the Desired Effects?' American Management Association, Personnel Series No. 134

Dudley, D. (1947) 'Molding public opinion through advertising', *Annals of the American Academy of Political and Social Sciences*, 250 (3), pp. 105–12

Dyson, V. (1978) 'Pilkington Advocates Advocacy Advertising', *Advertising News*, September 1, p. 8

'Economics for the People' (1955) *IPA Review*, January–March, pp. 11–17

Eden, A. (1960) *The Memoirs of Sir Anthony Eden: Full Circle*, Cassell, London

'Edward L. Bernays Intergroup Relations Award Meeting' (1949) *American Psychologist*, 4, p. 265

Ehrbar, A. F. (1978) 'The Backlash Against Business Advocacy', *Fortune*, August 28, pp. 62–8

Ellison, P. S. (1945) 'Is Your Advertising in Tune with Public Opinion?', *Printers' Ink*, November 16, pp. 25–32

Ellul, Jacques (1973) *Propaganda: The Formation of Men's Attitudes*, Vintage, New York (first published 1965)

'Enterprise Australia' (1975) Australian Free Enterprise Association Ltd, Sydney (n.p., n.d., but 1975)

'European War Unlikely, Mr. Menzies' Views' (1938) *SMH*, August 9

Fairhall, A. (1976). 'The Role of Free Enterprise in Present Day Australia', address to the Swiss-Australia Society, Sydney, June 23 (published by Enterprise Australia)

Fall, B. (1967) *The Two Vietnams*, Pall Mall, London

Faunce, W., ed. (1967) *Readings in Industrial Psychology*, Appleton-Century-Crofts, New York

Fein, M. (1976) 'Motivation for Work', in R. Dubin (ed.) *Handbook of Work, Organization and Society*, Rand McNally, Chicago, pp. 465–530

Ferguson, T., and J. Rogers (1979) 'The Knights of the Roundtable', *Nation*, December 15, pp. 620–5

Feulner, E. J. (1978) 'From Ideas to Political Reality — Working with Parliaments', in Ivens (ed.) *International Papers on the Revival of Freedom and Enterprise*, pp. 21–4

——— (1985) 'Ideas, Think-Tanks and Governments', *Quadrant*, November, pp. 22–6

Finnegan, W. (1984) Enterprise Australia: Its work and Influence in 'Economic Education', Appendix I, Interview with Personnel Operations Manager, IBM, unpublished paper, School of Psychology, University of NSW

Fisk, M., ed. (1974) *Encyclopedia of Associations: National Associations of the US*, vol. 1, Gale, Detroit

Fleming, D. F. (1966) 'The Costs and Consequences of the Cold War', *Annals of the American Academy of Political and Social Sciences*, 366, pp. 127–38

Forcey, C. (1961) *The Crossroads of Liberalism*, Oxford University Press, New York

Freeland, R. M. (1975) *The Truman Doctrine and the Origin of McCarthyism*, Knopf, New York

French, R., J. Israel and D. As (1960) 'An experiment in participation in a Norwegian factory', *Human Relations*, 13, pp. 3–19

Fullbright, F. W. (1954) *Reporter*, December 16, p. 10

Ghiselli, Edwin, and Clarence Brown (1948) *Personnel and Industrial Psychology*, McGraw Hill, New York

Gill, H. (1979) *Managers and Workers at the Cross-Roads—A critique*, Discussion Paper No. 2, Business Research Centre, North Brisbane College of Advanced Education

Ginsburg, B. (1954) 'Loyalty, Suspicion and the Tightening Chain', *Reporter*, July 6, pp. 10–14

Goldthorpe, J., et al. (1968) *The Affluent Worker: Industrial Attitudes and Behaviour*, Cambridge University Press, Cambridge

Golembiewski, R. T. (1960) 'O and M and the small group', *Public Administration Review*, 20 (Autumn), pp. 205–12

Gras, N. S. B. (1945), 'Shifts in Public Relations', *Bulletin of the Business Historical Society*, 19, pp.

97–148

Green, M., and A. Buchsbaum (1980) *The Corporate Lobbies: Political Profiles of the Business Roundtable and the Chamber of Commerce*, Public Citizen Gale Research Co., Washington

Gruber, K., ed. (1986) *Encyclopedia of Associations*, vol. 1, Gale Research Co., Detroit

Guzzardi, W. (1980) 'A New Public Face for Business', *Fortune*, June 30, pp. 48–52

Hale, William Harlan (1954) 'Big Brother in Foggy Bottom', *Reporter*, August 17

—— 'Let's Re-Re-Re-Reorganize the Foreign Service' (1954) *Reporter*, 11 (20 July), pp. 22–4

Harries, O. (1984) '12 Rules for Winning: A Primer for Polemicists', *Quadrant*, December, pp. 19–22

Harris, Herbert (1938) *American Labor*, Yale University Press, New Haven

Harris, R. (1978) 'The Conversion of the Intellectual', in Ivens (ed.) *International Papers on the Revival of Freedom and Enterprise*, pp. 10–12

Hartman, E. G. (1948) *The Movement to Americanize the Immigrant*, Columbia University Press, New York

Hartmann, G. W., and T. Newcombe, eds (1939) *Industrial Conflict*, New York, Cordon

Heller, Frank (1971) *Managerial Decisionmaking,* Van Gorcum, The Netherlands, in association with Tavistock, London

Henry, J. (1980) 'From Soap to Soapbox: The Corporate Merchandising of Ideas', *Working Papers for a New Society*, 7 (3), pp. 55–7

Herberg, W. (1951) 'When Social Scientists View Labor', *Commentary*, December, pp. 590–6

Herzberg, F. (1968) *Work and the Nature of Man,* Staples, London

Herzberg, F., et al. (1959) *The Motivation to Work*, Wiley, New York

Hines, G. (1973) *Cases in Organisational Behaviour,* Wiley, Sydney

Hollings, L. (1983) 'Current Affairs', *Australian Director*, August–September, pp. 20–8

Holsti, O. (1965) 'The Belief System and National Images; a Case Study', in D. Borrow (ed.) *Components of Defense Policy*, Princeton University Press, Princeton, pp. 378–89

Homans, G. C. (1968) 'The study of groups', *International Encyclopedia of the Social Sciences*, vol. 6, Macmillan, New York

Hook, E., and J. Harding, eds (1982) *The World of Business*, Jacaranda Wiley, Milton, Qld

Horowitz, D. (1967) *From Yalta to Vietnam*, Penguin, New York

Hughes, C. F. (1946) 'The merchants' point of view' *New York Times,* Business Section, November 9

'Human relations study is pressed' (1947) *New York Times*, Business Section, November 9

Hunt, John W. (1972) *The Restless Organisation,* Wiley, Sydney

'In the Name of All that is Sacred … We give you Enterprise Australia' (1982) *Queensland Teachers Journal*, April 22, p. 8

'Into the Eighties' (1980) Enterprise Australia, Sydney (n.p.)

'Is Anybody Listening?' (1950) *Fortune*, September, pp. 78–83

Ivens, M., ed. (1978) *International Papers on The Revival of Freedom and Enterprise*, Aims, London

Jacques, E. (1948) 'Field theory and industrial psychology', *Occupational Psychology*, 22 (April), pp. 126–33

James, W. (1907) *Pragmatism*, Longman Green, New York

Kariel, H. S. (1956) 'Democracy unlimited: Kurt Lewin's field theory', *American Journal of Sociology*, 63, pp. 280–9

Kasper, W. (1984) *Capital Xenophobia — Australian Controls of Foreign Investment*, CIS, Sydney

Keavney, J. T. (1977) 'Building for profit', Enterprise Australia, Sydney

—— (1978a) 'Advance Australia Fair', *Enterprise* (Washington), August, pp. 7–9

—— (1978b) 'Enterprise Australia: A Case Study in Mobilisation', in Ivens (ed.) *International Papers on the Revival of Freedom and Enterprise*, pp. 66–9

—— (1979) 'Reaching the Middle Ground', *Mining Review*, March, pp. 9–10

—— (1981a) 'Australia: Turning Away from Socialism', *Vital Speeches*, February 15, pp. 264–7

—— (1981b) 'Economic Literacy–Industry's Responsibility', Enterprise Australia, Sydney, July 14

—— (1982a) A Commentary by the Chief Executive of Enterprise Australia, September 2

—— (1982b) 'Your Organization Under Fire', *Special Bulletin*, Enterprise Australia, September (n.p.)

Kennan, G. (1958) *Soviet–American Relations, 1917–1920*, vol. 2, Princeton University Press, Princeton

Kerr, M. (1983) 'Economics in Primary Schools', *Economics* (Journal of the Economics and Commerce Teachers Association NSW), April, pp. 31–7

Key, V. O. (1958) *Politics, Parties and Pressure Groups*, Crowell, New York

Korman, A. K. (1971) *Industrial and Organisational Psychology*, Prentice-Hall, Eaglewood Cliffs, NJ

Kornhauser, A. W. (1934) 'Book Department', *Annals of the American Academy of Political and Social Sciences*, 172 (March), p. 171–

—— (1947) 'Industrial psychology as management technique and as social science', *American Psychologist*, 2 (7), pp. 224–9

Kristol, I. (1975) 'Business and the New Class', *Wall Street Journal*, May 19

Landsberger, Henry A. (1958) *Hawthorne Revisited*, Cornell University Press, Ithaca

Lane, E. (1950) 'Some Lessons From Past Congressional Investigations of Lobbying', *Public Opinion Quarterly*, 14 (1), pp. 14–32

Lasswell, H. D. (1930–35) 'Propaganda', *Encyclopedia of the Social Sciences*, Macmillan, New York (1954 reprint)

—— (1939) 'The Propagandist Bids For Power', *American Scholar*, 8 (Summer), pp. 350–7

—— (1953) 'The Theory of Political Propaganda', in B. Bardson and M. Janowitz (eds) *Reader in Public Opinion and Communication*, Free Press, New York

—— (1971) *Propaganda Techniques in World War I*, MIT Press, Cambridge (first published 1927)

Leavitt, H., and B. Bass (1964) 'Organisational psychology', *Annual Review of Psychology*, 15, pp. 371–98

Lesly, P. (1976) 'Why Economic Education Is Failing', *Management Review*, October, pp. 17–23

Lever, C. W. (1978) 'Fighting for Free Enterprise in America: the USIC Approach', in Ivens (ed.) *International Papers on the Revival of Freedom and Enterprise*, pp. 70–2

Levin, J. (1931) *Power Ethics*, Knopf, New York

Lewin, K., R. Lippitt and R. White (1939) 'Patterns of aggressive behaviour in experimentally created "social climates"', *Journal of Sociology*, 10, pp. 271–99

Link, H. C.(1946) 'The psychological corporation's index of public opinion', *Journal of Applied Psychology*, 30 (4), pp. 297–309

—— (1947a) 'American Opportunity: How to Sell America to Americans', *Vital Speeches*, 13 (15 June), pp538–9

—— (1947b) 'The Psychological Barometer of Public Attitudes', *Journal of Applied Psychology*, 31 (1), pp. 129–39

—— (1948) 'The Ninety-Fourth Issue of the Psychological Barometer and a Note on its Fifteenth Anniversary', *Journal of Applied Psychology*, 32 (2), pp. 105–6

—— (1950) 'To What Extent Have American People Accepted Socialism?', *Journal of Applied Psychology*, 34 (2), pp. 88–9

Link, H. C., and A. D. Freiberg (1949) 'The Psychological Barometer on Communism, Americanism and Socialism, *Journal of Applied Psychology*, 33 (1), pp. 6–14

Lippman, W. (1932) *Public Opinion*, Allen & Unwin, London (first published 1922)

—— (1955) *Essays in the Public Philosophy*, New York, Little Brown

Lowell, A. L. (1926) *Public Opinion and Popular Government*, Longman Green, New York (first published 1913, based on lectures at Johns Hopkins University in 1909)

Ludwig, S. (1973) 'Frederick Herzberg's recipe for motivation', *International Management*, September 18–22, pp. 18–23

Lupton, Tom (1971) *Management and the Social Sciences*, Penguin, Harmondsworth

Mock, James R., and C. Larson (1939) *Words that Won the War*, Princeton University Press, Princeton

MacDougall, A. K. (1980) 'Advocacy: Business Increasingly Uses (in Both Senses) Media to Push Views', *Los Angeles Times*, November 16

MacDougall, C. D. (1950) 'Is anybody listening?', editorial, *Fortune*, September 1950

—— (1952) *Understanding Public Opinion*, Macmillan, New York

Maier, N. R. F. (1946) *Industrial Psychology*, Harrap, London

Marsh, I. (1980) 'An Australian Think-Tank?', CEDA Study M61, University of NSW, Sydney

—— (1981) 'Business–Government Relations: Some Recent United States Developments', *Australian Director*, February, pp. 10–14

Mayo, Elton (1946) *The Human Problems of an Industrial Civilization*, Harvard Business School, Boston

McAdam, A. (1985) 'New Right: Where It Stands and What It Means', *Bulletin*, December 10, pp. 38–45

McDonald, F. (1962) *Insull*, University of Chicago Press, Chicago

McGregor, D. (1960) *The Human Side of Enterprise*, McGraw Hill, New York

McQuaid, K. (1981) 'The Roundtable: Getting Results in Washington', *Harvard Business Rev*
        May–June, pp. 114–23
Meagher, M. (1979) 'Spreading the Word for Free Enterprise', *Australian*, 4 April
Meier, Norman C. (1950) review of Thomas Bailey, *The Man in the Street*, *Public Opinion Quarte*
        Spring, pp. 160–3
Merson, M. (1954) 'My Education in Government', *The Reporter*, 7 Oct, pp.15–27
Miller, Arthur (1964) *The Crucible*, Viking, New York
Miller, Delbert, and William Form (1951) *Industrial Sociology*, Harper, New York
Miller, J. G. (1948) 'Psychological approaches to the prevention of war', in W. Dennis (ed.) *Cur*
        Trends in Social Psychology, University of Pittsburgh Press, Pittsburgh, pp. 274–99
Milliken, R. (1983) 'Ad Chiefs Give Thumbs Up to Policy Promotion', *National Times*, Febru
        6–12, p. 5
Mills, C. W. (1948) 'The Contribution of Sociology to Studies in Industrial Relations', *Proceed*
        of First Annual Meeting of Industrial Relations Research Association, December 29–30,
        199–209
——— (1970) *The Sociological Imagination*, Penguin, Harmondsworth
Mills, D. Q. (1979) 'Flawed Victory in Labor Law Reform', *Harvard Business Review*, May–J
        1979, pp. 92–101
Montgomery, P. L. (1981) 'Business Institutes on the Rise', *New York Times*, March, pp. C1, C
Moore, W. E. (1947) review of R. Dubin, 'Industrial and Social Order', *American Sociological Revi*
        52 (12), pp. 279–80
Moran, R. (1981) 'Business Wants to Tell the Truth', *TTW News*, 5, pp. 10–11
——— (1982) 'Fanatical Believers in Private Enterprise', *Australian Teacher*, 1, pp. 17–18
Morgenthau, H. J. (1951) *In Defense of the National Interest*, Knopf, New York
——— (1960) *The Purpose of American Politics*, Knopf, New York
Moulton, H. G., and C. W. McKee (1951) 'How Good is Economic Education?', *Fortune*, July,
        84–128
Moyes, A. G. (1984) Letter from Chairman of Enterprise Australia to corporate supporte
        February 16
Murphy, C. J. (1954) 'McCarthy and the Businessman', *Fortune*, April, pp. 156–8
Murray, R. K. (1955) *Red Scare: A Study in National Hysteria 1919–1920*, University
        Minneapolis Press, Minnesota
'NAM Gets the Story Across' (1945) *NAM News*, December 15, pp. 29–30
'NAM Propaganda' (1951) *New Republic*, March 5, p. 9
National Mutual Life Association of Australasia (1980) 'Curly and the Bald Hairy', *Natio*
        Mutuals Annual Report for Young People, Melbourne
'National Programme of Economic Education' (1979) *Enterprise News*, Enterprise Australia, Sydn
        (n.p.)
National Research Council Committee on Food Habits (1943) 'The problem of changing fo
        habits', *Bulletin of the National Research Council*, no. 108
Neal, A. C. (1962) Boobs and Booby Traps in Economic Education, address by Alfred C. Ne
        president, Committee for Economic Development at the 32nd Annual New Engla
        Bank Management Conference, Boston, Massachusetts, October 25
Niland, J., and D. Turner (1985) *Control, Consensus or Chaos*, Allen & Unwin, Sydney
Opinion Research Corporation (1946) *Aftermath of the Strikes, A Report of the Public Opinion Index*
        Industry, Princeton, New Jersey, April
Oshinsky, D. M. (1976) *Senator Joseph McCarthy and the American Labor Movement*, University
        Missouri Press, Columbia
'Overseas' (1978) *Newsletter*, Enterprise Australia, Sydney, May (n.p.)
Paech, P., ed. (1980) *The Social Responsibilities of Business in the 1980s*, Australian Council of Soc
        Service, Sydney
Paleman, C. (1970) *Participation and Democracy*, Cambridge University Press, Cambridge
Parenti, M. (1970) *The Anti-communist Impulse*, Random House, New York
Parker, W., and R. Kleemier (1951) *Human Relations in Supervision: Leadership in Managemen*
        McGraw Hill, New York
Pennock, George A. (1930) 'Industrial Research at Hawthorne', *Personnel Journal*, 8 (February), p
        296–313
Percy, C. H. (1977) 'Of Consumer Advocacy and a Highly Biased Poll', *New York Times*, June 9, p.

Peterson, W. H. (1980) 'Unbinding Prometheus', *The Freeman* (New York) 30 (11), pp. 663–72

Porter, R. (1946a) 'Hunt is sharpened for labor peace', *New York Times*, Business Section, May 20

―――― (1946b) 'Research in human relationships seen needed for reconversion', *New York Times*, Business Section, April 21

―――― (1947) 'Study of human relations viewed as industrial key', *New York Times*, Business Section, May 18

Post, L. (1970) *The Deportations Delirium of Nineteen-Twenty: A personal narrative of an historic official experience*, Da Capo, New York (first published 1923)

Preston, William (1963) *Aliens and Dissenters: The Federal Suppression of Radicals 1903–1933*, Harvard University Press, Cambridge, Mass.

'Private Enterprise: The Winning Way' (1984) Enterprise Australia, Sydney

'Programme For 1984' (1984) Enterprise Australia, Sydney

'Public Money, Private Goals' (1985) editorial, *SMH*, February 21

'Public Relations―First in the Order of Business' (1937) editorial, *Business Week*, January 23

'Publications in Print' (1981) Institute of Economic Affairs, London

Pugh, D. S., ed. (1971) *Organisation Theory*, Penguin, Harmondsworth

Putnam, Mark L. (1930) 'Improving Employee Relations', *Personnel Journal*, 8 (February), pp. 314–25

Pym, Denis (1971) 'Social change and the business firm', in D. Mills (ed.) *Australian Management and Society 1970–1985*, Penguin, Harmondsworth, pp. 199–209

'Radio Spots' (1978) *Newsletter*, Enterprise Australia, Sydney, May

Raven, B. (1968) 'Group performance', *International Encyclopedia of the Social Sciences*, vol. 6, Macmillan, New York, pp. 288–93

Rayback, J. G. (1966) *A History of American Labor*, Macmillan, New York

'Reaching Every Segment of Society' (1978) *Newsletter*, Enterprise Australia, Sydney, May

Rippa, S. (1958) Organized Business and Public Education: The Educational Policies and Activities of the Chamber of Commerce and the National Association of Manufacturers 1933–1956. D.Ed. thesis, Graduate School of Education, Harvard University

Roberts, C. M. (1954) *Reporter*, December 16, p. 13

Robinson, C. (1939) 'The New Science of Public Opinion Measurement and its Implications for Business', *Harvard Business School Bulletin*, 15 (4), pp. 232–37

Rockefeller, D. (1979) *David Rockefeller in Australia*, CEDA, Melbourne

Roethlisberger, F. J. (1941) *Management and Morale*, Harvard University Press, Cambridge

Roethlisberger, F. J., and William Dickson (1964) *Management and the Worker*, Wiley, New York; original 1939, Harvard University Press, Cambridge

Rosen, G. R. (1976) 'The New Conservative Idea Men', *Dun's Review*, April, pp. 39–45

Rovere, R. (1959) *Senator Joe McCarthy*, London, Methuen

Russell, B. (1945) *History of Western Philosophy*, Simon & Schuster, New York

Sampson, A. (1974) *The Sovereign State: The Secret History of ITT*, Coronet, London

Sawer, M. (1982) 'Political Manifestations of Libertarianism in Australia', in M. Sawer (ed.) *Australia and the New Right*, Allen & Unwin, Sydney, pp. 1–19

Schnapper, M. B., ed. (1948) *The Truman Programme*, Bureau of Public Affairs, Washington

Schriftgeisser, K. (1951) *The Lobbyists*, Little Brown, Boston

―――― (1960) *Business Comes of Age*, Harper, New York

Schumpeter, J. (1970) *Capitalism, Socialism and Democracy*, London: Allen & Unwin (first published 1943)

Scott, W. (1950) *Greater Production*, Law Book Co., Sydney

―――― (1962) *Human Relations in Management: A Behavioural Science Approach*, McGraw Hill, New York

Selvage, J. (1942) 'Selling the Free Enterprise System', *Vital Speeches*, November, pp. 142–7

Sentry Holdings (1978) *Managers and Workers at the Crossroads* Sentry Holdings Ltd, Sydney

Sethi, S. P. (1977) *Advocacy Advertising and Large Corporations*, Heath, Lexington

Shanahan, R. M. (1982) 'Enterprise Australia: Knowledge for Whom?', *South Australian Teachers Journal*, April 22

Sheehan, P. (1982) 'The Right Strikes Back', *SMH*, March 2

Shirer, W. L. (1960) *The Rise and Fall of the Third Reich*, Secker & Warburg, London

Simon, W. (1978a) *A Time for Truth*, McGraw-Hill, Sydney

―――― (1978b) 'Clearly this is Economic Insanity', *Enterprise* (Washington, NAM), April, pp. 3–7

'Simon: Preaching the Word for Olin' (1978) *New York Times*, July 16, p. 4

Smith, J. H. (1961) *The University Teaching of Social Sciences: Industrial Sociology*, UNESCO Paris

Snell, B. C. (1974) 'American Ground Transport ... ', US Senate Committee of the Judiciary Subcommittee on Antitrust and Monopoly, Washington (Snell Report)

Stagner, Ross (1956) *The Psychology of Industrial Conflict*, Wiley, New York

Streuben, J. (1950) *Strike Strategy*, Gaer, New York

Stewart, A. (1980) 'The Business Offensive in the United States—Will it Spread?', *Journal Industrial Relations*, December, pp. 484–91

Strauss, G. (1970) 'Organisational behaviour and personal relations', *A Review of Industrial Relatio Research*, 1, pp. 145–206

——— (1971) 'Human relations — 1968 style', in D. McFarlane (ed.) *Personnel Management* Penguin, Harmondsworth, pp. 107–27

Sward, K. (1939) 'The Johnstown Steel Strike of 1937: A Case Study of Large Scale Conflict', i Hartmann and Newcombe, *Industrial Conflict*, pp. 74–102

Sykes, A. J. (1965) 'Economic Interest and the Hawthorne Researches: A Comment', *Huma Relations*, 18 (August)

Tawney, R. H. (1938) *Religion and the Rise of Capitalism*, Penguin, Harmondsworth

Tedlow, R. S. (1976) 'The National Association of Manufacturers and Public Relations Durin The New Deal', *Business History Review*, pp. 25–45

'Television Documentary Series' (1978) *Newsletter*, Enterprise Australia, Sydney, July

Temporary National Economic Committee (1941) 'The Structure of Industry', in *Investigations Concentration of Economic Power*, Monograph No. 27: 'The Structure of Industry' Government Printing Office, Washington

'The Capitalist Crisis — Meeting the Challenge' (1983) Enterprise Australia, Sydney (n.p, n.d but early 1983)

'The Facts on the Enterprise Australia Schools and Colleges Programme' (1982) *A Special Bulleti for the Information of Members,* Enterprise Australia, Sydney, September

'The Fruitful Errors of Elton Mayo who Proposes to Management and Labor a Social Basis fo Industrial Peace' (1946) editorial, *Fortune*, November

The Psychological Corporation (1937) 'A Study of Public Relations and Social Attitudes', *Journa of Applied Psychology*, 21 (4), pp. 589–602

Thompson, E. P. (1968) *The Making of the English Working Class*, Penguin, Harmondsworth

Thompson, J. (1977) 'Waging guerrilla war for business on the campus', *In These Times*, April 2(

Thompson, V. (1961) *Modern Organisation*, Knopf, New York

Trevor-Roper, H. (1967) *The European Witch Craze of the Sixteenth and Seventeenth Centuries* Penguin, Harmondsworth

'Twenty-nine Largest Corporations Set Up Lobby Group', (1981) *Workforce*, 332, February 11

'Understanding Free Enterprise' (1956), *IPA Review*, January– March, pp. 9–17

United Nations (1973) Department of Social and Economic Affairs, *Multinational Corporations i World Development*, United Nations, New York

Urwick, L. F., and E. Brech (1948) *The Making of Scientific Management*, Part 3: *The Hawthorn Investigations*, Management Publications Trust, London

US Congress (1939) Committee on Education and Labor, *Violations of Free Speech and the Rights o Labor,* 76th Congress, First Session, Senate Report No. 6, Part 6, Section 3: 'Th National Association of Manufacturers', Government Printing Office, Washington

——— (1975) Oversight Hearings on Commerce Department Payment to the Nationa Advertising Council for Promotion of the Free Enterprise System ... ', Washingto DC, 94th Congress, First Session, July 30

'US Fondness For Our Agencies' (1980) *Advertising News*, March 14

'US Relations with China' (1949) State Department White Paper, August

Utz, J, (1984) Foreword to P. Burgess, *Economic Policy Research in Australia*, CEDA, Sydney

Vale, V. (1971) *Labour in American Politics*, Routledge & Kegan Paul, London

Vernon, Horace M. (1921) *Industrial Fatigue and Efficiency*, Dutton, London

Viteles, Morris S. (1932) *Industrial Psychology*, Norton, New York

——— (1953) *Motivation and Morale in Industry*, Staples, London

Vroom, V. H. (1964) *Work and Motivation*, Wiley, New York

Vroom, V., and N. Maier (1961) 'Industrial social psychology', *Annual Review of Psychology*, 12, pp. 413–45

Walker, S. H., and P. Sklar (1938) 'Business Finds Its Voice' Part 3, *Harper's*, March, pp. 428–31

Walsh, M. (1981) 'Media Perceptions of the Corporation', in *Corporate Risks In the Australian Political Environment*, AmCham, Sydney

Wardell, N. (1978) 'The Corporation', *Daedalus*, 107, pp. 97–110

Weaver, P. (1977) 'Corporations Are Defending Themselves with the Wrong Weapons' *Fortune*, June, p. 186–96

Weber, Max (1904) *The Protestant Ethic and the Spirit of Capitalism*, transl. T. Parsons, Allen & Unwin, London (first published 1930)

Weisner, P., ed. (1958) *Values in a Universe of Chance: Selected writings by C. S. Peirce*, Doubleday, New York

Werth, A. (1971) *Russia: The Cold War Years*, London, Hale

White, F. C. (1978). 'How to go on the political offensive', in Ivens (ed.) *International Papers on the Revival of Freedom and Enterprise*, pp. 1–2

White, R., and R. Lippitt (1960) *Autocracy and Democracy*, Harper, New York

—— (1962) 'Leader behaviour and member reaction in three "social climates"', in D. Cartwright and A. Zander (eds) *Group Dynamics*, Row Peterson, Evaston, pp. 527–53

Whitehead, T. North (1938a) *The Industrial Worker*, vol. 1, Oxford University Press, London

—— (1938b) *The Industrial Worker*, vol. 2, Oxford University Press, London

Whiting, A. (1960) *China Crosses the Yalu*, Macmillan, New York

'Who-What-Why' (1955) *Reporter*, January 27

'Why Too Many College Students Are Economic Illiterates' (1960) The *Public Opinion Index for Industry*, Opinion Research Corporation, Princeton, April

Whyte, W. H. (1950) 'Is Anybody Listening?', *Fortune*, September, pp. 78–83

—— (1956) *The Organisation Man*, Penguin, Harmondsworth

Wilcock, R. C. (1961) 'Industrial Managements' Policies Toward Unionism', in M. Derber and E. Young (eds) *Labor and the New Deal*, University of Wisconsin Press, Madison

Wilensky, J. L., and H. I. Wilensky (1951) 'Personal counselling: the Hawthorne case', *American Journal of Sociology*, 57, pp. 265–80

Willett, E. J. (1968) 'Management education in Australia' in D. Douglas (ed.) *Management Training: A Critical Assessment*, University of Sydney, Sydney, pp. 47–65

Williams, D., and S. Peterfreund (1954) *Management Education for Itself and Its Employees*, Part 4: *The Education of Employees: A Status Report*, AMA, New York

'Work and Wealth' (1978) *Newsletter*, Enterprise Australia, Sydney, July

Yankelovich, D. (1972) *The Changing Business Environment*, NAM, Washington

Yankelovich, D., and L. Kaagan (1981) 'Assertive America', *Foreign Affairs*, 59 (3), pp. 696–714

'Young Achievement Companies Fire Enthusiasm Among Youth and Adult Advisers in AmCham's Pilot Programme' (1977) *Commerce*, September–October

Young, Kimball (1945) *Social Psychology*, Appleton-Century-Crofts, New York

Yuill, Bruce (1966) *Organisational principles of management*, West, Sydney

Zipser, A. (1946) 'Business Studies Human Relations', *New York Times*, Business Section, September 22

INDEX